Get the eBook FREE!

(PDF, ePub, Kindle, and liveBook all included)

We believe that once you buy a book from us, you should be able to read it in any format we have available. To get electronic versions of this book at no additional cost to you, purchase and then register this book at the Manning website.

Go to https://www.manning.com/freebook and follow the instructions to complete your pBook registration.

That's it!
Thanks from Manning!

Troubleshooting Java

READ, DEBUG, AND OPTIMIZE JVM APPLICATIONS

LAURENŢIU SPILCĂ

MANNING
SHELTER ISLAND

For online information and ordering of this and other Manning books, please visit
www.manning.com. The publisher offers discounts on this book when ordered in quantity.
For more information, please contact

Special Sales Department
Manning Publications Co.
20 Baldwin Road
PO Box 761
Shelter Island, NY 11964
Email: orders@manning.com

Manning Publications Co.
20 Baldwin Road
PO Box 761
Shelter Island, NY 11964

Development editor:	Marina Michaels
Technical development editor:	Nick Watts
Review editor:	Marina Michaels
Production editor:	Deirdre S. Hiam
Copy editor:	Michele Mitchell
Proofreader:	Katie Tennant
Technical proofreader:	Jean-François Morin
Typesetter:	Gordan Salinovic
Cover designer:	Marija Tudor

ISBN 9781617299773
Printed in the United States of America

contents

preface

What does a software developer actually do for a living? "Implement software" is the most common answer to this question. But what does that mean? Is it only writing code? Well, no. While it is true that code is the result of everything a software developer does, the activity of writing code takes only a small part of a software developer's working time. Most of a software developer's time is actually used designing solutions, reading existing code, understanding how it executes, and learning new things. Writing code is the result of a software developer successfully accomplishing all of these tasks. Therefore, a programmer spends most of their time reading existing solutions rather than effectively writing new capabilities.

Clean coding as a subject has, in the end, the same purpose: teaching developers how to write easier-to-read solutions. Developers realize that it's more efficient to write an easier-to-read solution from the beginning than spend time trying to understand it later. But we need to be honest and admit that not all solutions are clean enough to quickly comprehend. We'll always face scenarios in which we will need to understand the execution of some foreign capability.

The reality is that software developers spend a lot of time investigating how apps work. They read and examine code in their app's codebases and associated dependencies to figure out why something doesn't work the way they expect. Developers sometimes read code only to learn about or better understand a given dependency. In many cases, reading code isn't enough, and you have to find alternative (sometimes more complicated) ways to figure out what your app does. To understand how the environment affects your app or the JVM instance your Java app runs on, you may use a combination of profiling, debugging, and log investigations. If you know your options well and how to choose from among them, you will save valuable time. Remember, this is what developers spend most of their time doing. This development activity can be very beneficial.

I designed this book to help people optimize the way they investigate software development challenges. In it, you'll find the most relevant investigation techniques, which are applied with examples. We'll discuss debugging, profiling, using logs, and efficiently combining these techniques. Throughout the book, I'll give you valuable tips and tricks that will help you to become more efficient and solve problems (even the most difficult of them) faster. In other words, this book's purpose, overall, is to make you more efficient as a developer.

I hope this book brings significant value to you and helps you to become more efficient in quickly finding the root causes of issues you investigate.

acknowledgments

This book wouldn't be possible without the many smart, professional, and friendly people who helped me out throughout its development process.

I want to say a big thanks to my wife Daniela, who was there for me, helped with valuable opinions, and continuously supported and encouraged me. I'd also like to send special thanks to all the colleagues and friends whose valuable advice helped me with the very first table of contents and proposal.

I'd like to thank the entire Manning team for their huge help in making this a valuable resource. I'd especially want to call out Marina Michaels, Nick Watts, and Jean-François Morin for being incredibly supportive and professional. Their advice brought great value to this book. Thans go as well to Deirdre Hiam, my project manager; Michele Mitchell, my copyeditor; and Katie Tennant, my proofreader.

I'd like to thank my friend Ioana Göz for the drawings she created for the book. She turned my thoughts into the cartoons you'll see throughout the book.

I'd also like to thank everyone who reviewed the manuscript and provided useful feedback that helped me improve the content of this book. I'd like to specifically call out the reviewers from Manning—Alex Gout, Alex Zuroff, Amrah Umudlu, Anand Natarajan, Andres Damian Sacco, Andriy Stosyk, Anindya Bandopadhyay, Atul Shriniwas Khot, Becky Huett, Bonnie Malec, Brent Honadel, Carl Hope, Cătălin Matei, Christopher Kardell, Cicero Zandona, Cosimo Damiano Prete, Daniel R. Carl, Deshuang Tang, Fernando Bernardino, Gabor Hajba, Gaurav Tuli, Giampiero Granatella, Giorgi Tsiklauri, Govinda Sambamurthy, Halil Karaköse, Hugo Figueiredo, Jacopo Biscella, James R. Woodruff, Jason Lee, Javid Asgarov, Jean-Baptiste Bang Nteme, Jeroen van Wilgenburg, Joel Caplin, Jürg Marti, Krzysztof Kamyczek, Latif Benzzine, Leonardo Gomes da Silva, Manoj Reddy, Marcus Geselle, Matt Deimel, Matt Welke, Michael Kolesidis, Michael Wall, Michal Owsiak, Oliver Korten, Olubunmi Ogunsan, Paolo Brunasti, Peter Szabós, Prabhuti Prakash, Rajesh Balamohan, Rajesh Mohanan, Raveesh Sharma, Ruben Gonzalez-Rubio, Aboudou SamadouSare, Simeon Leyzerzon, Simone Cafiero, SravanthiReddy, Sveta Natu, Tan Wee, Tanuj Shroff, Travis Nelson, Yakov Boglev, and Yuri Klayman—as well friends who advised me: Maria Chițu, Adrian Buturugă, Mircea Vacariuc, Cătălin Matei.

about this book

Who should read this book

Since you opened this book, I assume you are a developer using a JVM language. You might use Java, but you could also use Kotlin or Scala. Regardless of the JVM language you're using, you'll find this book's content valuable. It teaches you relevant investigation techniques you can use to identify the root causes of problems (i.e., bugs) and how to easily learn new technologies. As a software developer, you may have already noticed how much time you spend understanding what an app does. Like other developers, you probably spend more time reading code, debugging, or using logs than writing code. So why not become more efficient in what you do most during your working day?

In this book, we'll discuss, and apply examples to, the following topics:

- Simple and advanced debugging techniques
- Efficiently using logs to understand app behaviors
- Profiling CPU and memory resource consumption
- Profiling to find executing code
- Profiling to understand how an app works with persisted data
- Analyzing how apps communicate with one another
- Monitoring system events

Regardless of your experience, you will find this book helpful in learning new investigation techniques, or, if you're already an experienced developer, you will find this is a good refresher.

The prerequisite for reading this book is understanding the basics of the Java language. I intentionally designed all the examples with Java (even if they apply to any JVM language) for consistency. If you understand Java at a basic level (classes, methods, basic instructions such as decisional or repetitive instructions and declaring variables), you should be able to understand the discussions in the book.

How this book is organized: A roadmap

The book is divided into three parts that cover 12 chapters. We'll start our discussion (in the first part of the book) with debugging techniques. We'll discuss and apply both simple and more advanced debugging techniques and where you can use them to save time when investigating various scenarios. I chose to start our discussion with debugging because this is usually the first step in investigating how some capability of an app behaves during its development phase. Some people asked me why I didn't start with logs first, since they are the first investigation technique for production issues. While this is true, a developer has to deal with a debugger when they start implementing features, so I figured a better arrangement of the chapters would be to begin with debugging techniques.

In the first chapter, we discuss the relevance of the investigation techniques the book discusses and figure out a plan for learning them. Chapters 2, 3, and 4 focus on debugging and teach you relevant skills, from adding a simple breakpoint to debugging apps in remote environments. Chapter 5, which is the last chapter in part 1, discusses logging. Debugging and using logs are the simplest (and most frequently used) investigation techniques for building an application.

The second part of the book discusses profiling techniques. The popular opinion is that profiling is more advanced and less used with modern apps than debugging and researching logs. While I agree that profiling is more advanced, I demonstrate that you can use many profiling techniques to be more efficient when investigating issues in modern JVM apps or studying frameworks considered essential.

Chapter 6, which begins the book's second part, discusses identifying whether your app has faults in its management of CPU and memory resources. Chapter 7 goes into detail on this topic and shows you how to get to the part of the app that causes specific latencies and how to observe what your app executes at a given time. In chapters 6 and 7, we use VisualVM, a free tool. Chapter 8 continues the discussion from chapter 7 with more advanced visualization tools that you typically only get with a licensed profiling tool. For the details discussed in this chapter, we use JProfiler, which is not free to use.

Chapters 9 and 10 focus on more subtle profiling techniques. You'll learn skills that can save you time when dealing with issues deeply hidden in the multithreaded architecture behind an app's execution. Chapter 11 ends part 2 by addresssing how to investigate an app's memory management.

The book ends with part 3, which has just one chapter: chapter 12. In it, we go beyond an app's borders to discuss investigating issues in an extensive system composed of multiple apps.

The chapters are in the order in which I recommend you read them, but each focuses on a different topic. So, if you are interested in a specific topic, you can jump directly to that chapter. For example, if you're interested in investigating issues with memory management, you can go straight to chapter 11.

About the code

This book contains many examples of source code, both in numbered listings and in line with normal text. In both cases, source code is formatted in a `fixed-width` font `like this` to separate it from ordinary text. Sometimes code is also **in bold** to highlight code that has changed from previous steps in the chapter, such as when a new feature adds to an existing line of code.

In many cases, the original source code has been reformatted; we've added line breaks and reworked indentation to accommodate the available page space in the book. In rare cases, even this was not enough, and listings include line-continuation markers (➥). Additionally, comments in the source code have often been removed from the listings when the code is described in the text. Code annotations accompany many of the listings and highlight important concepts.

You can get executable snippets of code from the liveBook (online) version of this book at https://livebook.manning.com/book/troubleshooting-java. The complete code for the examples in the book is available for download from the Manning website at www.manning.com.

liveBook discussion forum

Purchase of *Troubleshooting Java* includes free access to liveBook, Manning's online reading platform. Using liveBook's exclusive discussion features, you can attach comments to the book globally or to specific sections or paragraphs. It's easy to make notes for yourself, ask and answer technical questions, and receive help from the author and other users. To access the forum, go to https://livebook.manning.com/book/troubleshooting-java/discussion. You can also learn more about Manning's forums and the rules of conduct at https://livebook.manning.com/discussion.

Manning's commitment to our readers is to provide a venue where a meaningful dialogue between individual readers and between readers and the author can take place. It is not a commitment to any specific amount of participation on the part of the author, whose contribution to the forum remains voluntary (and unpaid). We suggest you try asking him some challenging questions lest his interest stray! The forum and the archives of previous discussions will be accessible from the publisher's website as long as the book is in print.

Author online

I recommend you keep in touch with me online. You'll definitely find plenty of good learning material related to troubleshooting Java apps on my YouTube channel: youtube.com/c/laurentiuspilca, and you can follow me on Twitter @laurspilca.

about the author

LAURENȚIU SPILCĂ is a dedicated development lead and trainer at Endava, where he is responsible for leading and consulting on multiple projects from various locations in Europe, the United States, and Asia. He has been working in software development since 2007. Laurențiu believes it's essential to not only deliver high-quality software but to also share knowledge and help others upskill. This belief has driven him to design and teach courses related to Java technologies and deliver presentations and workshops. Laurențiu is also the author of *Spring Security in Action* (Manning, 2020), and he recently finished *Spring Start Here* (Manning, 2021).

about the cover illustration

The figure on the cover of *Troubleshooting Java* is "Homme de l'Istrie," or "Man from Istria," taken from a collection by Jacques Grasset de Saint-Sauveur, published in 1797. Each illustration is finely drawn and colored by hand.

In those days, it was easy to identify where people lived and what their trade or station in life was just by their dress. Manning celebrates the inventiveness and initiative of the computer business with book covers based on the rich diversity of regional culture centuries ago, brought back to life by pictures from collections such as this one.

Part 1

The basics of
investigating a codebase

As a software developer, working on real-world apps often involves investigating how your code works. You have to understand the app's behavior when fixing problems as well as when implementing new features. You use several techniques for this purpose, such as debugging, logging, profiling, and so on, which we will analyze deeply in this book.

In part 1, we start with the first techniques a developer is exposed to: debugging and logging. When working on an app, a developer must often engage in debugging. For example, say you have a small piece of code, and you need to understand how it works. You use the debugger to pause the application's execution and dive deep into how the app processes the data. Then, when your app runs in an environment, you can rely a lot on logs, which give you needed clues about where something could go wrong.

In chapter 1, we'll discuss the need for knowing investigation techniques and obtain a big-picture view of them, which we'll detail throughout the rest of the book. We'll then take these techniques in the order a developer is exposed to them. In chapters 2 through 4, we discuss debugging. In chapter 5, we go through essential details about implementing and using logs in investigations.

Starting to build an app

Reading code

```
profile.ifPresentOrElse(
      p ->
      {
        healthMetric.setProfile(p);
        healthMetricRepository.save(healthMetric);
      },
      () -> {
        throw new NonExistentHealthProfileException();
      });
```

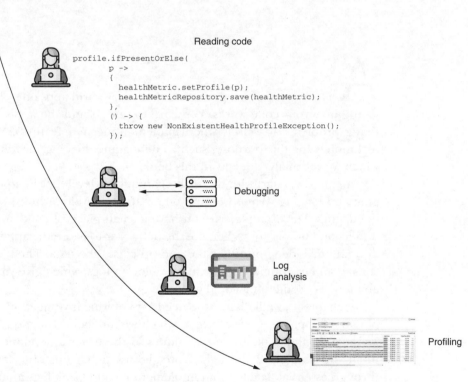

Debugging

Log
analysis

Profiling

Revealing an app's obscurities

1

This chapter covers

- The definition of a code investigation technique
- What code investigation techniques we use to understand Java apps

A software developer has various responsibilities—most of which depend on how they understand the code they are working with. Software developers spend much of their time analyzing code to figure out how to correct issues, implement new capabilities, and even learn new technologies. And time is precious, so developers need efficient investigation techniques to be productive. Learning how to be efficient in understanding your code is the main topic of this book.

NOTE Software developers generally spend more time understanding how the software works than writing code to implement new features or correct errors.

Often, software developers use the word *debugging* for any investigation techniques; however, this is only one of the various tools available for examining logic implemented as code. While debugging should mean "finding issues and solving them," developers use it to name different purposes for analyzing how code works:

- Learning a new framework
- Finding the root cause of a problem
- Understanding existing logic to extend it with new capabilities

1.1 How to more easily understand your app

First, it is important to understand what investigating code is and how developers do it. In this next section, we look at several commonly encountered scenarios in which you can apply the techniques you'll learn in this book.

I define *investigating code* as being the process of analyzing a software capability's specific behavior. You might wonder, "Why such a generic definition? What is the investigation's purpose?" Early in the history of software development, looking through code had one precise purpose: finding and correcting software errors (i.e., *bugs*). This is why many developers still use the term *debugging* for these techniques. Look at the way the word *debug* is formed:

$$\textbf{de-bug} = \text{take out bugs, eliminate errors}$$

In many cases today, we still debug apps to find and correct errors. But unlike the early days of software development, apps today are more complex. In many cases, developers find themselves investigating how a particular software capability works, simply to learn a specific technology or library. Debugging is no longer only about finding a particular issue; it is also about correctly understanding its behavior (figure 1.1; see also http://mng.bz/M012).

Figure 1.1   Code investigation is not only about finding problems in software. Today, apps are complex. We often use investigation techniques to understand an app's behavior or simply to learn new technologies.

Why do we analyze code in apps?

- To find a particular issue
- To understand how a particular software capability works so we can enhance it
- To learn a specific technology or library

Many developers also investigate code for fun, because exploring how code works is fun. It can sometimes become frustrating as well, but nothing compares to the feeling of finding the root cause of an issue or finally understanding how things work (figure 1.2).

Figure 1.2 Investigating code doesn't require much physical effort, but debugging sometimes makes you feel like Lara Croft or Indiana Jones. Many developers enjoy the unique sensation of solving the puzzle of a software issue.

There are various investigation techniques we can apply to investigate how software behaves. As we'll discuss later in the chapter, developers (especially beginners) often wrongly consider debugging equivalent to using a debugger tool. The debugger is a software program you can use to read and more easily understand the source code of an application, usually by pausing the execution on specific instructions and running the code step by step. It is a common way to investigate software behavior (and usually the first one a developer learns). But it is not the only technique you can use, and it doesn't help you in every scenario. We'll discuss both standard and more advanced ways of using a debugger in chapters 2 and 3. Figure 1.3 presents the various investigation techniques you'll learn throughout this book.

When a developer solves a bug, they spend most of their time on understanding a particular feature. The changes they end up making sometimes reduce the problem to a single line of code—a missing condition, a missing instruction, or a misused operator. It's not writing the code but rather understanding how the app works that occupies most of a developer's time.

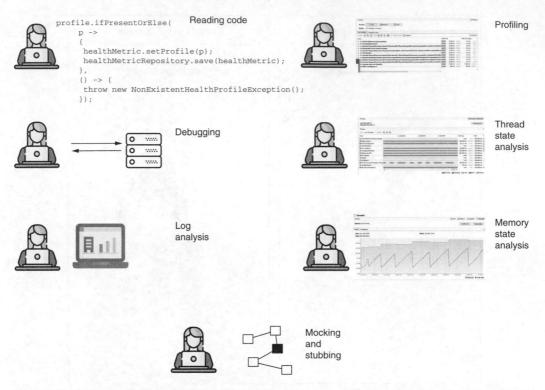

Figure 1.3   **Code investigation techniques. Depending on the case, a developer can choose from one or more of these techniques to understand how a certain capability works.**

In some cases, simply reading the code is enough to understand it, but reading code is not like reading a book. When we read code, we don't read nice short paragraphs written in a logical order from top to bottom. Instead, we step from one method to another, from one file to another; we sometimes feel like we advance in a vast labyrinth and get lost. (On this subject, I recommend the excellent book *The Programmer's Brain* by Felienne Hermans [Manning, 2021]).

In many cases, the source code is written in a way that doesn't make it easy to read. Yes, I know what you are thinking: it should be. And I agree with you. Today, we learn many patterns and principles for code design and how to avoid code smells, but let's be honest: developers still don't use these principles properly in too many cases. Moreover, legacy apps usually don't follow these principles, simply because the principles didn't exist many years ago when those capabilities were written. But you still need to be able to investigate such code.

Look at listing 1.1. Suppose you find this piece of code while trying to identify the root cause of a problem in an app you're working on. This code definitely needs refactoring. But before you can refactor it, you need to understand what it is doing. I know some developers out there can read through this code and immediately understand what it does, but I'm not one of them.

To easily understand the logic in listing 1.1, I use a *debugger*—a tool that allows me to pause the execution on specific lines and manually run each instruction while observing how the data changes—to go through each line to observe how it works with the given input (as we'll discuss in chapter 2). With a bit of experience and some tricks (that we'll discuss in chapters 2 and 3), you will find, by parsing this code a few times, that it calculates the maximum between the given inputs. This code is part of the project da-ch1-ex1 provided with the book.

Listing 1.1　Hard-to-read logic that requires use of a debugger

```
public int m(int f, int g) {
  try {
    int[] far = new int[f];
    far[g] = 1;
    return f;
  } catch(NegativeArraySizeException e) {
    f = -f;
    g = -g;
    return (-m(f, g) == -f) ? -g : -f;
  } catch(IndexOutOfBoundsException e) {
    return (m(g, 0) == 0) ? f : g;
  }
}
```

Some scenarios don't allow you to navigate through the code, or they make navigating it more challenging. Today, most apps rely on dependencies such as libraries or frameworks. In most cases, even when you have access to the source code (when you use an open source dependency), it's still difficult to follow the source code that defines a framework's logic. Sometimes, you don't even know where to start. In such cases, you must use different techniques to understand the app. For example, you could use a profiler tool (as you'll learn in chapters 6 through 9) to identify what code executes before deciding where to start the investigation.

Other scenarios will not give you the chance to have a running app. In some cases, you'll have to investigate a problem that made the app crash. If the application that encountered problems and stopped is a production service, you need to make it available again quickly. So, you need to collect details and use them to identify the problem and improve the app to avoid the same problem in the future. This investigation, which relies on collected data after the app crashes, is called a *postmortem investigation*. For such cases, you can use logs, heap dumps, or thread dumps—troubleshooting instruments that we'll discuss in chapters 10 and 11.

1.2　*Typical scenarios for using investigation techniques*

Let's discuss some common scenarios for using code investigation approaches. We must look at some typical cases from real-world apps and analyze them to emphasize the importance of this book's subject matter:

- To understand why a particular piece of code or software capability provides a different result than expected
- To learn how the technologies the app uses as dependencies work
- To identify causes for performance issues such as app slowness
- To find out root causes for cases in which an app suddenly stops

For each presented case, you'll find one or more techniques helpful in investigating the app's logic. Later, we'll dive into these techniques and demonstrate, with examples, how to use them.

1.2.1 *Demystifying the unexpected output*

The most frequent scenario in which you'll need to analyze code is when some logic ends up with a different output than expected. This might sound simple, but it isn't necessarily easy to solve.

First, let's define *output*. This term might have many definitions for an app. Output could be some text in the app's console, or it could be some records changed in a database. We can consider output an HTTP request the app sends to a different system or some data sent in the HTTP response to a client's request.

> **DEFINITION** Any result of executing a piece of logic that might result in data change, the exchange of information, or action against a different component or system is an *output*.

How do we investigate a case in which a specific part of the app doesn't have the expected execution result? We do so by choosing the proper technique based on the expected output. Let's look at some examples.

SCENARIO 1: THE SIMPLE CASE

Suppose an app should insert some records into a database. Yet, the app adds only part of the records. That is, you expected to find more data in the database than the app actually produces.

The simplest way to analyze this is to use a debugger tool to follow the code execution and understand how it works (figure 1.4). You'll learn about the main features of a debugger in chapters 2 and 3. The debugger adds a breakpoint to pause the app execution at a specific line of code of your choosing, and then it allows you to continue the execution manually. You run code instructions one by one so you can see how the values of the variables change and evaluate expressions on the fly.

This scenario is the simplest, and by learning how to use all the relevant debugger features properly, you can find solutions to such issues in no time. Unfortunately, other cases are more complex, and a debugger tool isn't always enough to solve the puzzle and find the cause of the problem.

You can mark an instruction with a breakpoint to tell
the debugger to pause the execution before executing.

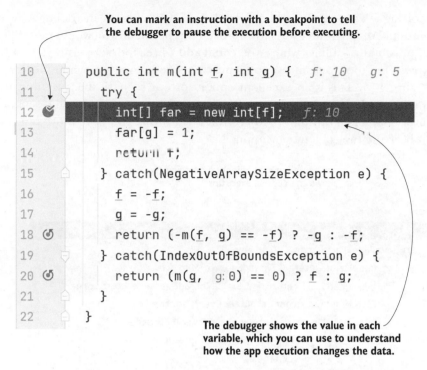

```
10    public int m(int f, int g) {   f: 10    g: 5
11      try {
12        int[] far = new int[f];   f: 10
13        far[g] = 1;
14        return f;
15      } catch(NegativeArraySizeException e) {
16        f = -f;
17        g = -g;
18        return (-m(f, g) == -f) ? -g : -f;
19      } catch(IndexOutOfBoundsException e) {
20        return (m(g, g: 0) == 0) ? f : g;
21      }
22    }
```

The debugger shows the value in each
variable, which you can use to understand
how the app execution changes the data.

Figure 1.4   Using a debugger, you can pause the execution before a particular instruction and then observe how the app's logic changes the data by manually running the instructions step by step.

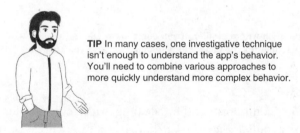

TIP In many cases, one investigative technique isn't enough to understand the app's behavior. You'll need to combine various approaches to more quickly understand more complex behavior.

SCENARIO 2: THE WHERE-SHOULD-I-START-DEBUGGING CASE?

Sometimes you won't be able to use a debugger simply because you don't know what to debug. Suppose your app is a complex service with many lines of code. You investigate an issue in which the app doesn't store the expected records in a database. It's definitely a problem of output, but out of the thousands of lines of code defining your app, you don't know what part implements the capability you need to fix.

I remember a colleague who was investigating such a problem. Stressed from not being able to find where to start, he exclaimed: "I wish debuggers had a way for you to add a breakpoint on all the lines of an app so you could see what it actually uses."

My colleague's statement was funny, but having such a feature in a debugger wouldn't be a solution. We have other ways to approach this problem. You would most likely narrow the possibilities of lines where you could add a breakpoint by using a profiler.

A *profiler* is a tool you can use to identify what code executes while the app is running (figure 1.5). This is an excellent option for our scenario because it would give you an idea of where to start the investigation with a debugger. We'll discuss using a profiler in chapters 6 through 9, where you'll learn that you have more options than simply observing the code in execution.

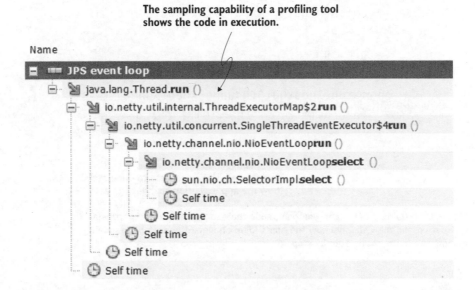

Figure 1.5 Identifying code in execution with a profiler. If you don't know where to start debugging, the profiler can help you to identify the code that is running and give you an idea of where you can use the debugger.

SCENARIO 3: A MULTITHREADED APP

Situations become even more complicated when dealing with logic implemented through multiple threads, or a *multithreaded architecture*. In many such cases, using a debugger is not an option because multithreaded architectures tend to be sensitive to interference.

In other words, the way the app behaves is different when you use the debugger. Developers call this characteristic a *Heisenberg execution* or *Heisenbug* (figure 1.6). The name comes from the twentieth-century physicist Werner Heisenberg, who formulated the uncertainty principle, which states that once you interfere with a particle, it behaves differently, so you cannot accurately predict both its velocity and position simultaneously (https://plato.stanford.edu/entries/qt-uncertainty/). A multithreaded architecture might change the way it behaves if you interfere with it, just like if you interfere with a quantum mechanics particle.

When nothing interferes with the app

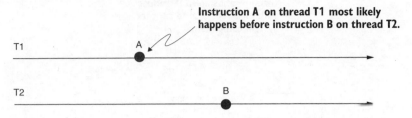

When a debugger interferes with the app

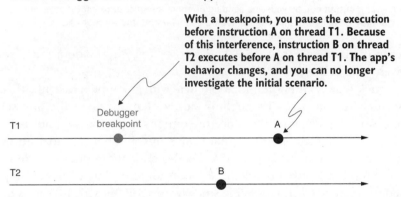

Figure 1.6   A Heisenberg execution. In a multithreaded app, when a debugger interferes with the app's execution, it might change how the app behaves. This change doesn't allow you to correctly investigate the initial app behavior that you wanted to research.

For multithreaded functionality, we have a large variety of cases. That's what makes such scenarios, in my opinion, the most difficult to test. Sometimes a profiler is a good option, but even the profiler might interfere with the app's execution, so that may not work either. Another alternative is to use logging (which we discuss in chapter 5) in the app. For certain issues, you can find a way to reduce the number of threads to one so that you can use a debugger for the investigation.

SCENARIO 4: SENDING THE WRONG CALLS TO A GIVEN SERVICE

You may need to investigate a scenario in which the app doesn't correctly interact with another system component or an external system. Suppose your app sends HTTP requests to another app. You get notified by the maintainers of the second app that the HTTP requests don't have the right format (maybe a header is missing or the request body contains wrong data). Figure 1.7 visually presents this case.

This is a *wrong output* scenario. How could you approach it? First, you need to identify what part of the code sends the requests. If you already know, you can use a debugger to investigate how the app creates the request and identify what is going wrong. If you need to find what part of the app sends a request, you may need to use a profiler,

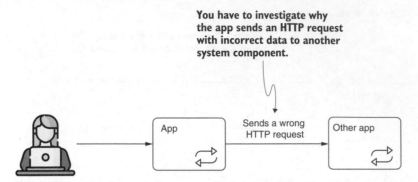

Figure 1.7   A wrong output can be your app sending erroneous requests to another system component. You may be asked to investigate such a behavior and find its root cause.

as you'll learn in chapters 6 through 9. You can use a profiler to determine what code acts at a given time in the execution process.

Here's a trick I always use when I have to deal with a complex case like this one, in which, for some reason, I can't straightforwardly identify where the app sends the request to/from: I replace the other app (the one my app wrongly sends requests to) with a stub. A *stub* is a fake application that I can control to help me identify the issue. For example, to determine what part of the code sends the requests, I can make my stub block the request so my app indefinitely waits for a response. Then, I simply use a profiler to determine what code is being stuck by the stub. Figure 1.8 shows the usage of a stub. Compare this figure to figure 1.7 to understand how the stub replaced the real app.

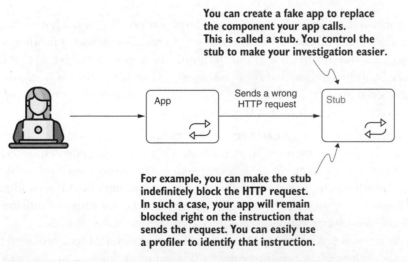

Figure 1.8   You can replace the system component your app calls with a stub. You control the stub to quickly determine where your app sends the request from. You can also use the stub to test your solution after you correct the issue.

1.2.2   Learning certain technologies

Another use of investigative techniques for analyzing code is learning how certain technologies work. Some developers joke that 6 hours of debugging can save 5 minutes of reading the documentation. While it's true that reading documentation is also essential when learning something new, some technologies are too complex to learn just from reading books or the specifications. I always advise my students to dive deeper into a specific framework or library to understand it properly.

TIP For any technology (framework or library) you learn, spend some time reviewing the code you write. Always try to go deeper and debug the framework's code.

I'll start with my favorite, Spring Security. At first glance, Spring Security may seem trivial. It's just implementing authentication and authorization, isn't it? In fact, it is—until you discover the variety of ways to configure these two capabilities into your app. You mix them wrong, and you may get in trouble. When things don't work, you have to deal with what isn't working, and the best choice to deal with what isn't working is by investigating Spring Security's code.

More than anything else, debugging helped me to understand Spring Security. To help others, I put my experience and knowledge into a book, *Spring Security in Action* (Manning, 2020). In it, I provide more than 70 projects for you to not only re-create and run, but also for you to debug. I invite you to debug all examples provided with books you read to learn various technologies.

The second example of a technology I learned mostly through debugging is Hibernate. Hibernate is a high-level framework used for implementing an app's capability to work with a SQL database. Hibernate is one of the best-known and most-used frameworks in the Java world, so it's a must-learn for any Java developer.

Learning Hibernate's basics is easy, and you can do this by simply reading books. But in the real world, using Hibernate (the how and the where) includes so much more than the basics. And for me, without digging deep into Hibernate's code, I definitely wouldn't have learned as much about this framework as I know today.

My advice for you is simple: for any technology (framework or library) you learn, spend some time reviewing the code you write. Always try to go deeper and debug the framework's code. This will make you a better developer.

1.2.3   Clarifying slowness

Performance issues occur now and then in apps, and, like any other problem, you need to investigate them before you know how to solve them. Learning the proper use of different debugging techniques to identify the causes of performance issues is vital.

In my experience, the most frequent performance issues that occur in apps are related to how quickly an app responds. However, even if most developers consider slowness and performance equal, that's not the case. Slowness problems (situations in which an app responds slowly to a given trigger) are just one kind of performance issue.

For example, I once had to debug a mobile app that was consuming the device's battery too quickly. I had an Android app using a library that connected to an external device via Bluetooth. For some reason, the library was creating lots of threads without closing them. These threads, which remain open and run without purpose, are called *zombie threads* and typically cause performance and memory issues. They are also usually challenging to investigate.

However, this type of issue in which the battery is being consumed too fast is also an app performance issue. An app using too much network bandwidth while transferring data over the network is another good example of a performance issue.

Let's stick to slowness problems, which are the most often encountered. Many developers fear slowness problems. Usually, that's not because those problems are difficult to identify, but because they can be challenging to solve. Finding the cause of a performance problem is usually an easy job with a profiler, as you'll learn in chapters 6 through 9. In addition to identifying which code executes, as discussed in section 1.2.1, a profiler also displays the time the app spends on each instruction (figure 1.9).

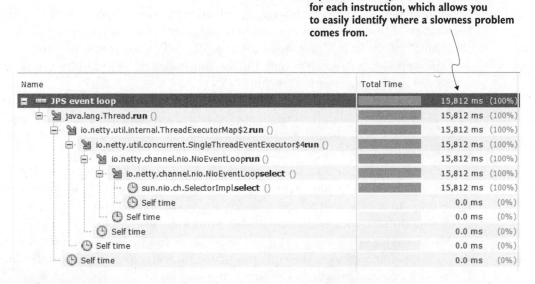

A profiler shows you the execution time for each instruction, which allows you to easily identify where a slowness problem comes from.

Name	Total Time	
JPS event loop	15,812 ms	(100%)
java.lang.Thread.**run** ()	15,812 ms	(100%)
io.netty.util.internal.ThreadExecutorMap$2**run** ()	15,812 ms	(100%)
io.netty.util.concurrent.SingleThreadEventExecutor$4**run** ()	15,812 ms	(100%)
io.netty.channel.nio.NioEventLoop**run** ()	15,812 ms	(100%)
io.netty.channel.nio.NioEventLoop**select** ()	15,812 ms	(100%)
sun.nio.ch.SelectorImpl.**select** ()	15,812 ms	(100%)
Self time	0.0 ms	(0%)
Self time	0.0 ms	(0%)
Self time	0.0 ms	(0%)
Self time	0.0 ms	(0%)
Self time	0.0 ms	(0%)

Figure 1.9   Investigating slowness problems with a profiler. The profiler shows you the time spent on each instruction during code execution. This profiler feature is excellent for identifying the root causes of performance problems.

In many cases, slowness problems are caused by I/O calls, such as reading or writing from a file or a database or sending data over the network. For this reason, developers often act empirically to find the cause of the problem. If you know what capability is affected, you can focus on the I/O calls that capability executes. This approach also helps in minimizing the scope of the problem, but you usually still need a tool to identify its exact location.

1.2.4   Understanding app crashes

Sometimes apps completely stop responding for various reasons. These kinds of problems are usually considered more challenging to investigate than others. In many cases, app crashes occur only under specific conditions, so you can't reproduce (make the problem happen on purpose) them in the local environment.

Every time you investigate a problem, you should first try to reproduce it in an environment where you can study the problem. This approach gives your investigation more flexibility and helps you to confirm your solution. However, we're not always lucky enough to be able to reproduce a problem. And app crashes are usually not easy to reproduce.

We find app crash scenarios in two main flavors:

- The app completely stops.
- The app still runs but doesn't respond to requests.

When the app completely stops, it's usually because it encountered an error from which it couldn't recover. Most often, a memory error causes such behavior. For a Java app, the situation in which the heap memory fills and the app no longer works is represented by an `OutOfMemoryError` message.

To investigate heap memory issues, we use *heap dumps*, which provide a snapshot of what the heap memory contains at a specific time. You can configure a Java process to automatically generate such a snapshot when an `OutOfMemoryError` message occurs and the app crashes.

Heap dumps are powerful tools that give you plenty of details about how an app internally processes the data. We'll discuss more about how to use them in chapter 11. But let's take a quick look at a short example.

Listing 1.2 shows you a small code snippet that fills the memory with instances of a class named `Product`. You can find this app in project da-ch1-ex2 provided with the book. The app continuously adds `Product` instances to a list, causing an intended `OutOfMemoryError` message.

> **Listing 1.2   An app example causing an `OutOfMemoryError` message**

```
public class Main {

    private static List<Product> products =      ⟵┐  We declare a list that stores
        new ArrayList<>();                              references of Product objects.
```

```
public static void main(String[] args) {
  while (true) {
    products.add(
      new Product(UUID.randomUUID().toString()));
    }
  }
}
```

We continuously add Product instances to the list until the heap memory completely fills.

Each Product instance has a String attribute. We use a unique random identifier as its value.

Figure 1.10 shows a heap dump created for one execution of this app. You can easily see that `Product` and `String` instances fill most of the heap memory. A heap dump is like a map of the memory. It gives you many details, including the relationships between instances as well as values. For example, even if you don't see the code, you can still notice a connection between the `Product` and the `String` instances based on how close the numbers of these instances are. Don't worry if these aspects look complex. We'll discuss in detail everything you need to know about using heap dumps in chapter 11.

Most of the memory is filled with String and Product objects.

The number of String instances is close to the number of Product instances, so a relationship between them is possible.

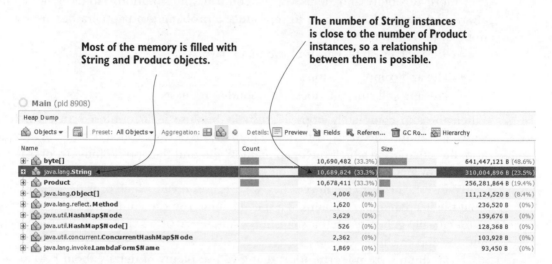

Figure 1.10   A heap dump is like a map of the heap memory. If you learn how to read it, it gives you invaluable clues about how the app internally processes data. A heap dump helps you investigate memory problems or performance issues. In this example, you can easily find which object fills most of the app's memory and that the `Product` and `String` instances are related.

If the app still runs but stops responding to requests, then a *thread dump* is the best tool to analyze what is happening. Figure 1.11 shows you an example of a thread dump and some of the details this tool provides. In chapter 10, we'll discuss generating and analyzing thread dumps to investigate code.

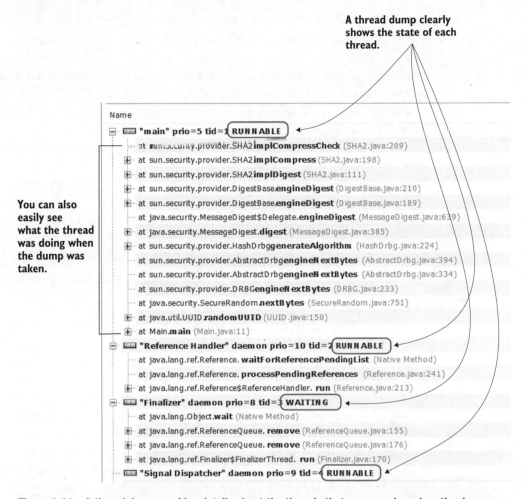

A thread dump clearly shows the state of each thread.

You can also easily see what the thread was doing when the dump was taken.

Figure 1.11 A thread dump provides details about the threads that were running when the dump was taken. It includes thread states and the stack traces, which tell you what the threads were executing or what blocked them. These details are valuable for investigating why an app is stuck or is having performance problems.

1.3 What you will learn in this book

This book is for Java developers with various levels of experience, from beginners to experts. You'll learn various code investigation techniques, the best scenarios in which to apply them, and how to apply them to save you troubleshooting and investigation time.

If you are a junior developer, you'll most likely learn many things from this book. Some developers master all these techniques only after years of experience; others never master them. If you are already an expert, you may find many things you already know, but you still have a good chance of finding new and exciting approaches you may not have had the opportunity to encounter.

When you finish the book, you will have learned the following skills:

- Applying different approaches to using a debugger to understand an app's logic or find an issue
- Investigating hidden functionality with a profiler to better understand how your app or a specific dependency of your app works
- Analyzing code techniques to determine whether your app or one of its dependencies causes a certain problem
- Investigating data in an app's memory snapshot to identify potential problems with how the app processes data
- Using logging to identify problems in an app's behavior or to identify security breaches
- Using remote debugging to identify problems you can't reproduce in a different environment
- Correctly choosing what app investigation techniques to use to make your investigation faster

Summary

- You can use various investigation techniques to analyze software behavior.
- Depending on your situation, one investigation technique may work better than another. You need to know how to choose the correct approach to make your investigation more efficient.
- For some scenarios, using a combination of techniques helps you to identify a problem faster. Learning how each analyzing technique works gives you an excellent advantage in dealing with complex problems.
- In many cases, developers use investigation techniques to learn new things rather than to solve problems. When learning complex frameworks such as Spring Security or Hibernate, simply reading books or the documentation isn't enough. An excellent way to accelerate your learning is to debug examples that use a technology you want to better understand.
- A situation is easier to investigate if you can reproduce it in an environment where you can study it. Reproducing a problem not only helps you find its root cause more easily, but it also helps you to confirm that a solution works when it is applied.

Understanding your app's logic through debugging techniques

2

This chapter covers
- When to use a debugger and when to avoid it
- Using a debugger to investigate code

Not long ago, during one of my piano lessons, I shared the sheet music of a song I wanted to learn with my piano teacher. I was so impressed when he just played the song while reading the music sheet for the first time. "How cool is that?" I thought. "How does someone gain this skill?"

Then, I remembered some years ago I was in a peer-programming session with one of the newly hired juniors in the company I was working for. It was my turn at the keyboard, and we were investigating a relatively large and complex piece of code using a debugger. I started navigating through the code, pressing relatively quickly the keyboard keys that allowed me to step over, into, and out of specific lines of code. I was focused on the code but was quite calm and relaxed, almost forgetting I had someone near me (rude of me). I heard this person say, "Wow, stop a bit. You're too fast. Can you even read that code?"

I realized that situation was similar to my experience with my piano teacher. How can you gain this skill? The answer is easier than you thought: work hard and gain experience. While practicing is invaluable and takes a lot of time, I have some tips to share with you that will help you to improve your technique much faster. In this chapter, we discuss one of the most important tools used in understanding code: the debugger.

DEFINITION A debugger is a tool that allows you to pause the execution on specific lines and manually execute each instruction while observing how the data changes.

Using a debugger is like navigating with Google Maps: it helps you find your way through complex logic implemented in your code. It's also the most used tool for understanding code.

A debugger is usually the first tool a developer learns to use to help them understand what code does. Fortunately, all IDEs come with a debugger, so you don't have to do anything special to have one. In this book, I use IntelliJ IDEA Community in my examples, but any other IDE is quite similar and offers (sometimes with a different look) the same options we'll discuss. Although a debugger seems to be a tool most developers know how to use, you may find, in this chapter and in chapter 3, some new techniques for using one.

We'll start in section 2.1 by discussing how developers read code and why, in many cases, simply reading the code isn't enough to understand it. Enter the debugger or a profiler (which we discuss later, in chapters 6–9). In section 2.2, we continue the discussion by applying the simplest techniques for using a debugger with an example.

If you are an experienced developer, you might already know these techniques. But, you may still find it useful to read through the chapter as a refresher, or you could go straight to the more advanced techniques for using a debugger that we'll discuss in chapter 3.

OK! Let's see!

2.1 *When analyzing code is not enough*

Let's start by discussing how to read code and why sometimes reading just the logic isn't enough to understand it. In this section, I'll explain how reading code works and how it is different from reading something else, like a story or a poem. To observe this difference and understand what causes the complexity in deciphering code, we'll use a code snippet that implements a short piece of logic. Understanding what's behind the way our brain interprets code helps you to realize the need for tools such as a debugger.

Any code investigation scene starts with reading the code. But reading code is different from reading poetry. When reading a verse, you move through text line by line in a given linear order, letting your brain assemble and picture the meaning. If you read the same verse twice, you might understand different things.

With code, however, it's the opposite. First, code is not linear. When reading code, you don't simply go line by line. Instead, you jump in and out of instructions to understand how they affect the data being processed. Reading code is more like a maze than a straight road. And, if you're not attentive, you might get lost and forget where you started. Second, unlike a poem, the code always and for everyone means the same thing. That meaning is the objective of your investigation.

Just like you'd use a compass to find your path, a debugger helps you more easily identify what your code does. As an example, we'll use the `decode(List<Integer> input)` method. You can find this code in project da-ch2-ex1 provided with the book.

Listing 2.1 An example of a method to debug

```java
public class Decoder {

  public Integer decode(List<String> input) {
    int total = 0;
    for (String s : input) {
      var digits = new StringDigitExtractor(s).extractDigits();
      total += digits.stream().collect(Collectors.summingInt(i -> i));
    }

    return total;
  }
}
```

If you read from the top line to the bottom line, you have to assume how some things work to understand it. Are those instructions really doing what you think they're doing? When you are not sure, you have to dive deeper and observe what the code actually does—you have to analyze the logic behind it. Figure 2.1 points out two of the uncertainties in the given code snippet:

- What does the `StringDigitExtractor()` constructor do? It might just create an object, or it might also do something else. It could be that it somehow changes the value of the given parameter.

- What is the result of calling the `extractDigits()` method? Does it return a list of digits? Does it also change the parameter inside the object we used when creating the `StringDigitsExtractor` constructor?

Does this constructor only create an object, or does it also do something else?

```
public class Decoder {

  public Integer decode(List<String> input) {
    int total = 0;
    for (String s : input) {
      var digits = new StringDigitExtractor(s).extractDigits();
      total += digits.stream().collect(Collectors.summingInt(i -> i));
    }

    return total;
  }
}
```

What does this method really do? Does it use the String parameter value?

Figure 2.1   When reading a piece of code, you often need to figure out what happens behind the scenes in some of the instructions composing that logic. The method names are not always suggestive enough, and you can't totally rely on them. Instead, you need to go deeper into what these methods do.

Even with a small piece of code, you may have to dive deeper into the instructions. Each new code instruction you examine creates a new investigation plan and adds to its cognitive complexity (figures 2.2 and 2.3). The deeper you go into the logic and the more plans you open, the more complex the process becomes.

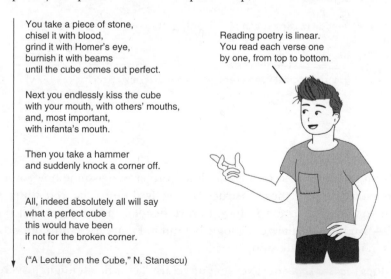

You take a piece of stone,
chisel it with blood,
grind it with Homer's eye,
burnish it with beams
until the cube comes out perfect.

Next you endlessly kiss the cube
with your mouth, with others' mouths,
and, most important,
with infanta's mouth.

Then you take a hammer
and suddenly knock a corner off.

All, indeed absolutely all will say
what a perfect cube
this would have been
if not for the broken corner.

("A Lecture on the Cube," N. Stanescu)

Reading poetry is linear.
You read each verse one
by one, from top to bottom.

Figure 2.2   Compare how you read poetry with how you read code. You read poetry line by line, but when you read code, you jump around.

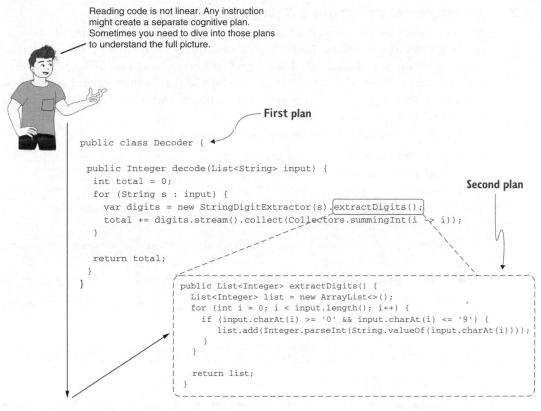

Reading code is not linear. Any instruction might create a separate cognitive plan. Sometimes you need to dive into those plans to understand the full picture.

First plan

```java
public class Decoder {

  public Integer decode(List<String> input) {
    int total = 0;
    for (String s : input) {
      var digits = new StringDigitExtractor(s).extractDigits();
      total += digits.stream().collect(Collectors.summingInt(i -> i));
    }

    return total;
  }
}
```

Second plan

```java
public List<Integer> extractDigits() {
  List<Integer> list = new ArrayList<>();
  for (int i = 0; i < input.length(); i++) {
    if (input.charAt(i) >= '0' && input.charAt(i) <= '9') {
      list.add(Integer.parseInt(String.valueOf(input.charAt(i))));
    }
  }

  return list;
}
```

Figure 2.3 Reading code is different from reading poetry and is much more complex. You can imagine reading code as reading in two dimensions. One dimension is reading a piece of code top to bottom. The second dimension is going into a specific instruction to understand it in detail. Trying to remember how things work for each plan and how it assembles makes understanding code just by reading it very difficult.

Reading poetry always has one path. Code analysis instead creates many paths through the same piece of logic. The fewer new plans you open, the less complex the process is. You must choose between skipping over a certain instruction, making the overall investigation process simpler, or going into detail to better understand each individual instruction and raise the process complexity.

TIP Always try to shorten the reading path by minimizing the number of plans you open for investigation. Use a debugger to help you more easily navigate the code, keep track of where you are, and observe how the app changes the data while executing.

2.2   *Investigating code with a debugger*

In this section, we discuss a tool that can help you to minimize the cognitive effort of reading code to understand how it works—a debugger. All IDEs provide a debugger, and even if the interface might look slightly different from one IDE to another, the options are generally the same. I'll use IntelliJ IDEA Community in this book, but I encourage you to use your favorite IDE and compare it with the examples in the book. You'll find they are pretty similar.

A debugger simplifies the investigation process by

- Providing you with a means to pause the execution at a particular step and execute each instruction manually at your own pace
- Showing you where you are and where you came from in the code's reading path; this way, the debugger works as a map you can use, rather than trying to remember all the details
- Showing you the values that variables hold, making the investigation easier to visualize and to process
- Allowing you to try things on the fly by using watchers and evaluating expressions

Let's take the example in project da-ch2-ex1 again and use the most straightforward debugger capabilities to understand the code.

Listing 2.2   **A piece of code we want to understand**

```java
public class Decoder {

  public Integer decode(List<String> input) {
    int total = 0;
    for (String s : input) {
      var digits = new StringDigitExtractor(s).extractDigits();
      total += digits.stream().collect(Collectors.summingInt(i -> i));
    }

    return total;
  }
}
```

I'm sure you're wondering, "How do I know when to use a debugger?" This is a fair question I want to answer before going any further. The main prerequisite is *knowing what piece of logic you want to investigate*. As you'll learn in this section, the first step in using a debugger is selecting an instruction where you want the execution to pause.

NOTE Unless you already know which instruction you need to start your investigation from, you can't use a debugger.

In the real world, you'll find cases in which you don't know up front the specific piece of logic you want to investigate. In this case, before you can use a debugger, you need to apply different techniques to find the part of the code you want to investigate using the debugger (which we'll address in later chapters). In this chapter and chapter 3, we'll focus only on using the debugger, so we'll assume you somehow found the piece of code you want to understand.

Going back to our example, where do we start? First, we need to read the code and figure out what we do and don't understand. Once we identify where the logic becomes unclear, we can execute the app and "tell" the debugger to pause the execution. We can pause the execution on those lines of code that are not clear to observe how they change the data. To "tell" the debugger where to pause the app's execution, we use *breakpoints*.

 **DEFINITION**   A breakpoint is a marker we use on lines where we want the debugger to pause the execution so that we can investigate the implemented logic. The debugger will pause the execution before executing the line marked with the breakpoint.

In figure 2.4, I shaded the code that is pretty easy to understand (considering you know the language fundamentals). As you can see, this code takes a list as an input, parses the list, processes each item in it, and somehow calculates an integer that the method returns in the end. Moreover, the process the method implements is easy to ascertain without a debugger.

**1. The method takes a list
   of strings as a parameter.**

```
public class Decoder {

  public Integer decode(List<String> input) {
    int total = 0;
    for (String s : input) {
      var digits = new StringDigitExtractor(s).extractDigits();
      total += digits.stream().collect(Collectors.summingInt(i -> i));
    }

    return total;
  }
}
```

**2. The method iterates
   over the List parameter.**

**3. The method returns an
   integer value, which is a sum
   of something calculated for each
   string in the List parameter.**

Figure 2.4   Assuming you know the language fundamentals, you can easily see that this code takes a collection as an input and parses the collection to calculate an integer.

In figure 2.5, I shaded the lines that usually cause difficulties in understanding what the method does. These lines of code are more challenging to decipher because they hide their own implemented logic. You may recognize `digits.stream().collect(Collectors.summingInt(i -> i))` as it's been part of the Stream API provided with the JDK since Java 8. But we can't say the same thing about `new StringDigit-Extractor(s).extractDigits()`. Because this is part of the app we are investigating, this instruction might do anything.

The way a developer chooses to write the code may also add additional complexity. For example, starting with Java 10, developers can infer the type of a local variable using `var`. Inferring the variable type is not always a wise choice because it can make the code even more difficult to read (figure 2.5), bringing one more scenario in which using the debugger would be useful.

TIP When investigating code with a debugger, start from the first line of code that you can't figure out.

While training junior developers and students over the past many years, I have observed that in many cases they start debugging on the first line of a specific code block. While you certainly can do this, it's more efficient if you first read the code without the debugger and try to figure out whether you can understand the code. Then, start debugging directly from the point that causes difficulties. This approach will save you time since you may find out you don't need the debugger to understand what happens in a specific piece of logic. After all, even if you use the debugger, you only need to go over the code you don't understand.

In some scenarios, you add a breakpoint on a line because its intent is not obvious. Sometimes your app throws an exception; you see that in the logs, but you don't know which previous line is causing the problem. In this case, you can add a breakpoint to pause the app's execution just before it throws the exception. But the idea stays the same: avoid pausing the execution of the instructions you understand. Instead, use breakpoints for the lines of code you want to focus on.

For this example, we will start by adding a breakpoint on line 11, presented in figure 2.6:

```
var digits = new StringDigitExtractor(s).extractDigits();
```

Generally, to add a breakpoint on a line in any IDE, you click on or near the line number (or even better, use a keyboard shortcut; for IntelliJ, you can use Ctrl-F8 for Windows/Linux, or Command-F8 for macOS). The breakpoint will be displayed with a

What happens for every string in the list? How is the String turned into a number?

```java
public class Decoder {

  public Integer decode(List<String> input) {
    int total = 0;
    for (String s : input) {
      var digits = new StringDigitExtractor(s).extractDigits();
      total += digits.stream().collect(Collectors.summingInt(i -> i));
    }

    return total;
  }
}
```

Figure 2.5 In this piece of code, I shaded the lines of code that are more difficult to understand. When you use a debugger, add the first breakpoint on the first line that makes the code more challenging to understand.

circle, as presented in figure 2.6. Make sure you run your application with the debugger. In IntelliJ, look for a button represented as a small bug icon near the one you use to start the app. You can also right-click the main class file and use the Debug button in the context menu. When the execution reaches the line you marked with a breakpoint, it pauses, allowing you to navigate further manually.

1. Add a breakpoint on the line where you want the debugger to stop the execution. This line should be the first instruction that creates concerns.

2. Run the app with the debugger.

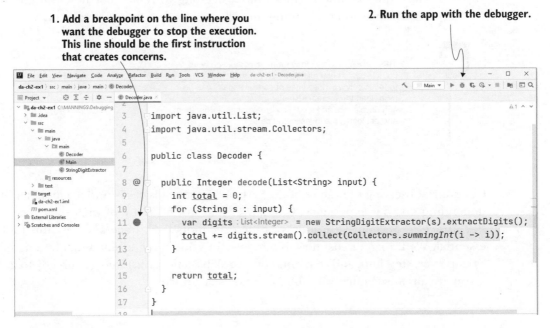

Figure 2.6 Click near the line number to add a breakpoint on a specific line. Then, run the app with the debugger. The execution pauses on the line you marked with a breakpoint and allows you to control it manually.

Since the shortcuts can change and differ depending on the operating system you use (some developers even prefer to customize them), I'm not usually going to discuss them. However, I advise you to check your IDE's manual and learn to use the keyboard shortcuts.

> **NOTE**   Remember, you always need to execute the app using the Debug option to have an active debugger. If you use the Run option, the breakpoints won't be considered since the IDE doesn't attach the debugger to the running process. Some IDEs may run your app by default as well as attach the debugger, but if that's not the case (like for IntelliJ or Eclipse), then the app execution won't pause at the breakpoints you define.

When the debugger pauses the code execution on a specific instruction from the line you mark with a breakpoint, you can use the valuable information the IDE displays. In figure 2.7, you can see that my IDE displays two essential pieces of information:

- *The value of all the variables in scope*—Knowing all the variables in scope and their values helps you understand what data is being processed and how the logic affects the data. Remember that the execution is paused before the execution of the line marked with a breakpoint, so the data state remains the same.
- *The execution stack trace*—This shows you how the app executes the line of code where the debugger paused the execution. Each line in the stack trace is a method involved in the calling chain. The execution stack trace helps you to visualize the execution path, without needing to remember how you got to a specific instruction when using the debugger to navigate through code.

TIP You can add as many breakpoints as you want, but it is best to use a limited number at a time and to focus only on those lines of code. I usually use no more than three breakpoints at the same time. I often see developers add too many breakpoints, forget them, and get lost in the investigated code.

Generally, observing the values of the variables in scope is easily understandable. But, depending on your experience, you may or may not be aware of what the execution stack trace is. Section 2.2.1 addresses the execution stack trace and why this tool is essential. We'll then discuss how to navigate the code using essential operations such as step over, step into, and step out. You can skip section 2.2.1 and go directly to 2.2.2 if you are already familiar with the execution stack trace.

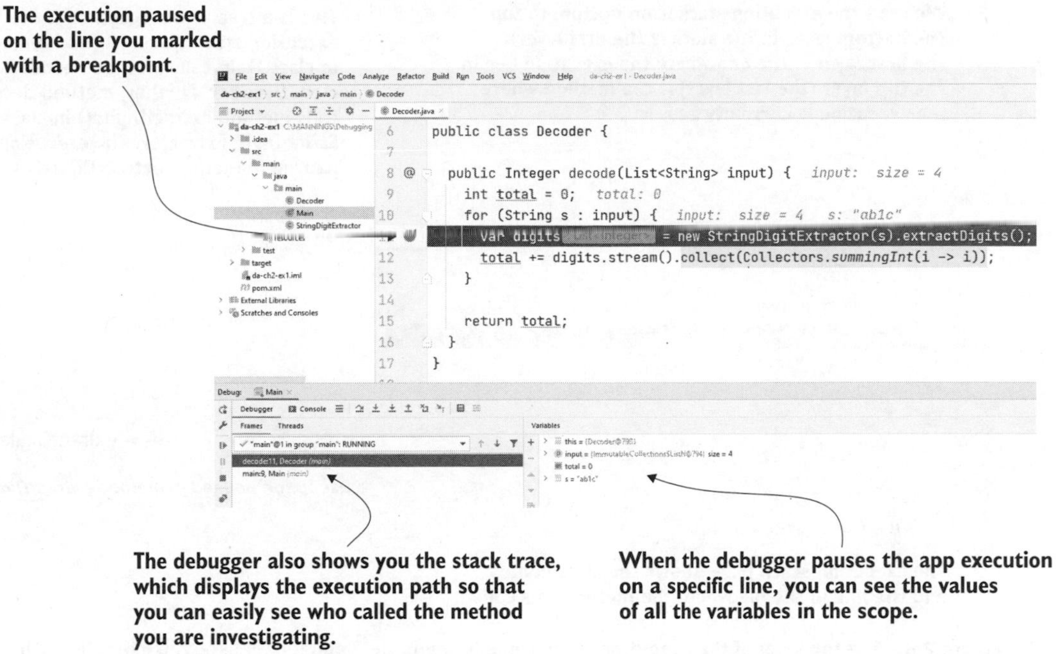

The execution paused on the line you marked with a breakpoint.

The debugger also shows you the stack trace, which displays the execution path so that you can easily see who called the method you are investigating.

When the debugger pauses the app execution on a specific line, you can see the values of all the variables in the scope.

Figure 2.7 When the execution is paused on a given line of code, you can see all the variables in scope and their values. You can also use the execution stack trace to remember where you are as you navigate through the lines of code.

2.2.1 What is the execution stack trace, and how do I use it?

The execution stack trace is a valuable tool you use to understand the code while debugging it. Just like a map, the execution stack trace shows you the execution's path to the specific line of code where the debugger paused it and helps you to decide where to navigate further.

Figure 2.8 provides a comparison of the execution stack trace and the execution in a tree format. The stack trace shows how methods called one another up to the point where the debugger paused the execution. In the stack trace, you can find the method names, the class names, and the lines that caused the calls.

One of my favorite uses of the execution stack trace is finding hidden logic in the execution path. In most cases, developers use the execution stack trace simply to understand where a certain method has been called from. But you also need to consider that apps that use frameworks (such as Spring, Hibernate, etc.) sometimes alter the execution chain of the method.

For example, Spring apps often use code that is decoupled in what is called *aspects* (in Java/Jakarta EE terminology, they are named *interceptors*). These aspects implement logic that the framework uses to augment the execution of specific methods in certain conditions. Unfortunately, such logic is often difficult to observe since you

We read the execution stack from bottom to top.
The bottom layer in the stack is the first layer.
The first layer is the one where the execution began.
The top layer (the last layer) is the method where
the execution is currently paused.

This is a tree representation of the
execution stack trace. Method main()
in class Main calls method decode() in
class Decoder. Further, method decode()
calls method extractDigits() in class
StringDigitsExtractor. The execution is
paused in method extractDigits().

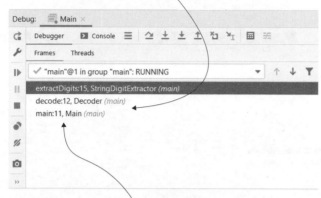

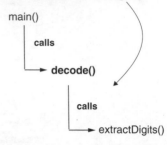

Execution paused in method extractDigits()

The execution stack trace shows the class names
and the line in the file where the method was called.

Figure 2.8   The top layer of the execution stack trace is where the debugger paused the execution. All other layers in the execution stack trace are where the methods represented by the above layers were called. The bottom layer of the stack trace (the first layer) is where the execution of the current thread began.

can't see the aspect code directly in the call chain when reading the code (figure 2.9). This characteristic makes it challenging to investigate a given capability.

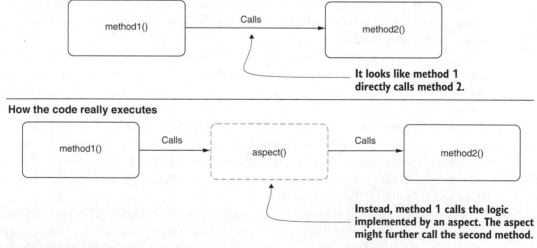

Figure 2.9   An aspect logic is completely decoupled from the code. For this reason, when reading the code, it is difficult to see that there's more logic that will execute. Such cases of hidden logic executing can be confusing when investigating a certain capability.

Let's take a code example to examine this behavior and how the execution stack trace is helpful in such cases. You can find this example in project da-ch2-ex2 provided with the book (appendix B provides a refresher for opening the project and starting the app). The project is a small Spring app that prints the value of the parameter in the console.

Listings 2.3, 2.4, and 2.5 show the implementation of these three classes. As presented in listing 2.3, the `main()` method calls `ProductController`'s `saveProduct()` method, sending the parameter value `"Beer"`.

Listing 2.3   The main class calls the `ProductController`'s `saveProduct()` method

```
public class Main {

  public static void main(String[] args) {
    try (var c =
      new AnnotationConfigApplicationContext(ProjectConfig.class)) {
      c.getBean(ProductController.class).saveProduct("Beer");
    }
  }
}
```

> We call the saveProduct() method with the parameter value "Beer".

In listing 2.4, you can see that `ProductController`'s `saveProduct()` method simply calls the `ProductService`'s `saveProduct()` method with the received parameter value.

Listing 2.4   `ProductController` calling `ProductService`

```
@Component
public class ProductController {

  private final ProductService productService;

  public ProductController(ProductService productService) {
    this.productService = productService;
  }

  public void saveProduct(String name) {
    productService.saveProduct(name);
  }
}
```

> ProductController calls the service and sends the parameter value.

Listing 2.5 shows the `ProductService`'s `saveProduct()` method that prints the parameter value in the console.

Listing 2.5   `ProductService` printing the value of the parameter

```
@Component
public class ProductService {

  public void saveProduct(String name) {
```

```
        System.out.println("Saving product " + name);
    }
}
```
                                                                    Prints the parameter
                                                                    value in the console

As presented in figure 2.10, the flow is quite simple:

1   The main() method calls the saveProduct() method of a bean named Pro-
    ductController, sending the value "Beer" as a parameter.

2   Then, the ProductController's saveProduct() method calls the savePro-
    uct() method of another bean, ProductService.

3   The ProductService bean prints the value of the parameter in the console.

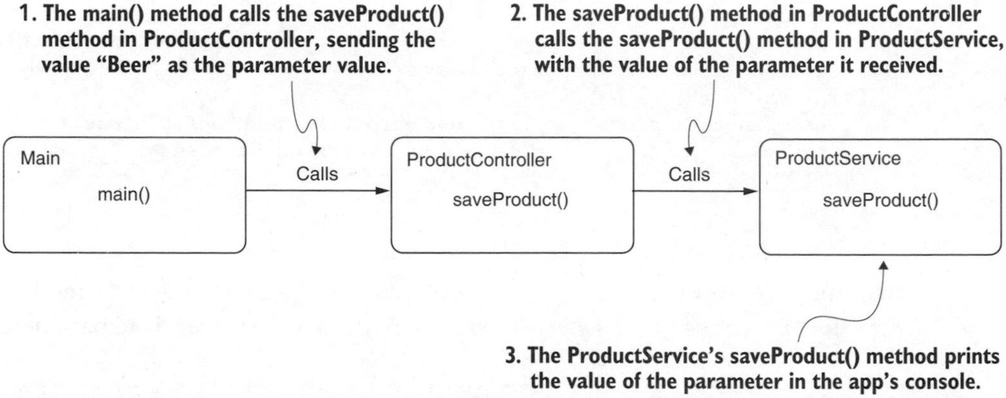

1. The main() method calls the saveProduct()
method in ProductController, sending the
value "Beer" as the parameter value.

2. The saveProduct() method in ProductController
calls the saveProduct() method in ProductService,
with the value of the parameter it received.

3. The ProductService's saveProduct() method prints
the value of the parameter in the app's console.

Figure 2.10   Method main() calls saveProduct() of bean ProductController, sending the
value "Beer" as the parameter value. The ProductController's saveProduct() method calls
the ProductService bean, sending the same parameter value as the one it receives. The Product-
Service bean prints the parameter value in the console. The expectation is that "Beer" will be printed
in the console.

Naturally, you would assume the following message is printed when you run the app:

```
Saving product Beer
```

However, when you run the project, the message is different:

```
Saving product Chocolate
```

How is that possible? To answer this question, the first thing to do is use the execution
stack trace to find out who changed the parameter value. Add a breakpoint on the line
that prints a different value than you expect, run the app with the debugger, and
observe the execution stack trace (figure 2.11). Instead of having the ProductService's
saveProduct() method from the ProductController bean, you find that an aspect
alters the execution. If you review the aspect class, you will, indeed, see that the aspect
is responsible for replacing "Beer" with "Chocolate" (listing 2.6).

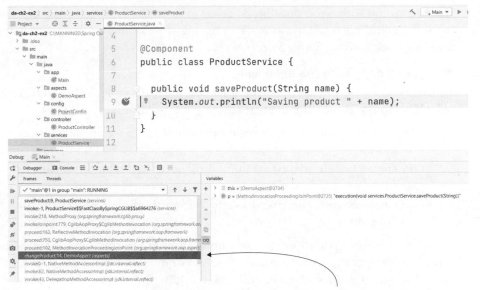

**The execution stack trace is much larger than you would expect
when reading the code. It clearly shows that ProductService's
saveProduct() method is not called directly from ProductController.
Somehow, an aspect executes in between the two methods.**

Figure 2.11 The execution stack trace shows that an aspect has altered the execution. This aspect
is the reason that the value of the parameter changes. Without using the stack trace, finding why the
app has a different behavior than expected would be more difficult.

The following code shows the aspect that alters the execution by replacing the value
`ProductController` sends to `ProductService`.

Listing 2.6   The aspect logic that alters the execution

```
@Aspect
@Component
public class DemoAspect {

  @Around("execution(* services.ProductService.saveProduct(..))")
  public void changeProduct(ProceedingJoinPoint p) throws Throwable {
    p.proceed(new Object[] {"Chocolate"});
  }
}
```

Aspects are quite a fascinating and useful feature in Java application frameworks
today. But if you don't use them properly, they can make apps difficult to understand
and maintain. Of course, in this book, we are discussing relevant techniques that can
help you to identify and understand code even in such cases. But, trust me, if you
need to use this technique for an application, it means the application is not easily

maintainable. A clean-coded app (without technical debt) is always a better choice than an app in which you must invest effort to debug later. If you're interested in better understanding how aspects work in Spring, I recommend you read chapter 6 of another book I wrote, *Spring Start Here* (Manning, 2021).

2.2.2 *Navigating code with the debugger*

In this section, we discuss the basic ways you navigate code with a debugger. You'll learn how to use three fundamental navigation operations:

- *Step over*—Continue the execution with the next line of code in the same method.
- *Step into*—Continue the execution inside one of the methods called on the current line.
- *Step out*—Return the execution to the method that called the one you are investigating.

To start the investigation process, you must identify the first line of code where you want the debugger to pause the execution. To understand the logic, you need to navigate through the lines of code and observe how the data changes when different instructions execute.

There are buttons on the GUI and keyboard shortcuts to use the navigation operations in any IDE. Figure 2.12 shows you how these buttons appear in the IntelliJ IDEA Community GUI, the IDE I use.

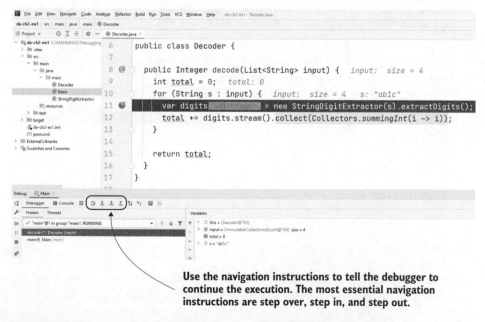

Use the navigation instructions to tell the debugger to continue the execution. The most essential navigation instructions are step over, step in, and step out.

Figure 2.12   The navigation operations help you "walk" through the app logic in a controlled way to identify how the code works. To navigate through code, you can use the buttons on the IDE's GUI or use the keyboard shortcuts associated with these operations.

TIP Even if at the beginning you find it easier to use the buttons on the IDE's GUI, I recommend you use the keyboard shortcuts instead. If you get comfortable using the keyboard shortcuts, you'll see they are much faster than a mouse.

Figure 2.13 visually describes the navigation operations. You can use the step over operation to go to the next line in the same method. Generally, this is the most commonly used navigation operation.

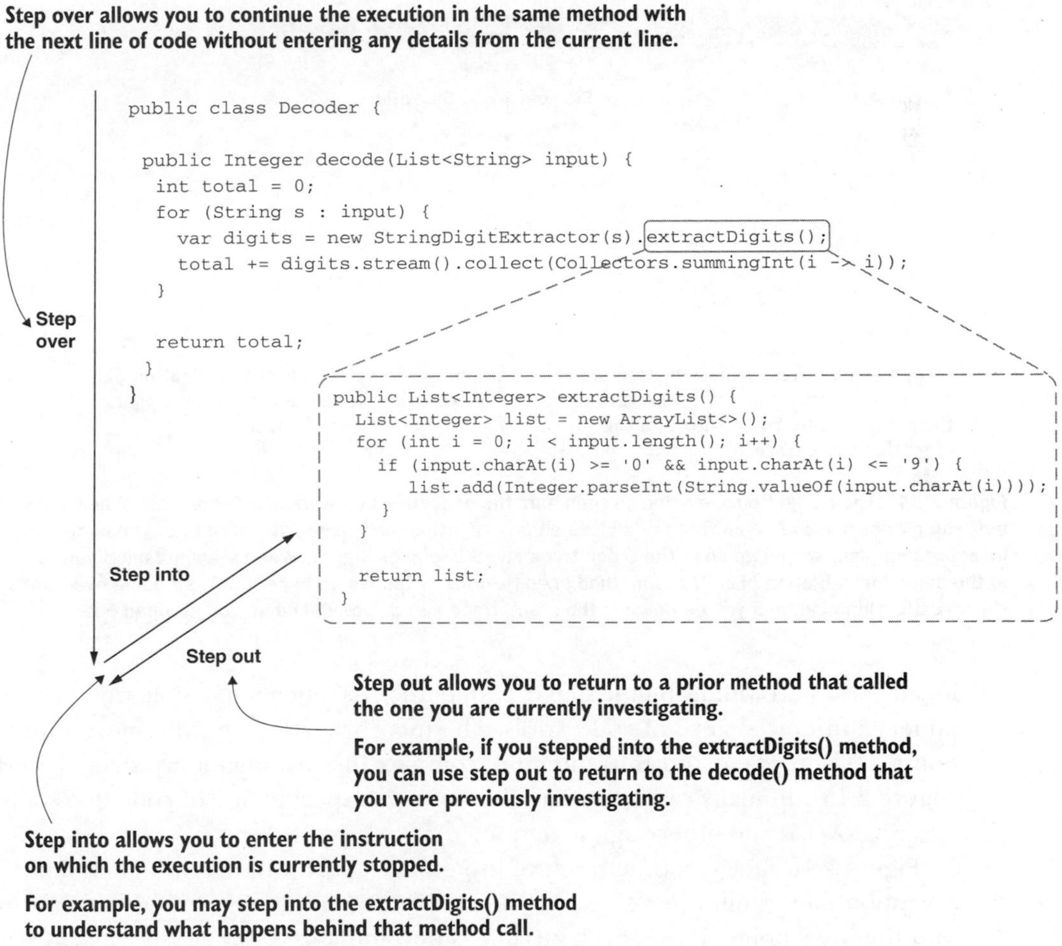

Step over allows you to continue the execution in the same method with the next line of code without entering any details from the current line.

```
public class Decoder {

  public Integer decode(List<String> input) {
    int total = 0;
    for (String s : input) {
      var digits = new StringDigitExtractor(s).extractDigits();
      total += digits.stream().collect(Collectors.summingInt(i -> i));
    }

    return total;
  }
}
```

Step over

```
  public List<Integer> extractDigits() {
    List<Integer> list = new ArrayList<>();
    for (int i = 0; i < input.length(); i++) {
      if (input.charAt(i) >= '0' && input.charAt(i) <= '9') {
        list.add(Integer.parseInt(String.valueOf(input.charAt(i))));
      }
    }

    return list;
  }
```

Step into

Step out

Step out allows you to return to a prior method that called the one you are currently investigating.

For example, if you stepped into the extractDigits() method, you can use step out to return to the decode() method that you were previously investigating.

Step into allows you to enter the instruction on which the execution is currently stopped.

For example, you may step into the extractDigits() method to understand what happens behind that method call.

Figure 2.13 Navigation operations. Stepping over allows you to go to the next instruction in the same method. When you want to start a new investigation plan and go into detail in a specific instruction, you can use the step into operation. You can go back to the previous investigation plan with the step out operation.

Sometimes you need to better understand what happens with a particular instruction. In our example, you may need to enter the extractDigits() method to clearly understand what it does. For such a case, you use the step into operation. When you want to return to the decode() method, you can use step out.

You can also visualize the operations on the execution stack trace, as presented in figure 2.14.

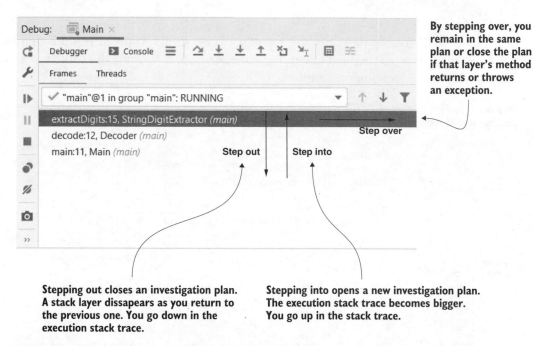

Figure 2.14   The navigation operation as seen from the execution stack trace point of view. When you step out, you go down in the stack trace and close an investigation plan. When you step into, you open a new investigation plan, so you go up in the stack trace and it becomes bigger. When stepping over, you remain in the same investigation plan. If the method ends (returns or throws an exception), stepping over closes the investigation plan, and you go down in the stack trace just as you did when you stepped out.

Ideally, you start with using the step over operation as much as possible when trying to understand how a piece of code works. The more you step into, the more investigation plans you open, and thus the more complex the investigation process becomes (figure 2.15). In many cases, you can deduce what a specific line of code does only by stepping over it and observing the output.

Figure 2.16 shows you the result of using the step over navigation operation. The execution pauses on line 12, one line below where we initially paused the debugger with the breakpoint. The digits variable is now initialized as well, so you can see its value.

Figure 2.15   The movie *Inception* (2010) portrays the idea of dreaming in a dream. The more layers deep you dream, the longer you stay there. You can compare this idea with stepping into a method and opening a new investigation layer. The deeper you step in, the more time you'll spend investigating the code.

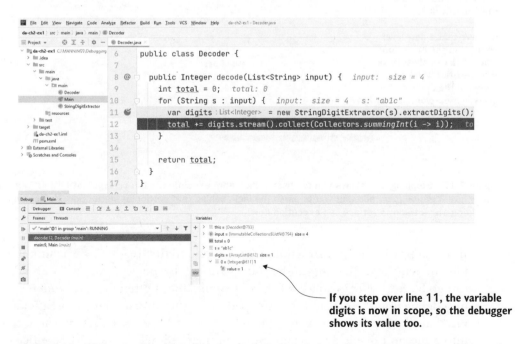

If you step over line 11, the variable digits is now in scope, so the debugger shows its value too.

Figure 2.16   When you step over a line, the execution continues in the same method. In our case, the execution paused on line 12, and you can see the value of the `digits` variable that was initialized by line 11. You can use this value to deduce what line 11 does without having to go into more detail.

Try continuing the execution multiple times. You'll observe that, on line 11, for each string input, the result is a list that contains all the digits in the given string. Often, the logic is easy enough to understand simply by analyzing the outputs for a few executions. But what if you can't figure out what a line does just by executing it?

If you don't understand what happens, you need to go into more detail on that line. This should be your last option since it requires that you open a new investigation plan, which complicates your process. But, when you have no other choice, you can step into an instruction to get more details on what the code does. Figure 2.17 shows you the result of stepping into line 11 of the `Decoder` class:

```
var digits = new StringDigitExtractor(s).extractDigits();
```

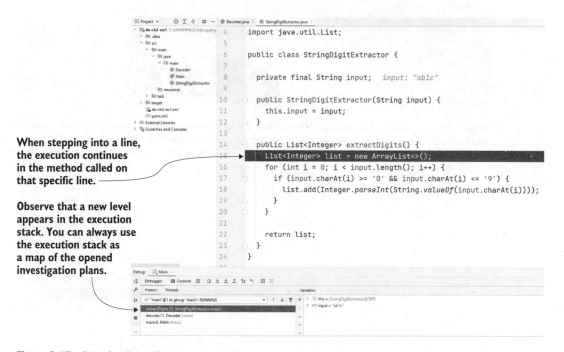

When stepping into a line, the execution continues in the method called on that specific line.

Observe that a new level appears in the execution stack. You can always use the execution stack as a map of the opened investigation plans.

Figure 2.17 Stepping into allows you to observe the entire execution of the current instruction. This opens a new investigation plan, allowing you to parse the logic behind that particular instruction. You can use the execution stack trace to retrace the execution flow.

If you stepped into an instruction, take the time to first read what's behind that code line. In many cases, looking at the code is enough to spot what happens, and then you can go back to where you were before stepping into. I often observe students rushing into debugging the method they stepped into without first taking a breath and reading that piece of code. Why is it important to read the code first? Because stepping into a method opens another investigation plan, so, if you want to be efficient, you have to redo the investigation steps:

1. Read the method and find the first line of code you don't understand.
2. Add a breakpoint on that line of code, and start the investigation from there.

Often, if you stop and read the code, you'll find that you don't need to continue that investigation plan. If you already understand what happens, you simply need to return to where you were previously. And you can do this using the step out operation. Figure 2.18 shows you what happens when using step out from the extractDigits() method: the execution returns to the previous investigation plan in the decode(List <String> input) method.

TIP The step out operation can save you time. When entering a new investigation plan (by stepping into a code line), first read the new piece of code. Step out of the new investigation plan once you understand what the code does.

When you step out of the extractDigits() method, the execution returns to the previous investigation plan.

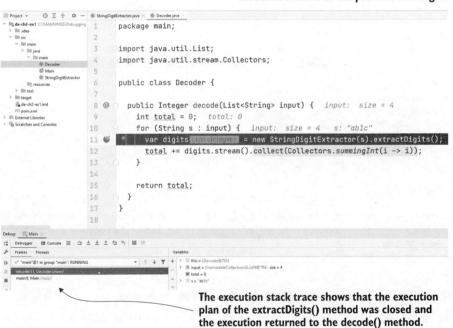

The execution stack trace shows that the execution plan of the extractDigits() method was closed and the execution returned to the decode() method.

Figure 2.18 The step out operation allows you to close an investigation plan and return to the previous one in the execution stack trace. Using step out is helpful to save time since you don't have to step over each instruction until the current execution plan closes by itself. Stepping out offers you a shortcut to return to the previous execution plan you were investigating.

Why is the next execution line not always the next line?

When discussing code navigation with a debugger, I often talk about the "next execution line." I want to make sure I'm clear about the difference between the "next line" and the "next execution line."

The next execution line is the line of code the app executes next. When we say the debugger paused the execution on line 12, the *next line* is always line 13, but the *next execution line* can be different. For example, if line 12 doesn't throw an exception, as shown in the following figure, the next execution line will be 13, but if line 12 throws an exception, the next execution line is line 18. You find this example in project da-ch2-ex3.

When using the step over operation, the execution will continue to the *next execution line*.

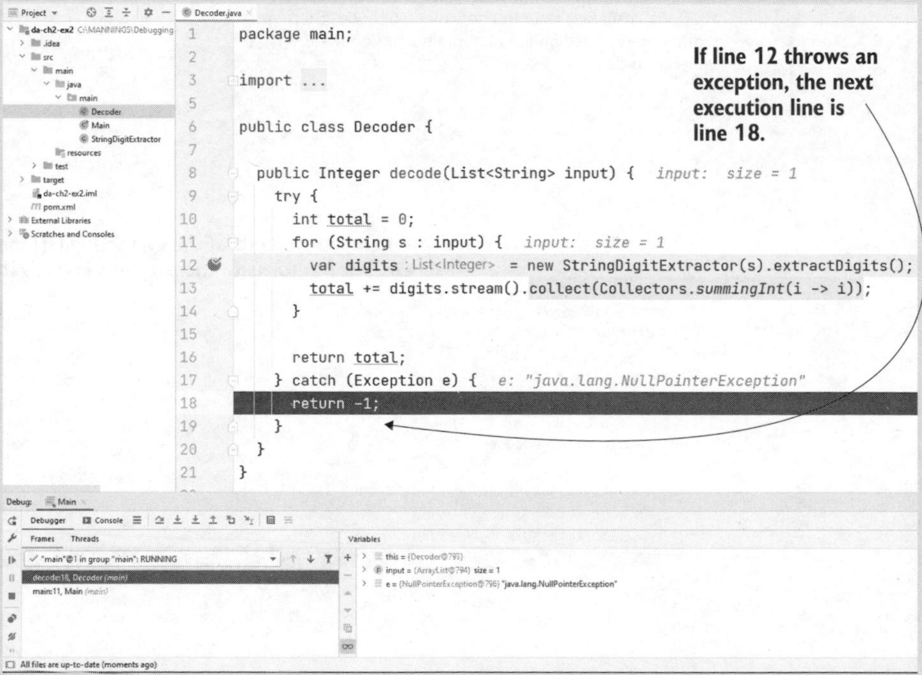

In this figure, we step over from line 12, and line 12 throws an exception; the execution continues on line 18, which is the next execution line. In other words, the next execution line is not always the next line.

2.3   *When using the debugger might not be enough*

The debugger is an excellent tool that can help you to analyze code by navigating through the code to understand how it works with data. But not all code can be investigated with a debugger. In this section, we discuss some scenarios in which using a debugger is not possible or not enough. You need to be aware of these cases so that you don't waste time using a debugger.

Here are some of the most often encountered investigation scenarios when using a debugger (or only a debugger) is usually not the right approach:

- Investigating output problems when you don't know which part of the code creates the output
- Investigating performance problems
- Investigating crashes where the entire app fails
- Investigating multithreaded implementations

 **TIP**   Remember that a critical prerequisite for using a debugger is knowing where to pause the execution.

Before you start debugging, you need to find the part of the code that is generating the wrong output. Depending on the app, it may be easier to find where something happens in the implemented logic. If the app has a clean class design, it is relatively easy to find the part of the app responsible for the output. If the app lacks a class design, it may be more challenging to discover where things happen and thus where to use the debugger. In the upcoming chapters, you'll learn several other techniques. Some of these techniques, such as profiling the app or using stubs, will help you to identify where to start the investigation with a debugger.

Performance problems are a particular set of issues you usually can't investigate with a debugger. Slow applications or those that stick completely are frequent performance issues. In most cases, profiling and logging techniques (that we'll discuss in chapters 5–9) will help you to troubleshoot such scenarios. For the particular instances in which the app blocks entirely, getting and analyzing a thread dump is usually the most straightforward investigation path. We'll discuss analyzing thread dumps in chapter 10.

If the app encountered an issue and the execution stopped (the app crashed), you cannot use a debugger on the code. A debugger allows you to observe the app in execution. If the application no longer executes, a debugger clearly won't help. Depending on what happened, you might need to audit logs, as we'll discuss in chapter 5, or investigate thread or heap dumps, which you'll learn about in chapters 10 and 11.

Most developers find *multithreaded implementations* the most challenging to investigate. Such implementations can be easily influenced by your interference with tools such as a debugger. This interference creates a Heisenberg effect (discussed in chapter 1): the app behaves differently when you use the debugger than when you don't interfere with it. As you'll learn, you can sometimes isolate the investigation to one thread and use the debugger. But in most cases, you'll have to apply a set of techniques that include debugging, mocking and stubbing, and profiling to understand the app's behavior in the most complex scenarios.

Summary

- Every time you open a new piece of logic (e.g., entering a new method that defines its own logic), you open a new investigation plan.

- Unlike a text paragraph, reading code is not linear. Each instruction might create a new plan you need to investigate. The more complex the logic you explore, the more plans you need to open. The more plans you open, the more complex the process becomes. One trick to speeding up a code investigation process is to open as few plans as possible.

- A debugger is a tool that allows you to pause the app's execution on a specific line so that you can observe the app's execution, step by step, and the way it manages data. Using a debugger can help you to reduce some of the cognitive load of reading code.

- You can use breakpoints to mark the specific lines of code where you want the debugger to pause an app's execution so you can evaluate the values of all the variables in the scope.

- You can step over a line, which means continuing to the next execution line in the same plan, or step into a line, which means going into detail on the instruction on which the debugger paused the execution. You should minimize the number of times you step into a line and rely more on stepping over. Every time you step into a line, the investigation path gets longer and the process more time consuming.

- Even though using the mouse and the IDE's GUI to navigate through the code is initially more comfortable, learning to use the keyboard shortcuts for these operations will help you debug faster. I recommend you learn the keyboard shortcuts of your favorite IDE and use them instead of triggering the navigation with the mouse.

- After stepping into a line, first read the code and try to understand it. If you can figure out what happens, use the step out operation to return to the previous investigation plan. If you don't understand what happens, identify the first unclear instruction, add a breakpoint, and start debugging from there.

Finding problem root causes using advanced debugging techniques

This chapter covers

- Using conditional breakpoints to investigate specific scenarios
- Using breakpoints to log debug messages in the console
- Changing data while debugging to force the app to act in a specific way
- Rerunning a certain part of the code while debugging

In chapter 2, we started discussing the most common ways to use a debugger. When debugging a certain piece of implemented logic, developers often use code navigation operations such as stepping over, stepping into, and stepping out of a line. Knowing how to properly use these operations helps you to investigate a piece of code to better understand or find an issue.

But a debugger is a more powerful tool than many developers are aware of. Developers sometimes struggle when debugging code using only the basic navigation, whereas they could save a lot of time if they used some of the other (lesser-known) approaches a debugger offers.

In this chapter, you'll learn how to get the most out of the features a debugger offers:

- Conditional breakpoints
- Breakpoints as log events
- Modifying in-memory data
- Dropping execution frames

We'll discuss some beyond-basic ways to navigate the code you are investigating, and you'll learn how and when to use these approaches. We'll use code examples to discuss these investigation approaches so that you understand how you can use them to save time and when to avoid them.

3.1   *Minimizing investigation time with conditional breakpoints*

In this section, we discuss the use of *conditional breakpoints* to pause the app's execution on a line of code under specific conditions.

> **DEFINITION**   A conditional breakpoint is a breakpoint you associate with a condition, so that the debugger only pauses the execution if the condition is fulfilled. Conditional breakpoints are helpful in investigation scenarios when you are only interested in how a part of the code works with given values; using conditional breakpoints where appropriate saves you time and helps you to more easily understand how your app works.

Let's look at an example to understand how conditional breakpoints work and typical cases in which you'll want to use them. Listing 3.1 presents a method that returns the sum of the digits in a list of String values. You might already be familiar with this method from chapter 2. We'll use this piece of code here as well to discuss conditional breakpoints. We'll then compare this simplified example with similar situations you may encounter in real-world cases. This example can be found in project da-ch3-ex1 provided with the book.

> **Listing 3.1   Using conditional breakpoints for investigation**

```
public class Decoder {

  public Integer decode(List<String> input) {
    try {
      int total = 0;
      for (String s : input) {
        var digits = new StringDigitExtractor(s).extractDigits();
        var sum = digits.stream().collect(Collectors.summingInt(i -> i));
        total += sum;
      }
```

```
        return total;
    } catch (Exception e) {
        return -1;
    }
  }
}
```

When debugging a piece of code, you are often only interested in how the logic works for specific values. For example, say you suspect the implemented logic doesn't work well in a given case (e.g., some variable has a certain value), and you want to prove it. Or you simply want to understand what happens in a given situation to have a better overview of the entire functionality.

Suppose that, in this case, you only want to investigate why the variable sum is sometimes zero. How can you only work on this specific case? You could use the step over operation to navigate the code until you observe that the method returns zero. This approach is likely acceptable in a demo example such as this one (small enough). But in a real-world case, you may have to step over a lot of times until you reach the case you expect. In fact, in a real-world scenario, you may not even know when the specific case you want to investigate appears.

Using conditional breakpoints is more efficient than navigating through code until you get to the conditions you want to research. Figure 3.1 shows you how to apply a condition to a breakpoint in IntelliJ IDEA. Right-click the breakpoint you want to add

In IntelliJ, right-click on the breakpoint to define its condition. In this example, the debugger stops only on this breakpoint when the variable "sum" is zero.

You can add a condition on certain breakpoints. The debugger considers these breakpoints only if their condition evaluates to true.

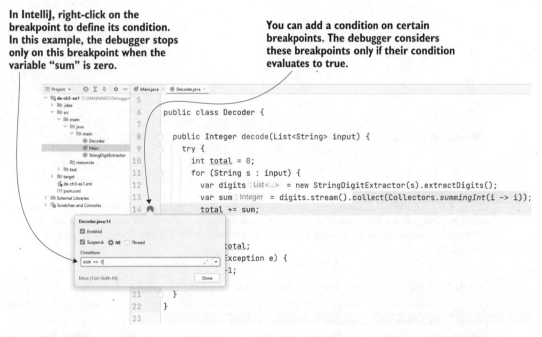

Figure 3.1   Using a conditional breakpoint to pause the execution just for specific cases. In this figure, we want to pause the execution on line 14 only if sum is zero. We can apply a condition on the breakpoint that instructs the debugger to consider that breakpoint only if the given state is true. This helps you more quickly get to a scenario you want to investigate.

the condition for and write the condition to which the breakpoint applies. The condition needs to be a Boolean expression (it should be something that can be evaluated as true or false). Using the sum == 0 condition on the breakpoint, you tell the debugger to consider that breakpoint and pause the execution only when it reaches a case where the variable sum is zero.

When you run the app with the debugger, the execution pauses only when the loop first iterates on a string that contains no digits, as you observe in figure 3.2. This situation causes the variable sum to be zero, and thus the condition on the breakpoint is evaluated as true.

Figure 3.2   A conditional breakpoint. Line 14 in the figure was executed multiple times, but the debugger only paused the execution when the variable sum was zero. This way, we skipped over all the cases we were not interested in so that we can start with the conditions relevant to our investigation.

A conditional breakpoint saves you time since you don't have to search for the specific case you want to investigate. Instead, you allow the app to run, and the debugger pauses the execution when a certain condition is met, allowing you to begin your investigation at this point. Although using conditional breakpoints is easy, many developers seem to forget about this approach and waste a lot of time investigating scenarios that could be simplified with conditional breakpoints.

Setting conditional breakpoints is an excellent way to investigate code. However, they have their downside. Conditional breakpoints can dramatically affect the performance of the execution since the debugger must continuously intercept the values of the variables in the scope you use, and evaluate the breakpoint conditions.

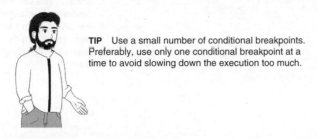

TIP   Use a small number of conditional breakpoints. Preferably, use only one conditional breakpoint at a time to avoid slowing down the execution too much.

Another way to use conditional breakpoints is to log specific execution details such as various expression values and the stack traces for particular conditions (figure 3.3).

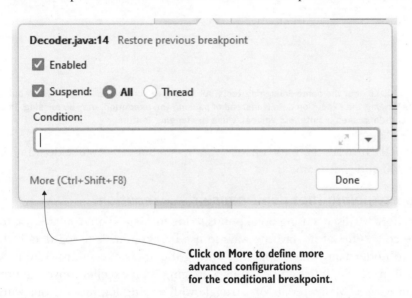

Click on More to define more advanced configurations for the conditional breakpoint.

Figure 3.3   To apply advanced configuration on the breakpoint in IntelliJ, you can click the More button.

Unfortunately, this feature only works in certain IDEs. For example, even though you can use conditional breakpoints in Eclipse in the same way as described here, Eclipse does not allow you to use breakpoints just for logging execution details (figure 3.4).

You might ask yourself whether you should only use IntelliJ IDEA for these examples. Even if most examples in this book use IntelliJ IDEA, that doesn't mean this IDE is better than others. I've used many IDEs with Java, such as Eclipse, Netbeans, and JDeveloper. My recommendation is that you shouldn't become too comfortable with

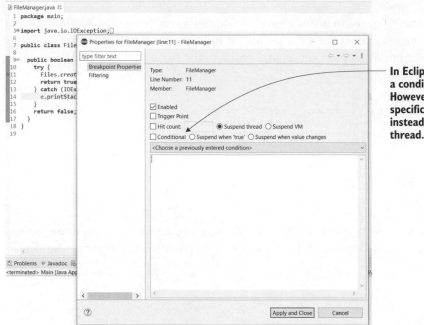

Figure 3.4   Not all IDEs offer the same debugging tools. All IDEs give you the basic operations, but some features, such as logging the execution details instead of pausing the execution, may be missing. In Eclipse, you can define conditional breakpoints, but you can't use the logging feature.

using one IDE. Instead, try to use various options so that you can decide which is a better fit for you and your team.

3.2   *Using breakpoints that don't pause the execution*

In this section, we discuss using breakpoints to log messages you can later use to investigate the code. One of my favorite ways to use breakpoints is to log details that can help me to understand what happened during the app's execution without pausing the execution. As you'll learn in chapter 5, logging is an excellent investigation practice in some cases. Many developers struggle with adding log instructions when they could have simply used a conditional breakpoint.

Figure 3.5 shows you how to configure a conditional breakpoint that doesn't pause the execution. Instead, the debugger logs a message every time the line marked with the breakpoint is reached. In this case, the debugger logs the value of the `digits` variable and the execution stack trace.

Figure 3.6 shows the result of running the app with the conditional breakpoint configured. Notice that the debugger logged the execution stack trace in the console, and the value of the `digits` variable is an empty list: `[]`. This kind of information can help you to solve the puzzles of the code you investigate in real-world scenarios.

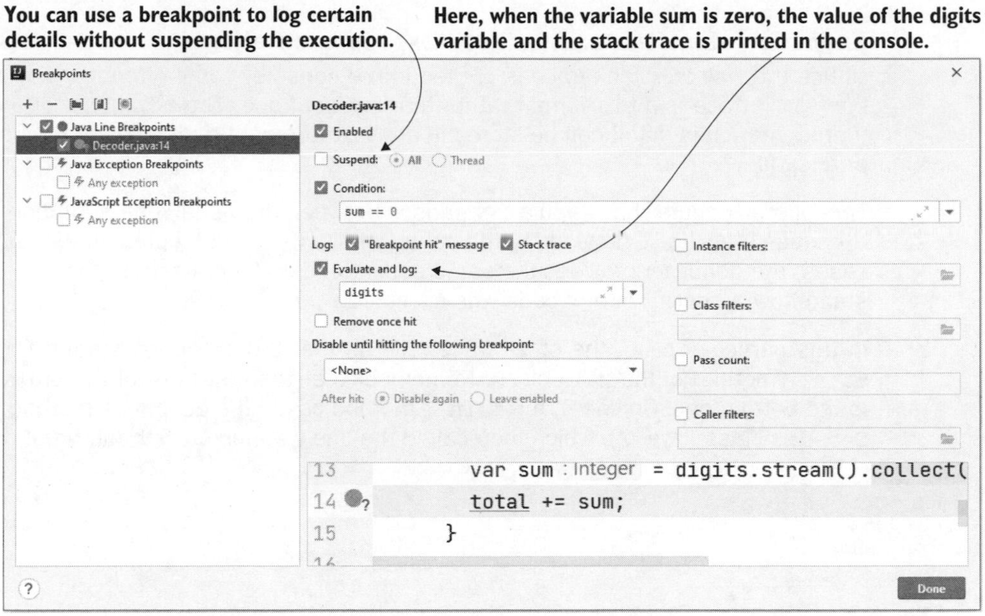

You can use a breakpoint to log certain details without suspending the execution.

Here, when the variable sum is zero, the value of the digits variable and the stack trace is printed in the console.

Figure 3.5 Conditional breakpoint advanced configuration. In addition to specifying a condition for the breakpoint, you can instruct the debugger to not suspend the execution for the given breakpoint. Instead, you can simply log the data you need to understand your case.

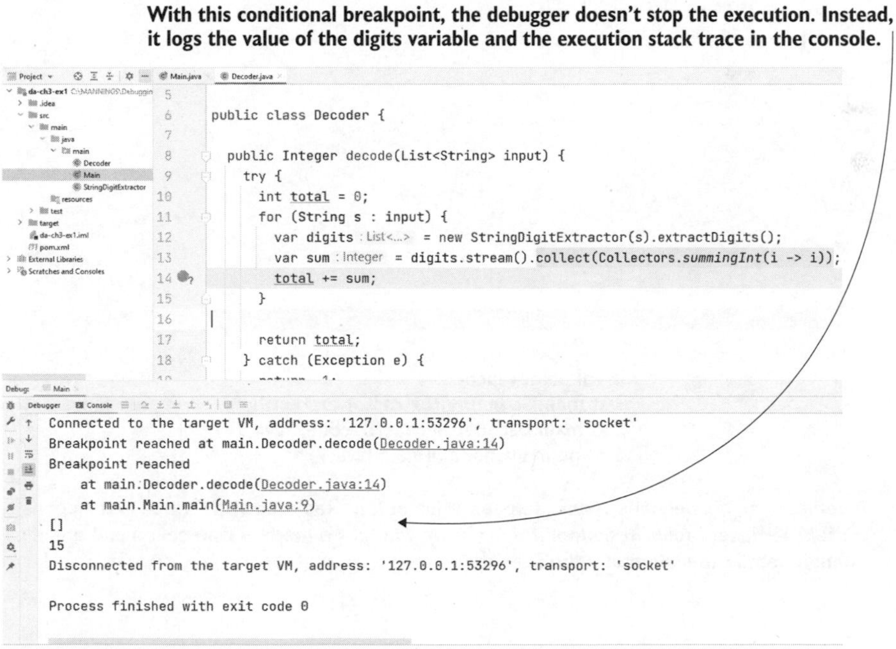

With this conditional breakpoint, the debugger doesn't stop the execution. Instead, it logs the value of the digits variable and the execution stack trace in the console.

Figure 3.6 Using breakpoints without pausing the execution. Instead, the debugger logs a message when the line has been reached. The debugger also logs the value of the `digits` variable and the execution stack trace.

Execution stack trace: Visual vs. text representation

Notice the way the stack trace is printed in the console. You'll often find the execution stack trace in a text format rather than a visual one. The advantage of the text representation is that it can be stored in any text format output, such as the console or a log file.

The following figure shows you a comparison between the visual representation of the execution stack trace provided by the debugger and its textual representation. In both cases, the debugger provides the same essential details that can help you to understand how a specific line of code was executed.

In this particular case, the stack trace tells us that the execution started from the `main()` method of the `Main` class. Remember that the first layer of the stack trace is the bottom one. On line 9, the `main()` method called the `decode()` method in the `Decoder` class (layer 2), which then called the line we marked with the breakpoint.

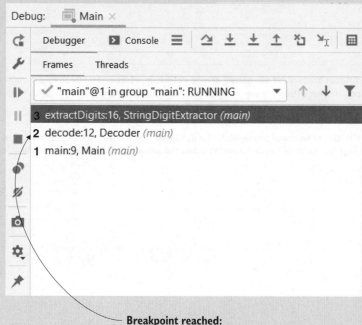

Breakpoint reached:
3 at main.StringDigitExtractor.extractDigits(StringDigitExtractor.java:16)
2 at main.Decoder.decode(Decoder.java:12)
1 at main.Main.main(Main.java:9)

A comparison between the visual representation of the execution stack trace in the debugger and its text representation. The stack trace shows you how a method was called and provides you enough details to understand the execution path.

3.3 *Dynamically altering the investigation scenario*

In this section, you'll learn another valuable technique that will make your code investigations easier: changing the values of the variables in scope while debugging. In some cases, this approach can save a significant amount of time. We'll begin with discussing the scenarios in which changing variables' values on the fly is the most effective approach. Then I will demonstrate how to use this approach with an example.

Earlier in this chapter, we discussed conditional breakpoints. Conditional breakpoints allow you to tell the debugger to pause the execution under specific conditions (e.g., when a given variable has a certain value). Often, we investigate logic that executes in a short time, and using conditional breakpoints is enough. For cases such as debugging a piece of logic called through a REST endpoint (especially if you have the right data to reproduce a problem in your environment), you would simply use a conditional breakpoint to pause the execution when appropriate. That's because you know it won't take long to execute something called through an endpoint. But consider the following scenarios:

- You investigate an issue with a process that takes a long time to execute. Say it's a scheduled process that sometimes takes over an hour to complete its execution. You suspect that some given parameter values are causing the wrong output, and you want to confirm your suspicion before you decide how to correct the problem.
- You have a piece of code that executes quickly, but you can't reproduce the issue in your environment. The problem appears only in the production environment to which you don't have access due to security constraints. You believe the issue appears when certain parameters have specific values. You want to prove your theory is right.

In scenario 1, breakpoints (conditional or not) aren't so helpful. Unless you investigate some logic that happens at the very beginning of the process, running the process and waiting for the execution to pause on a line marked with a breakpoint would take too much time (figure 3.7).

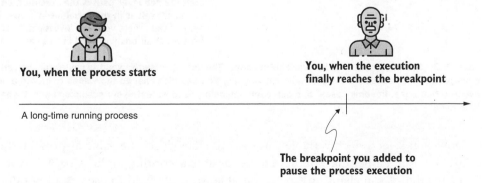

You, when the process starts

You, when the execution finally reaches the breakpoint

A long-time running process

The breakpoint you added to pause the process execution

Figure 3.7 Usually, when investigating issues in a long-running process, using breakpoints is not really an option. It can take a long time for the execution to reach the part of code you are investigating, and if you have to rerun the process several times, you will definitely spend too much time on it.

For scenario 2, using breakpoints may sometimes be possible. In chapter 4, we'll discuss remote debugging, and you'll learn how and when remote debugging is a helpful investigation technique. But let's assume for the moment (since we haven't discussed it yet) that you can't apply remote debugging in this case. Instead, if you have an idea of what causes the problem and you just need to prove it but don't have the right data, you can use on-the-fly changes in variables' values.

Figure 3.8 shows you how to change the data in one of the variables in the scope when the debugger pauses the execution. In IntelliJ IDEA, you right-click the variable whose value you want to change. You complete this action in the frame where the debugger shows the current values of the variables in scope. Let's look at the our previous example, da-ch3-ex1.

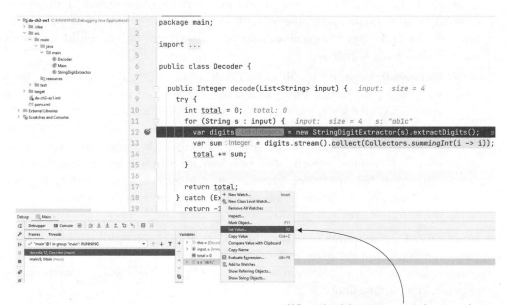

When the debugger pauses the execution on a line, you can set values in the variables in scope. This way, you can create you own investigation scenario with the conditions you need in this case.

Figure 3.8   Setting a new value in a variable in scope. The debugger shows you the values for the variables in scope when it pauses the execution on a given line. You can also change the values to create a new investigation case. In some cases, this approach can help you to validate your suspicions about what the code does.

Once you select which variable you want to change, set the value as presented in figure 3.9. Remember that you have to use a value according to the variable's type. That means that if you change a String variable, you still need to use a String value; you cannot use a long or a Boolean value.

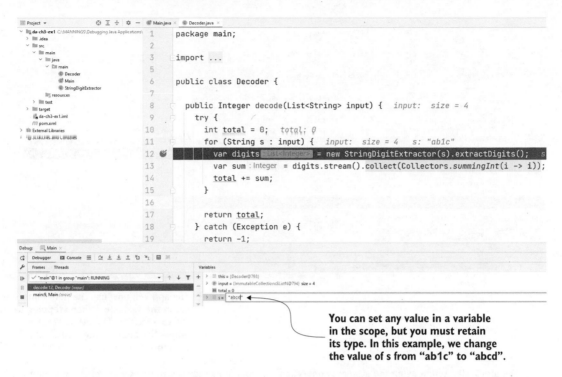

Figure 3.9 Change the variable's value to observe how the app's execution behaves in different conditions.

When you continue the execution, as presented in figure 3.10, the app now uses the new value. Instead of calling `extractDigits()` for value `"ab1c"`, the app used the value `"abcd"`. The list the method returns is empty because the string `"abcd"` doesn't contain digits.

Let's compare the conditional breakpoints approach we discussed in section 3.1 to changing data on the fly. In both cases, you need to first have an idea of the part of the code that is potentially causing the problem. You can use conditional breakpoints if

- You have the data that causes the scenario you want to investigate. In our example, we need the value necessary to execute the behavior in the provided list.
- The code you're investigating doesn't take too long to execute. For example, suppose we have a list with many elements, and for each element it takes several seconds for the app to process it. In this case, using a conditional breakpoint may mean you will have to invest a lot of time to investigate your case.

You can use the approach of changing a variable's value if

- You don't have the data necessary to cause the scenario you want to investigate.
- Executing the code takes too long.

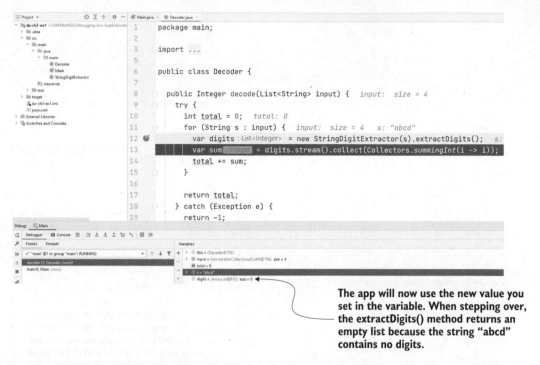

The app will now use the new value you set in the variable. When stepping over, the extractDigits() method returns an empty list because the string "abcd" contains no digits.

Figure 3.10   When using the step over operation, the app uses the new value you set to the s variable. `extractDigits()` returns an empty list because string `"abcd"` doesn't contain digits. Setting values in variables on the fly allows you to test different scenarios even if you don't have the input data you need.

I know what you are thinking now: why are we using conditional breakpoints at all? It might look like you should avoid using conditional breakpoints entirely since you can create any environment you need to investigate simply by changing the variables' values on the fly.

Both techniques have advantages and disadvantages. Changing the values of the variables may be an excellent approach if you only need to change a couple of values. But when your changes become more extensive, the complexity of the scenario becomes increasingly challenging to manage.

3.4   *Rewinding the investigation case*

We can't go back in time. However, with debugging, rewinding the investigation is sometimes possible. In this section, we discuss when and how we can "go back in time" while investigating code with a debugger. We call this approach *dropping frames, dropping execution frames,* or *quitting execution frames.*

We'll look an example using IntelliJ IDEA. We'll compare this approach with the ones we discussed in the previous sections of this chapter, and then we'll also determine when this technique can't be used.

Dropping an execution frame is, in fact, going back one layer in the execution stack trace. For example, suppose you stepped into a method and want to go back; you can drop the execution frame to return to where the method was called.

Many developers confuse dropping a frame with stepping out, most likely because the current investigation plan closes in both cases, and the execution returns to where the method is called. However, there's a big difference. When you step out of a method, the execution continues in the current plan until the method returns or throws an exception. Then, the debugger pauses the execution right after the current method exits.

Figure 3.11 shows you how stepping out works using the example in project da-ch3-ex1. You are in the `extractDigits()` method, which, as you can see from the execution stack trace, has been called from the `decode()` method in the `Decoder` class. If you use the step out operation, the execution continues in the method that called `extractDigits()` until the method returns. Then, the debugger pauses the execution in the `decode()` method. In other words, stepping out is like fast-forwarding this execution plan to close it and return to the previous one.

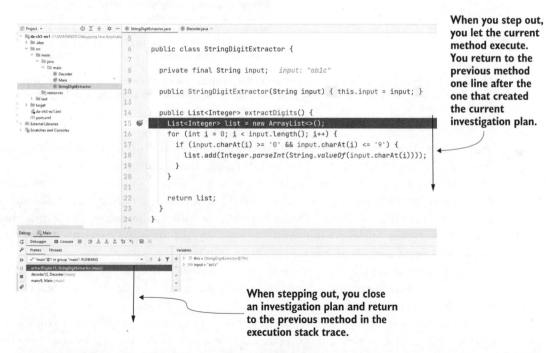

When you step out, you let the current method execute. You return to the previous method one line after the one that created the current investigation plan.

When stepping out, you close an investigation plan and return to the previous method in the execution stack trace.

Figure 3.11 Stepping out closes the current investigation plan by executing the method and then pausing the execution right after the method call. This operation allows you to continue the execution and return one layer in the execution stack.

When you drop an execution frame, the execution returns in the previous plan before the method is called, unlike stepping out. This way, you can replay the call. If the step out operation is like fast-forwarding, dropping an execution frame (figure 3.12) is like rewinding.

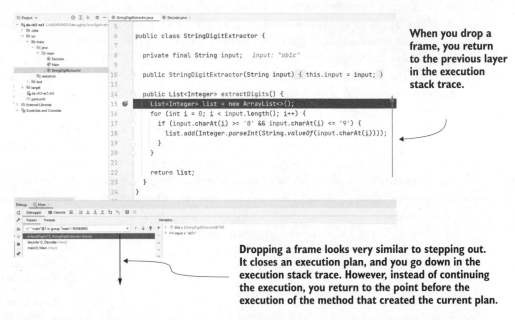

When you drop a frame, you return to the previous layer in the execution stack trace.

Dropping a frame looks very similar to stepping out. It closes an execution plan, and you go down in the execution stack trace. However, instead of continuing the execution, you return to the point before the execution of the method that created the current plan.

Figure 3.12   When you drop a frame, you return to the previous layer in the execution stack trace before the method call. This way, you can replay the method execution either by stepping into it again or stepping over it.

Figure 3.13 shows you, relative to our example, a comparison between stepping out from the extractDigits() method and dropping the frame created by the extract-Digits() method. If you step out, you'll go back to line 12 in the decode() method, from where extractDigits() is called, and the next line the debugger will execute is line 13. If you drop the frame, the debugger goes back to the decode() method, but the next line that will execute is line 12. Basically, the debugger returns to the line before the execution of the extractDigits() method.

Figure 3.14 shows you how to use the drop frame functionality in IntelliJ IDEA. To drop the current execution frame, right-click the method's layer in the execution stack trace and select Drop Frame.

Why is the drop frame useful, and how does it help save time? Whether you use an endpoint to find a specific case you want to investigate or create one by changing the values of the variables, as discussed in section 3.3, you'll still sometimes find it useful to repeat the same execution several times. Understanding a certain piece of code is not always trivial, even if you use the debugger to pause the execution and take it step by step. But going back now and then to review the steps and how specific code instructions change the data may help you to understand what's going on.

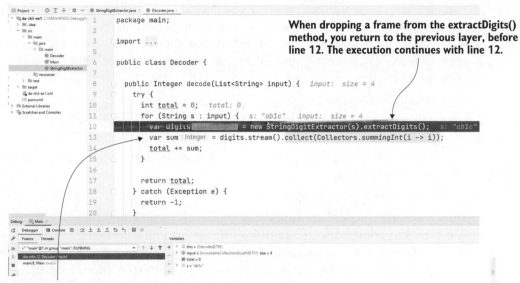

When dropping a frame from the extractDigits() method, you return to the previous layer, before line 12. The execution continues with line 12.

When stepping out from the extractDigits() method, you return to the previous layer, at line 12. The execution continues with line 13.

Figure 3.13 Dropping a frame versus stepping out. When you drop a frame, you return to the line before the method's execution. When you step out, you continue the execution but close the current investigation plan (represented by the current layer in the execution stack).

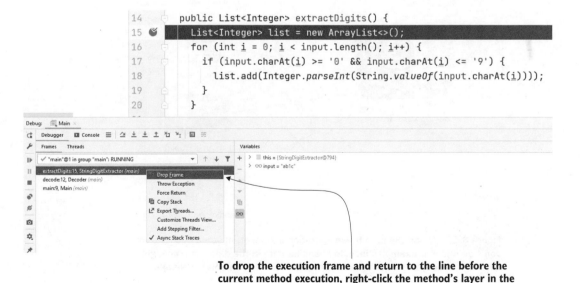

To drop the execution frame and return to the line before the current method execution, right-click the method's layer in the execution stack. Then, select Drop Frame.

Figure 3.14 When using IntelliJ IDEA, you can drop a frame by right-clicking the method's layer in the execution stack trace and then selecting Drop Frame.

You also need to pay attention when you decide to repeat particular instructions by dropping the frame. This approach can sometimes be more confusing than helpful. Remember that if you run any instruction that changes values outside of the app's internal memory, you can't undo that change by dropping the frame. Examples of such cases are (figure 3.15) as follows:

- Modifying data in a database (insert, update, or delete)
- Changing the filesystem (creating, removing, or changing files)
- Calling another app, which changes the data for that app
- Adding a message into a queue that is read by a different app, which changes data for that app
- Sending an email message

You can drop a frame that results in committing a transaction that changes data in a database, but going back to a previous instruction won't undo the changes made by the transaction. If the app calls an endpoint that posts something into a different service, the changes resulting from the endpoint call cannot be undone by dropping the frame. If the app sends an email message, dropping the frame cannot take back the message, and so on (figure 3.15).

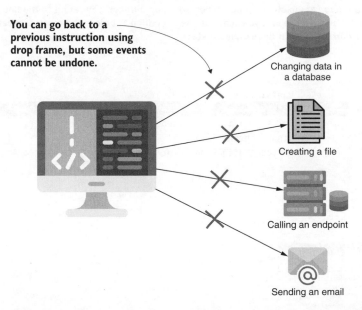

You can go back to a previous instruction using drop frame, but some events cannot be undone.

Changing data in a database

Creating a file

Calling an endpoint

Sending an email

Figure 3.15   Using the drop frame operation can result in some events that can't be undone. Examples include changing data in the database, changing data in the filesystem, calling another app, or sending an email message.

You need to be careful when data is changed outside the app, as sometimes repeating the same code won't have the same result. Take as an example a simple piece of code (listing 3.2, which you can find in project da-ch3-ex2). What happens if you drop the frame after the execution of the line that creates a file?

```
Files.createFile(Paths.get("File " + i));
```

The created file remains in the filesystem, and after the second time you execute the code after dropping the frame, you get an exception (because the file already exists). This is a simple example of when going back in time while debugging is not helpful. The worst part is that, in real-world cases, it's not this obvious. My recommendation is to avoid repeating the execution of large pieces of code and, before deciding to use this approach, make sure that part of the logic doesn't make external changes.

If you notice differences that seem unusual after running a dropped frame again, it may be because the code changed something externally. Often in large apps, observing such behavior is not straightforward. For example, your app may use a cache or log data that accesses a certain library to observe or execute code that is completely decoupled through interceptors (aspects).

Calling the `Files.createFile()` method creates a new file in the filesystem. If you drop the frame after running this line, you'll return to the line before the `create-File()` method is called. However, this doesn't undo the file creation.

> **Listing 3.2   A method that makes changes outside the app when executing**

```
public class FileManager {

  public boolean createFile(int i) {
    try {
      Files.createFile(Paths.get("File " + i));    <-- Creating a new file
      return true;                                      in the filesystem.
    } catch (IOException e) {
      e.printStackTrace();
    }
    return false;
  }
}
```

Summary

- A conditional breakpoint is a breakpoint associated with a Boolean condition. The debugger pauses the execution only if the provided condition is true—that is, only when particular conditions apply. This way, you save the time of navigating through code until you get to the desired point to begin your investigation.
- You can use breakpoints to log the values of certain variables in the console that don't suspend the app's execution. This approach is quite helpful because you can add log messages without changing the code.
- When the debugger pauses the execution on specific lines of code, you can alter the data on the fly to create custom scenarios according to what you want

to investigate. This way, you don't have to wait until the execution gets to a conditional breakpoint. In some cases, when you don't have an appropriate environment, changing data while debugging saves you time you would have needed to prepare the data in the environment.

- Changing variables' values to create a custom investigation scenario can be an efficient technique when trying to understand just a piece of the logic of a long-running process or when you don't have the desired data in the environment where you run the app. However, changing more than one or two variable values at a time may add considerable complexity and make your investigation more challenging.

- You can step out of an investigation plan and return to the point before the method was called. This is called dropping a frame, but it can sometimes introduce an unwanted side effect. If the app changed anything externally (e.g., committed a transaction and changed some database records, changed a file in the filesystem, or made a RESTful call to another app), returning to a previous execution step won't undo these changes.

Debugging apps remotely

One of my friends recently had a problem where a particular part of the software he was implementing was very slow. Generally, when we have these types of performance issues, we suspect that an I/O interface is the cause (e.g., a connection to a database or reading or writing in a file). Remember from chapter 1 that such interfaces often slow down apps, so they are a likely suspect. But in my friend's case, interfaces were not the issue.

The performance issue was caused by the simple generation of a random value (a universally unique identifier [UUID] stored in the database). The operating system uses hardware sources (e.g., mouse movements, the keyboard, etc.) to collect randomness, referred to as *entropy*. The app uses this randomness to generate random values. But when we deploy the app in a virtualized environment such as a virtual machine or a container (which is pretty common for app deployments today), the operating system has fewer sources to create its entropy. Thus, sometimes there's not enough entropy for the app to create the random values it needs. This situation causes performance problems and, in some cases, can have a negative impact on the app's security.

This type of problem can be really challenging to investigate without connecting directly to the environment in which the problem occurs. For such scenarios, remote debugging can be the solution. You can only examine certain cases in particular environments. Suppose your client observes an issue, but the problem doesn't occur when you run the app on your computer. You definitely cannot solve it by simply telling your client, "It works on my machine."

You need to connect to the environment in which the problem occurs when you cannot reproduce the issue on your computer. Although sometimes you don't have any other options, and you have to take the challenging path of trying to fix a problem you can't re-create, at other times, the environment is open for remote debugging. *Remote debugging*, or debugging an app installed in an external environment, is the subject of this chapter (see figure 4.1).

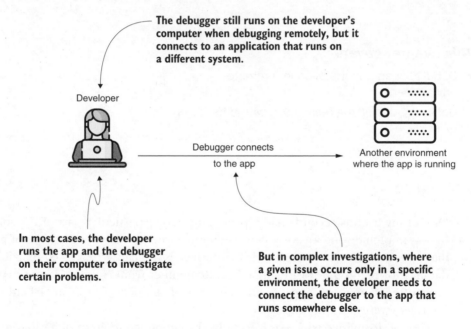

The debugger still runs on the developer's computer when debugging remotely, but it connects to an application that runs on a different system.

Developer

Debugger connects to the app

Another environment where the app is running

In most cases, the developer runs the app and the debugger on their computer to investigate certain problems.

But in complex investigations, where a given issue occurs only in a specific environment, the developer needs to connect the debugger to the app that runs somewhere else.

Figure 4.1 Remotely debugging an app. The developer can run the debugger tool locally but connect it to an app instance running in a different environment. This approach allows the developer to investigate problems that only occur in specific environments.

We'll start the chapter by discussing what remote debugging is and when you can expect to use it, as well as when you should not use this method. Then, to apply this technique, we'll look at an issue to investigate. You'll learn how an app needs to be configured to remotely debug it and how to connect and use the debugger for a remote environment.

4.1 *What is remote debugging?*

In this section, we discuss what remote debugging is, when to use it, and when to avoid it. Remote debugging is nothing more than applying the debugging techniques you learned in chapters 2 and 3 on an app that doesn't run locally on your system but instead runs in an outside environment. Why would you need to use such techniques in a remote environment? To answer this question, let's briefly review a typical software development process.

When developers implement an app, they don't write it for their local systems. The final purpose of an app is to deploy it in a production environment where it helps users solve various business problems. Moreover, when implementing the software, we often don't deploy the app directly in users' environments, or *production environments.* Instead, we use similar environments to roughly test the capabilities and fixes we need to implement before installing them in an environment where they are officially used with real data.

As described in figure 4.2, a development team uses at least three environments when developing an app:

- *The development environment (dev)*—An environment similar to where the app will be deployed. Developers mainly use this environment to test new capabilities and fixes they implement after developing them on their local system.
- *The user acceptance test environment (UAT)*—Once successfully tested in the development environment, the app is installed in the user acceptance test environment. Users can test the new implementations and fixes and confirm they work before the app is delivered to an environment with real data.
- *The production environment (prod)*—After users confirm a new implementation works as expected and they feel comfortable using it, the app is installed in the production environment.

But what if an implementation works on your local computer but behaves differently in another environment? You might wonder how an app can work differently. Even when using the same compiled app, we can observe differences in the app's behavior between two different environments. Some reasons for these differences include the following:

- The data available in the app's environments is different. Different environments use different database instances, different configuration files, and so on.
- The operating systems in which the app is installed are not the same.
- The way the deployment is orchestrated may be different. For example, one environment may use virtual machines for the deployment, while another uses a containerized solution.
- Permission setup may be different in each environment.
- The environments may have different resources (allocated memory or CPU).

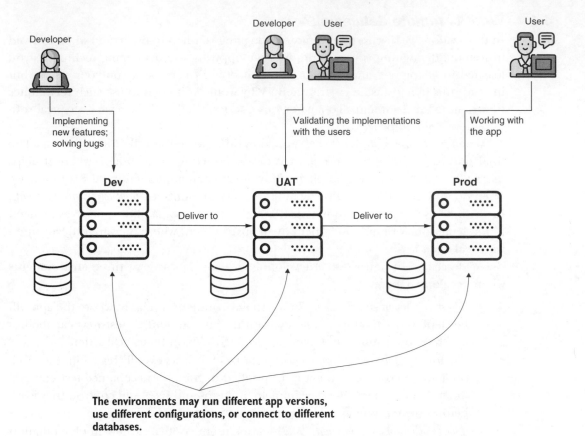

Developer

Developer   User

User

Implementing
new features;
solving bugs

Validating the implementations
with the users

Working with
the app

Dev

UAT

Prod

Deliver to

Deliver to

**The environments may run different app versions,
use different configurations, or connect to different
databases.**

**Figure 4.2   When building a real-world app, developers often use multiple environments. First, they build the
app in development (dev) environments. Then, once a feature or a solution is ready, they present it to users (or
stakeholders of the app) using a user acceptance test (UAT) environment. Finally, after the stakeholders
confirm that the implementation works, they install it in a production (prod) environment.**

These are just some of the many things that can make a given output or behavior different. The last time I had such a problem (not long ago), the app produced a different output due to a request that was being sent to a web service the app used in the implemented use case. Because of security issues, we couldn't use the same endpoint in the dev environment, and we couldn't connect to the one the app used in the environment with the problem. These conditions made the investigation challenging (honestly, we didn't even consider that an endpoint was the cause of our issue until we started debugging).

Remote debugging can really help you to understand the software behavior faster in these types of cases. However, keep one crucial piece of advice in mind: never use remote debugging in the production environment (figure 4.3). Also, make sure you always understand the main differences between the environments you use.

TIP Paying attention to how the environments differ from one another gives you clues as to what could go wrong. It can even spare you the time of investigating an issue in which simply knowing these details will empirically give you the answer to a problem.

As you'll learn, you need to attach a piece of software we name *agent* to the app execution to enable remote debugging. Some of the consequences of attaching the debugging agent (and why you shouldn't do this in a production environment) include these:

- The agent can slow the app's execution; this slowness can cause performance problems.
- The agent needs to communicate with the debugger tool through the network. To enable this, you need to make specific ports available, which can cause vulnerability issues.
- Debugging a specific piece of code can interfere with functionality if the same part of the app is being used elsewhere simultaneously.
- Sometimes debugging can block the app indefinitely and force you to restart the process.

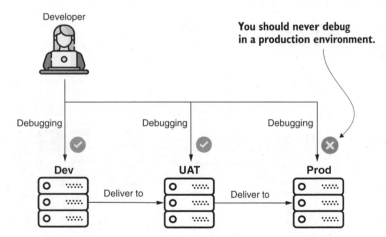

Figure 4.3 Developers implement the app using the dev and UAT environments. It's OK to debug apps in these environments. But remember, never debug apps in the prod environment, as this can affect the app's execution, interfere with users' actions, and even expose sensitive data, creating a security vulnerability.

4.2 *Investigating in remote environments*

In this section, we consider debugging an app that runs in a remote environment. I'll start by describing the scenario in section 4.2.1. Then, in section 4.2.2, using an app provided with this book (project da-ch4-ex1), we will discuss how to start an app for remote debugging and how to attach a debugger to the remotely running app using the techniques you learned in chapters 2 and 3.

4.2.1   *The scenario*

Suppose you work on a team that implements and maintains a large application many clients use to manage their product inventory. Recently, your team implemented a new capability that helps your clients easily manage their costs. The team successfully tested the behavior in the dev environment and installed the app in the UAT environment to allow users to validate the feature before moving it to production. However, the person responsible for testing the new capability informs you that the web interface where the new data should be displayed shows nothing.

Concerned, you take a look and quickly see that the problem is not the frontend. But an endpoint on the backend seems to behave weirdly. When the endpoint is called in the UAT environment, the HTTP response status code is 200 OK, but the app doesn't return the data in the HTTP response (figure 4.4). You check the logs, but nothing shows there either. Since you can't observe the problem locally or in the dev environment, you decide to remotely connect your debugger in the UAT environment to find the cause of this issue.

> **NOTE** Even if we discuss debugging an app running in a remote environment, to make the example simpler, we use the local system to run the app, to which we connect remotely. For this reason, you'll see in the figures that I use "localhost" to access the environment running the app. In a real-world scenario, the app would run on a different system, which would be identified with an IP address or DNS name.

By calling the **HTTP GET endpoint**, the app exposes the local system at port 8080.

Click the **Send button** to send the **HTTP request.**

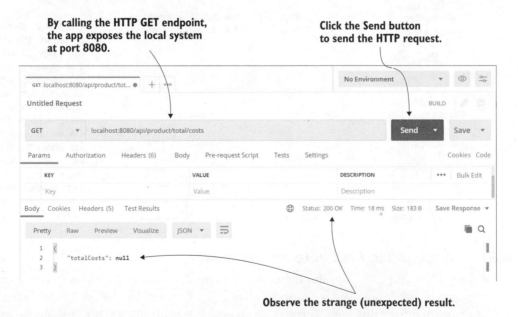

Observe the strange (unexpected) result.

Figure 4.4   The scenario you have to investigate. The `/api/product/total/costs` endpoint should return the total costs from the database. Instead, when a request is sent to the endpoint, the app behaves oddly. The HTTP status is 200 OK, but the total costs, which you expected to be a list of values, comes back null.

4.2.2 Finding issues in remote environments

In this section, we use remote debugging to investigate the case study described in section 4.2.1. We start by configuring and running the app to connect to a remote debugger and then attach the debugger to start our investigation.

The app would already be running in a real-world case and most likely wouldn't be already configured to allow remote debugging. Therefore, we begin with starting the app so that you are aware of the full picture of remote debugging and know the prerequisites of such an approach.

When starting the app that you want to remotely debug, you need to make sure you attach a debugger agent to the execution. To attach a debugger agent to a Java app execution, you add the `-agentlib:jdwp` parameter to the `java` command line, as in figure 4.5. You must specify the port number to which you'll attach the debugger tool. Basically, the debug agent acts as a server, listening for a debugger tool to connect on the configured port and allowing the tool to run the debug operations (pausing the execution on a breakpoint, stepping over, stepping into, etc.).

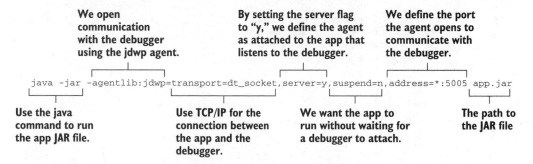

Figure 4.5 When debugging an app locally, the IDE attaches the debugger. But when running an app in a remote environment, you must attach a debugger agent at the app start yourself.

You can copy this command:

```
java -jar -agentlib:jdwp=transport=dt_socket,
    server=y,suspend=n,address=*:5005 app.jar
```

Notice the few configurations specified in the command:

- `transport=dt_socket` configures the way the debugger tool communicates with the debugger agent. The `dt_socket` configuration means we use TCP/IP to establish the communication over a network. This is always how you establish the communication between the agent and the tool.
- `server=y` means the agent acts as a server after attaching to the app execution. The agent waits for a debugger tool to connect to it and control the app execution through it. You would use the `server=n` configuration to connect to a debugger agent rather than starting one.

- suspend=n tells the app to start without waiting for a debugger tool to connect. If you want to prevent the app from starting until you connect a debugger, you need to use suspend=y. In our case, we have a web app, and the problem appears when calling one of its endpoints, so we need the app to start before it can call the endpoint. If we were investigating a problem with the server boot process, we would most likely need to use suspend=y to allow the app to start only after we have the debugger tool connected.

- address=*:5005 tells the agent to open port 5005 on the system, the port to which the debugger tool will connect to communicate with the agent. The port value must not already be in use on the system, and the network needs to permit the communication between the debugger tool and the agent (the port needs to be opened in the network).

Figure 4.6 shows the app, starting with the debugger agent attached. Notice the message printed in the console right after the command tells us the agent is listening on the configured port 5005.

You can use the command line to start the application. When you start the app, you must make it available to connect to a debugger on a given port.

```
$ java -jar -agentlib:jdwp=transport=dt_socket,server=y,suspend=n,address=*:5005 da-ch4-ex1-0.0.1-SNAPSHO
T.jar
Listening for transport dt_socket at address: 5005
```

```
 :: Spring Boot ::                (v2.4.1)

2021-08-21 08:59:12.122  INFO 83884 --- [           main] com.example.Main                     : Star
ting Main v0.0.1-SNAPSHOT using Java 11.0.12 on EN1310832 with PID 83884 (C:\MANNINGS\Debugging Java Appl
ications\CODE\spilca3\code\da-ch4-ex1\target\da-ch4-ex1-0.0.1-SNAPSHOT.jar started by lspilca in C:\MANNI
NGS\Debugging Java Applications\CODE\spilca3\code\da-ch4-ex1\target)
```

Figure 4.6   When you run the command to start the app, you can see that the app begins executing. At the same time, you can see that the debugging agent printed a line showing that it is listening for a debugger to attach on the configured port 5005.

Once your remote app has a debugger agent attached, you can connect the debugger to start investigating the issue. Remember, we assume that the network is configured to allow communication between the two apps (the debugger tool and the debugger agent). We run both on the localhost for our example, so for our demonstration, such networking configurations are not an issue.

But in a real-world scenario, you should always make sure you can establish the communication before you start to debug. In most cases, you'll likely need someone on the infrastructure team to help you open the needed port if communication is not allowed. Remember that, usually, ports are, by default, closed for communication for security reasons.

Next, we'll examine how to attach the debugger to a remote app using IntelliJ IDEA Community. The steps to run the debugger on the app running in a remote environment are as follows:

1 Add a new running configuration.
2 Configure the remote address (IP address and port) of the debugger agent.
3 Start debugging the app.

Figure 4.7 shows you how to open the Edit Configurations section to add a new running configuration.

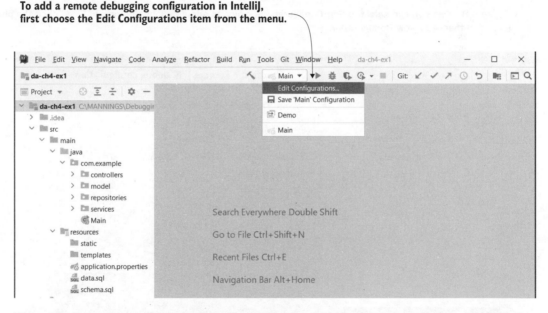

To add a remote debugging configuration in IntelliJ, first choose the Edit Configurations item from the menu.

Figure 4.7   You can use an IDE to configure the debugger to attach to an already running app in a particular environment, as long as the app has a debugger agent attached to it. In IntelliJ IDEA Community, you need to create a new running configuration to tell the debugger to attach to an already running app. You can add a new run configuration by selecting Edit Configurations.

Figure 4.8 shows you how to add a new running configuration.

Since we want to connect to a remote debugger agent, we need to add a new remote debugging configuration, as presented in figure 4.9.

Once you click Edit Configurations, IntelliJ presents this window. Click the small plus icon, and then choose Add New Configuration.

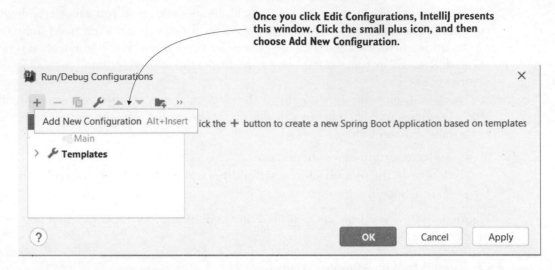

Figure 4.8   Once you've selected Edit Configurations, you can add a new configuration. First, click the plus icon, and then Add New Configuration.

Choose the Remote JVM Debug configuration from the list of configurations.

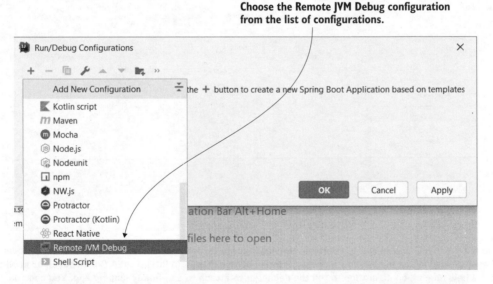

Figure 4.9   Since we want to attach the debugger to an app running in a remote environment, select the Remote JVM Debug configuration type.

Configure the address of the debugger agent, as shown in figure 4.10. In our case, we are running the app on the same system as the debugger, so we use localhost. In a real-world setting, if the app runs on a different system, you'd have to use the IP address of that system. We use port 5005 for the agent to listen and connect with a debugger tool.

1. **Choose a name for the new configuration.**

2. **Set the address of the system where the app runs (in our case, localhost) and the port you configure to attach a debugger.**

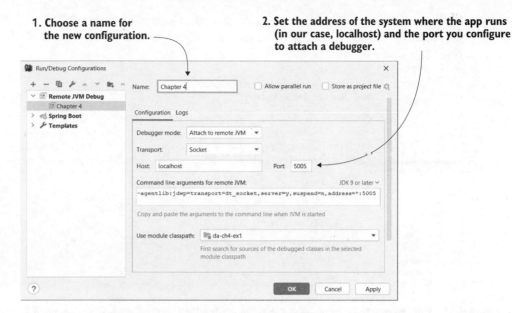

Figure 4.10   Give a name to the new configuration you add and specify the address of the environment and port you configured the debugger agent to listen on (here, port 5005 when starting the app).

Remember that we connect the debugger tool to the debugger agent, which opens port 5005 (figure 4.11). Don't confuse the port opened by the debugger agent (5005) with our web app's port (8080).

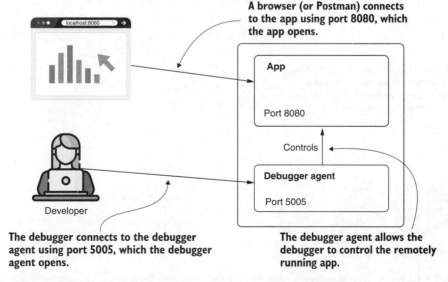

A browser (or Postman) connects to the app using port 8080, which the app opens.

The debugger connects to the debugger agent using port 5005, which the debugger agent opens.

The debugger agent allows the debugger to control the remotely running app.

Figure 4.11   The debugger tool that runs on the developer's computer connects to the debugger agent on port 5005. The debugger agent allows the debugger tool to control the app. The app also opens a port, but this port is for its clients (the browser, in the case of a web app).

Once you have a configuration in place, start the debugger (figure 4.12). The debugger will start "talking" with the debugger agent attached to the app and allow you to control the execution.

Choose the newly added configuration and click the Debug button.

Figure 4.12   You can now run the debugger using the newly added configuration. Click the small bug icon to start the debugger.

Now you can use the debugger the same way you learned in chapters 2 and 3. It is important to be careful with the version of the code you use (figure 4.13). When locally debugging an application, you know that the IDE compiles the app and then attaches the debugger to the freshly compiled code. However, when you connect to a remote app, you can no longer be sure that the source code you have corresponds to the compiled code of the remote app to which you attach the debugger. If the team started on new tasks, code that you need to investigate may have potentially been

To correctly view the app execution, the developer needs to have the same source code version that generated execution in the remote environment.

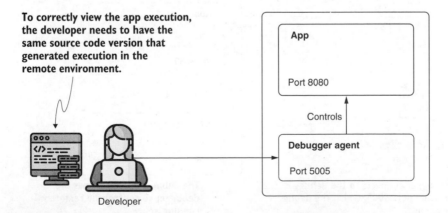

Figure 4.13   The developer needs to make sure they have the same version of source code as the one used to generate the app's executable run in the remote environment. Otherwise, the debugger's actions could become inconsistent with the code the developer investigates, which would create more confusion than it would help the developer understand the app's behavior.

changed, added, or removed in the same classes involved. Using a different source code version can lead to strange and confusing debugger behavior. For example, the debugger may show that you are navigating empty lines, even lines outside the methods or classes. The execution stack trace can also become inconsistent with the expected execution.

Fortunately, today we use source code versioning software such as Git or SVN, so we can always figure out which version of the source code created the app we deployed. Before debugging, you need to make sure you have the same source code as the one compiled into the app you want to investigate remotely. Use your source code versioning tool to find the exact source code version.

Here's an exercise for you!
Take a break from reading here
and try to solve the problem.

What is causing the app's strange behavior,
and how would you solve the problem?

Let's add a breakpoint on the first line that raises concerns: line 23 in the `Product-Service` class, as presented in figure 4.14. Here, the app should select the data from the database to return in the HTTP response. First, I want to determine whether the data is correctly retrieved from the database, so I pause the execution on this line and step over to see the result.

**After starting the debugger, you can use it just
as you did when investigating a local app. Add
breakpoints and navigate through the code.**

```
da-ch4-ex1 ) src ) main ) java ) com ) example ) services ) ⓒ ProductService ) ⓜ getTotalCosts        Chapter 4 ▾ ▶ ...
Project ▾                            ⓒ ProductService.java
  da-ch4-ex1  C:\MANNINGS\Debuggin
  > .idea                          16  public ProductService(ProductRepository productRepository) {
  ∨ src                            17      this.productRepository = productRepository;
    ∨ main                         18  }
      ∨ java
        ∨ com.example              19
          > controllers            20  public TotalCostResponse getTotalCosts() {
          ∨ model                  21      TotalCostResponse response = new TotalCostResponse();
            > dtos                 22      try {
            > entities             23        var products :List<Product>  = productRepository.findAll();
          > repositories
          ∨ services               24
            ⓒ ProductService       25      var costs :Map<String, BigDecimal>  = products.stream()
          ⓜ Main                   26          .collect(Collectors.toMap(
        ∨ resources                27              Product::getName,
          static                   28              p -> p.getPrice().multiply(new BigDecimal(p.getQuantity(
          templates
          application.properties   29
          data.sql                 30      response.setTotalCosts(costs);
          schema.sql
    > test
  > target
    mvnw
    mvnw.cmd
    pom.xml
  > External Libraries
  > Scratches and Consoles
```

**Figure 4.14 Just as when debugging an app locally, you can add breakpoints and use navigation
operations. Add a new breakpoint on line 23 in the `ProductService` class.**

After adding the breakpoint, use Postman (or a similar tool) to send the HTTP request with the unexpected behavior (figure 4.15). Postman (which you can download from https://www.postman.com/downloads/) is a simple tool you can use to call a given endpoint, and lately it has become one of developers' favorite tools for this purpose. Postman has a user-friendly GUI, but if you prefer the command line, you can choose another tool such as cURL. To make the example simple, I use Postman.

Using a tool such as Postman, send a request to the endpoint. You can see that the request doesn't finish, and it remains in a pending state because the debugger paused the app on the line you marked with a breakpoint.

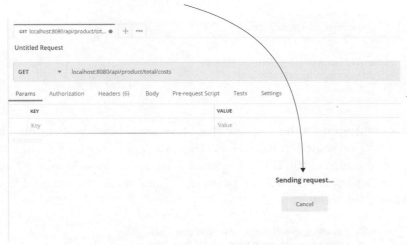

Figure 4.15   When using Postman to send the request, the response doesn't come back immediately. Instead, Postman waits indefinitely for the response because the app paused the execution on the line you marked with a breakpoint.

Note that Postman doesn't immediately show the HTTP response. Instead, you see that the request remains pending because the debugger paused the app on the line you marked with a breakpoint, as shown in figure 4.16. You can now start using the navigation operations to investigate the problem.

The execution paused on the line you marked with a breakpoint. You can now start navigating the code to investigate the issue.

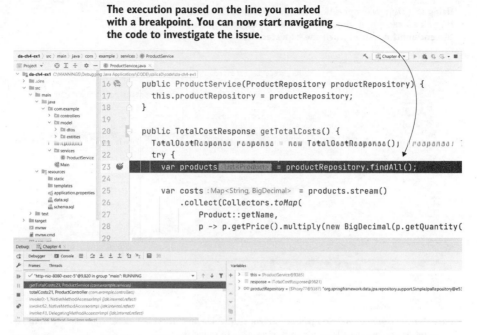

Figure 4.16   The IDE shows that the debugger did indeed pause the execution on the line you marked with a breakpoint. Thus, you can use navigation operations to continue your investigation.

Using a step over operation, you see that instead of returning the data from the database, the app throws an exception (figure 4.17). Now you can start to discern the problem:

1 The developer who implemented this functionality used a primitive type to represent a column that could take null values in a database. Since a primitive in Java is not an object type and cannot hold the value null, the app throws an exception.

2 The developer used the `printStackTrace()` method to print the exception message, which is not helpful because you can't easily configure the output for various environments. This is likely the reason you couldn't see anything in the logs in the first place (to be discussed further in chapter 5).

3 The problem did not happen locally or in the dev environment because there were no null values for that field in the database.

Clearly, the code needs to be refactored, and maybe an enhancement of the code review process should be discussed with the team in the next retrospective meeting. Nonetheless, you are happy that you found the cause of the issue and know how to solve it.

Using the step over operation, you can see that the code
throws an exception. Now you have a clue as to why
the endpoint doesn't return the expected result.

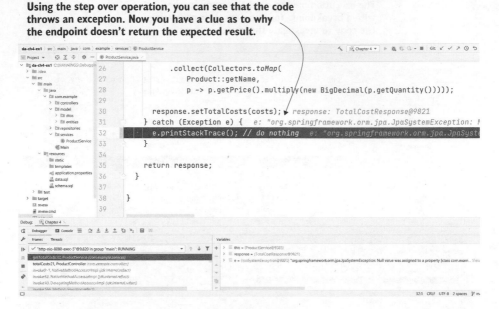

Figure 4.17   The step over operation shows that the app throws an exception. Now you have an idea of what the problem is and can decide how to solve it.

Creating a remote configuration in Eclipse IDE

I use IntelliJ IDEA as the primary IDE for the examples of the book. But, as I stated in earlier chapters, this book isn't about using a certain IDE. You can apply the techniques we discuss with a variety of tools of your choosing. For example, you can do remote debugging with other IDEs, such as Eclipse.

The following figure shows you how to add a new debugging configuration in Eclipse IDE.

To add a new debugging configuration in Eclipse IDE,
choose Run > Debug Configurations.

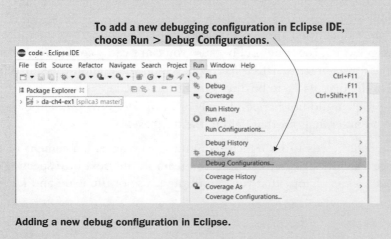

Adding a new debug configuration in Eclipse.

To add a new debug configuration in Eclipse IDE, choose Run > Debug Configurations. You can configure the debug configuration to attach it to the debugging agent controlling the remote app.

Just as in IntelliJ IDEA, you need to configure the debugging agent's address (IP address and port) to which the debugger tool connects.

Set the debugging agent address (IP address and port) and save the configuration.

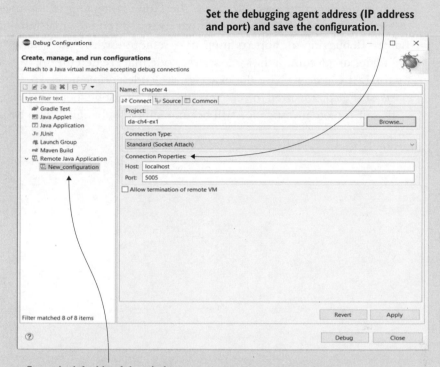

From the left side of the window, add a new Remote Java Application configuration.

Add a new Remote Java Application debug configuration and set the address of the debugger agent. You can then save the configuration and use the debugging feature to connect to the app remotely for debugging.

Once you've added the configuration, start the debugger and add the breakpoints to pause the execution where you want to start investigating your code.

Summary

- Sometimes the specific unexpected behavior of a running app happens only in certain environments in which the app executes. When this happens, debugging becomes more challenging.

- You can use a debugger with a Java app that executes in a remote environment with some conditions:
  - The app should be started with a debugger agent attached.
  - The network configuration should allow communication between the debugger tool and the debugger agent attached to the app in the remote environment.
- Remote debugging allows you to use the same debugging techniques as local debugging by attaching to a process that runs in a remote environment.
- Before debugging an app running in a remote environment, make sure the debugger uses a copy of the same source code that created the app you are investigating. If you don't have the exact source code and changes are made in the parts of the app involved in your investigation, the debugger may behave oddly, and your remote investigation will become more challenging than helpful.

Making the most
of logs: Auditing
an app's behavior

5

This chapter covers

- Effectively using logs to understand an app's behavior
- Correctly implementing log capabilities in your app
- Avoiding issues caused by logs

In this chapter, we will discuss using log messages that an app records. The concept of logging didn't first appear with software. For centuries, people used logs to help them understand past events and processes. People have used logging since writing was invented, and we still use it today. All ships have logbooks. Sailors record decisions (direction, speed increase or decrease, etc.) and given or received orders, along with any encountered event (figure 5.1). If something happens to the onboard equipment, they can use the logbook notes to understand where they are and navigate to the nearest shore. If an accident happens, the logbook notes can be

Figure 5.1   Sailors store events in logs that they can use to determine their route or analyze the crew's response to a given event. In the same way, apps store log messages so that developers can later analyze a potential issue or discover breaches in the app.

used in the investigation to determine how the unfortunate event could have been avoided.

If you've ever watched a chess game, you know that both players write down each piece's movement. Why? These logs help them re-create the entire game afterward. They study both their and their opponent's moves to spot potential mistakes or vulnerabilities.

For similar reasons, applications also log messages. We can use those messages to understand what happens when an app executes. By reading the log messages, you can re-create the execution in the same way that a chess player re-creates a whole chess game. We can use logs when we investigate a strange or unwanted behavior or more hard-to-see issues such as security vulnerabilities.

I'm sure you already know what logs look like. You've seen log messages, at least when running your app with an IDE (figure 5.2). All IDEs have a *log console*. It's one of the first things all software developers learn. But an app doesn't just display log messages in the IDE's console. Real-world apps store logs to allow developers to investigate a specific app behavior at a given time.

When running an app on your local system using the IDE, you find the log messages in the console.

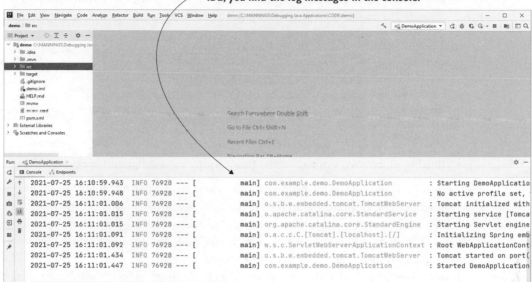

Figure 5.2   IDE log console. All IDEs have a log console. While logging messages in the console is useful when running the app locally, real-world apps also store logs that are needed to understand how the app behaved at a given time.

Figure 5.3 shows the anatomy of a standard-formatted log message. A log message is just a string, so theoretically it can be any sentence. However, clean and easy-to-use

Timestamp. When did the app write the message? The timestamp shows when a message was logged, and is a vital detail that allows us to chronologically order the messages. For this reason, the timestamp should always be at the beginning of the message.

Severity. How critical is the message? Severity indicates whether it's a highly important message that requires immediate attention or a message with details about an execution event.

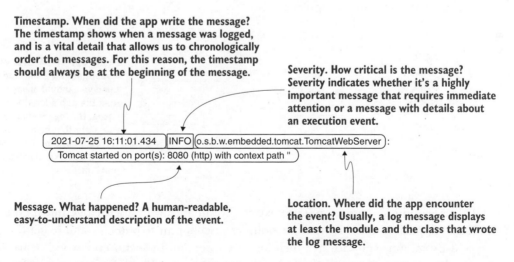

Message. What happened? A human-readable, easy-to-understand description of the event.

Location. Where did the app encounter the event? Usually, a log message displays at least the module and the class that wrote the log message.

Figure 5.3   The anatomy of a well-formatted log message. In addition to describing a situation or an event, a log message should also contain several other relevant details: the timestamp of when the app logged the message, the event's severity, and where the message was written. Using the details in these logs allows you to more easily investigate a problem.

logs need to follow some best practices (that you'll learn throughout this chapter). For example, in addition to a description, a log message contains a timestamp of when the app wrote the message, a description of the severity, and a notation for the part of the app that wrote the message (figure 5.3).

In many cases, logs are an efficient way to investigate an app's behavior. Some examples include the following:

- Investigating an event or a timeline of events that already happened
- Investigating issues where interfering with the app changes the app's behavior (Heisenbugs)
- Understanding the application's behavior over the long term
- Raising alarms for critical events that require immediate attention

We generally don't use just one technique when investigating how a particular app capability behaves. Depending on the scenario, a developer may combine several techniques to understand a particular behavior. In some cases, you'll use the debugger with logs as well as other techniques (which you'll learn in the following chapters) to figure out why something works the way it does.

I always recommend that developers check the logs before doing anything else when investigating an issue (figure 5.4). Logs often allow you to immediately identify strange behavior that helps you to pinpoint where to begin your investigation. The logs won't necessarily answer all your questions, but having a starting point is extremely important. If the log messages show you where to begin, you've already saved a lot of time!

Before deciding which investigation technique to use, you should read the log messages.

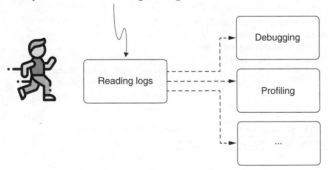

Figure 5.4   Whenever you investigate an issue, the first thing you should always do is read the app's logs. In many cases, the log messages give you a starting point or offer valuable hints on what you should do next to solve the problem.

In my opinion, logs are not just extremely valuable; they are, in fact, indispensable for any application. In the next section, we discuss how to use logs and learn the typical investigation scenarios in which logs are essential. In section 5.2, you'll learn how to properly implement logging capabilities in your app. We'll discuss using logging levels to help you more easily filter events and issues caused by logs. In section 5.3, we'll talk about the differences between using logs and remote debugging.

I also recommend reading part 4 of *Logging in Action* by Phil Wilkins (Manning, 2022). This chapter focuses more on investigation techniques with logs, while *Logging in Action* dives more deeply into logs' technicalities. You'll also find logging demonstrated using a different language than Java (Python).

5.1 Investigating issues with logs

Like any other investigation technique, using logs makes sense in some situations and doesn't in others. In this section, we examine various scenarios in which using logs can help you to more easily understand software's behavior. We'll begin by discussing several key points of log messages and then analyze how these characteristics assist developers in their investigation of app issues.

One of the biggest advantages of log messages is that they allow you to visualize the execution of a certain piece of code at a given time. When you use a debugger, as we discussed in chapters 2 through 4, your attention is mainly on the present. You look at how the data looks while the debugger pauses the execution on a specific line of code. A debugger doesn't give you many details on the execution history. You can use the execution stack trace to identify the execution path, but everything else is focused on the present.

In contrast, logs focus on the app's execution over a past period (figure 5.5). Log messages have a strong relationship with time.

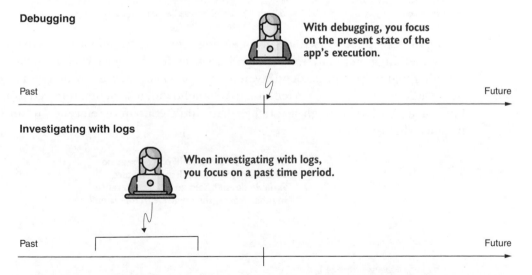

Figure 5.5   When investigating an issue with the debugger, you focus on the present. When you use log messages, you focus on a given period in the past. This difference can help you to decide which to use.

Remember to consider the time zone of the system on which your app is running. The log time may be shifted by a few hours because of different time zones (e.g., between where the app runs and where the developer is), and this can be confusing.

NOTE Always include the timestamp in a log message. You'll use the timestamp to easily identify the order in which messages were logged, which will give you an idea of when the app wrote a certain message. I recommend the timestamp be in the first part (at the beginning) of the message.

5.1.1   *Using logs to identify exceptions*

Logs help you to identify a problem after it occurred and investigate its root cause. Often, we use logs to decide where to start an investigation. We then continue exploring the problem using other tools and techniques, such as the debugger (as discussed in chapters 2–4) or a profiler (as discussed in chapters 6–9). You can often find exception stack traces in the logs. The next snippet shows an example of a Java exception stack trace:

```
java.lang.NullPointerException
at java.base/java.util.concurrent.ThreadPoolExecutor
➥   runWorker(ThreadPoolExecutor.java:1128) ~[na:na]
at java.base/java.util.concurrent.ThreadPoolExecutor$Worker
➥   run(ThreadPoolExecutor.java:628) ~[na:na]
at org.apache.tomcat.util.threads.TaskThread$WrappingRunnable
➥   run(TaskThread.java:61) ~[tomcat-embed-core-9.0.26.jar:9.0.26]
at java.base/java.lang.Thread.run(Thread.java:830) ~[na:na]
```

Seeing this exception stack trace, or something similar, in the application's log tells you that something potentially went wrong with a given feature. Each exception has its own meaning that helps you to identify where the app encountered a problem. For example, a `NullPointerException` tells you that somehow an instruction referred to an attribute or a method through a variable that didn't contain a reference to an object instance (figure 5.6).

If the app throws a NullPointerException on this line, it means that the invoice variable doesn't hold an object reference. In other words, the invoice variable is null.

```
var invoice = getLastIssuedInvoice();

if (client.isOverdue()) {
  invoice.pay();  ◄──
}
```

Figure 5.6   A `NullPointerException` indicates the app execution encountered a behavior that was called without the behaving instance. But that doesn't mean that the line that produced the exception is also the cause of the problem. The exception could be a consequence of the root cause. You should always look for the root cause instead of locally treating a problem.

NOTE   Remember that where an exception occurs is not necessarily the location of the root cause of the problem. An exception tells you where something went wrong, but the exception itself can be a consequence of a problem elsewhere. It is not necessarily the problem itself. Don't make a decision about solving the exception locally by adding a `try-catch-finally` block or an `if-else` statement too quickly. First, make sure you understand the root cause of the problem before looking for a solution to solve it.

I often find that this concept confuses beginners. Let's take a simple `NullPointer-Exception`, which is probably the first exception any Java developer encounters and one of the simplest to understand. However, when you find a `NullPointerException` in the logs, you need first to ask yourself: why is that reference missing? It could be missing because a particular instruction that the app executed earlier didn't work as expected (figure 5.7).

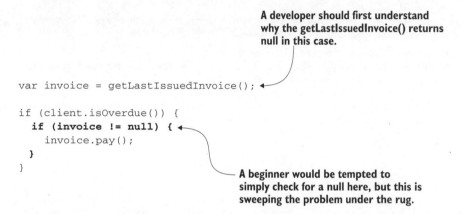

A developer should first understand why the getLastIssuedInvoice() returns null in this case.

```
var invoice = getLastIssuedInvoice();

if (client.isOverdue()) {
  if (invoice != null) {
    invoice.pay();
  }
}
```

A beginner would be tempted to simply check for a null here, but this is sweeping the problem under the rug.

Figure 5.7   Locally solving the problem is in many cases equivalent to sweeping it under the rug. If the root cause remains, more issues can appear later. Remember that an exception in the logs doesn't necessarily indicate the root cause.

5.1.2   *Using exception stack traces to identify what calls a method*

One of the techniques developers consider unusual, but that I find advantageous in practice, is logging an exception stack trace to identify what calls a specific method. Since starting my career as a software developer, I've worked with messy codebases of (usually) large applications. One of the difficulties I frequently encounter is figuring out who calls a given method when an app is running in a remote environment. If you just read the app's code, you will discover hundreds of ways that method could've been called.

Of course, if you are lucky enough, and have access, you can use remote bugging as discussed in chapter 4. You can then access the execution stack trace the debugger provides. But what if you can't use a debugger remotely? In this case, you can use a logging technique instead!

Exceptions in Java have a capability that is often disregarded: they keep track of the execution stack trace. When discussing exceptions, we often call the execution stack trace an *exception* stack trace. But they are, in the end, the same thing. The exception stack trace displays the chain of method calls that cause a specific exception, and you have access to this information even without throwing that exception. In code, it's enough to use the exception:

```
new Exception().printStackTrace();
```

Consider the method in listing 5.1. If you don't have a debugger, you can simply print the exception stack trace, as I did in this example, as the first line in the method to find the execution stack trace. Keep in mind that this only prints the stack trace and doesn't throw the exception, so it doesn't interfere with the executed logic. This example is in project da-ch5-ex1.

Listing 5.1   Printing the execution stack trace in logs using an exception

```
public List<Integer> extractDigits() {
  new Exception().printStackTrace();        ⟵——— Prints the exception stack trace
  List<Integer> list = new ArrayList<>();
  for (int i = 0; i < input.length(); i++) {
    if (input.charAt(i) >= '0' && input.charAt(i) <= '9') {
      list.add(Integer.parseInt(String.valueOf(input.charAt(i))));
    }
  }

  return list;
}
```

The next snippet shows how the app prints the exception stack trace in the console. In a real-world scenario, the stack trace helps you to immediately identify the execution flow, which leads to the call you want to investigate, as we discussed in chapters 2 and 3. In this example, you can see from the logs that the extractDigits() method was called on line 11 of the Decoder class from within the decode() method:

```
java.lang.Exception at main.StringDigitExtractor
➡ extractDigits(StringDigitExtractor.java:15)
    at main.Decoder.decode(Decoder.java:11)
    at main.Main.main(Main.java:9)
```

5.1.3   *Measuring time spent to execute a given instruction*

Log messages are an easy way to measure the time a given set of instructions takes to execute. You can always log the difference between the timestamp before and after a given line of code. Suppose you are investigating a performance issue in which some given capability takes too long to execute. You suspect that the cause is a query the app executes to retrieve data from the database. For some parameter values, the query is slow, which is decreasing the app's overall performance.

To find which parameter is causing the problem, you can write the query and the query execution time in logs. Once you identify the troublesome parameter values, you can start looking for a solution. Maybe you need to add one more index to a table in the database, or perhaps you can rewrite the query to make it faster.

Listing 5.2 shows you how to log the time spent by the execution of a specific piece of code. For example, let's figure out how much time it takes the app to run the operation of finding all the products from the database. Yes, I know, we have no parameters here; I simplified the example to allow you to focus on the discussed syntax. But in a real-world app, you would most likely investigate a more complex operation.

> **Listing 5.2   Logging the execution time for a certain line of code**

```
public TotalCostResponse getTotalCosts() {
  TotalCostResponse response = new TotalCostResponse();

  long timeBefore = System.currentTimeMillis();
  var products = productRepository.findAll();
  long spentTimeInMillis =
     System.currentTimeMillis() - timeBefore;

  log.info("Execution time: " + spentTimeInMillis);

  var costs = products.stream().collect(
        Collectors.toMap(
           Product::getName,
           p -> p.getPrice()
             .multiply(new BigDecimal(p.getQuantity()))));

  response.setTotalCosts(costs);

  return response;
}
```

Logs the timestamp before the method's execution

Executes the method for which we want to calculate the execution time

Calculates the time spent between the timestamp after execution and the timestamp before the execution

Prints the execution time

Precisely measuring how much time an app spends executing a given instruction is a simple but effective technique. However, I would only use this technique temporarily when investigating an issue. I don't recommend you keep such logs in the code for long since they most likely will not be needed later, and they make the code more difficult to read. Once you've solved the problem and no longer need to know the execution time for that line of code, you can remove the logs.

5.1.4   *Investigating issues in multithreaded architectures*

A multithreaded architecture is a type of capability that uses multiple threads to define its functionality and is often sensitive to external interference (figure 5.8). For example, if you use a debugger or a profiler (tools that interfere with the app's execution), the app's behavior may change (figure 5.9).

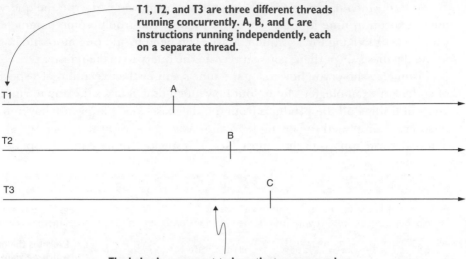

T1, T2, and T3 are three different threads running concurrently. A, B, and C are instructions running independently, each on a separate thread.

The behavior you want to investigate appears when instructions A, B, and C run in this order.

Figure 5.8   A multithreaded architecture. An app with the capability to use multiple threads running concurrently to process data is a multithreaded app. Unless explicitly synchronized, instructions running on independent threads (A, B, and C) can run in any order.

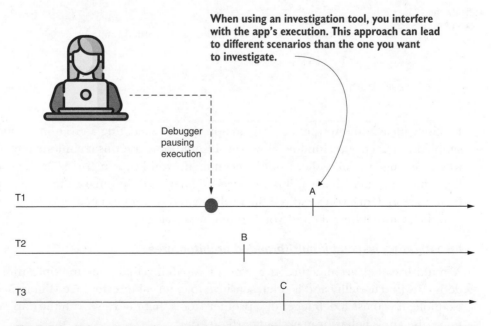

When using an investigation tool, you interfere with the app's execution. This approach can lead to different scenarios than the one you want to investigate.

Debugger pausing execution

Figure 5.9   Using a tool such as a debugger or a profiler interferes with the execution, making some (or all) threads slower. Because of this, the execution often changes, and some instructions may execute in a different order than the scenario you wanted to investigate. In such a case, the tool is no longer useful since you can't research the behavior you're interested in.

However, if you use logs, there's a smaller chance the app will be affected while running. Logs can also sometimes interfere in multithreaded apps, but they don't have a big enough impact on the execution to change the app's flow. Thus, they can be a solution for retrieving the data needed for your investigation.

Since log messages contain a timestamp (as discussed earlier in the chapter), you can order the log messages to find the sequence in which the operations execute. In a Java app, it is sometimes helpful to log the thread's name that executes a certain instruction. You can get the name of the current thread in execution using the following instruction:

```
String threadName = Thread.currentThread().getName();
```

In Java apps, all threads have a name. The developer can name them, or the JVM will identify the threads using a name with the pattern Thread-x, where x is an incremented number. For example, the first thread created will be named Thread-0; the next one, Thread-1; and so on. As we'll discuss in chapter 10 when we address thread dumps, naming your app's threads is good practice so that you can identify them easier when investigating a case.

5.2 Implementing logging

In this section, we discuss best practices for implementing logging capabilities in apps. To make your app's log messages ready for investigations and avoid causing trouble with the app's execution, you need to take care of some implementation details.

We'll start by discussing how apps persist logs in section 5.2.1—specifically the advantages and disadvantages of these practices. In section 5.2.2, you'll learn how to use the log messages more efficiently by classifying them based on severity and thus make the app perform better. In section 5.2.3, we'll discuss the problems log messages can cause and how to avoid them.

5.2.1 Persisting logs

Persistence is one of the essential characteristics of log messages. As discussed earlier in this chapter, logging is different from other investigation techniques because it focuses more on the past than the present. We read logs to understand something that happened, so the app needs to store them so that we can read them later. How log messages are stored can affect the logs' usability and the app's performance. I've worked with many apps and have had the chance to see various ways developers implement log message persistence:

- Storing logs in a nonrelational database
- Storing logs in files
- Storing logs in a relational database

These can all be good choices depending on what your app does. Let's look at some of the main things you need to consider to make the right decision.

STORING LOGS IN NONRELATIONAL DATABASES

Nonrelational (NoSQL) databases help you to make compromises between performance and consistency. You can use a NoSQL database to store logs in a more performant way, which gives the database a chance to miss log messages or not store them in the exact chronological order in which the app wrote them. But, as we discussed earlier in this chapter, a log message should always contain the timestamp when the message was stored, preferably at the beginning of the message.

Storing log messages in NoSQL databases is common. In most cases, apps use a complete engine that stores the logs and has the capability to retrieve, search, and analyze the log messages. Today's two most-used engines are the ELK stack (https://www.elastic .co/what-is/elk-stack) and Splunk (https://www.splunk.com/).

STORING LOGS IN FILES

In the past, apps stored logs in files. You may still find older applications that write log messages directly in files, but this approach is less common today because it is generally slower, and searching for logged data is more difficult. I bring this to your attention because you'll find many tutorials and examples in which apps store their logs in files, but with more current apps, you should avoid this.

STORING LOGS IN A RELATIONAL DATABASE

We rarely use relational databases to store log messages. A relational database mainly guarantees data consistency, which ensures log messages are not lost. Once they are stored, you can retrieve them. But consistency comes with a compromise in performance.

In most apps, losing a log message is not a big deal, and performance is generally preferred over consistency. But, as always, in real-world apps, there are exceptions. For example, governments worldwide impose log message regulations for financial apps, especially for payment capabilities. Such capabilities should generally have specific log messages that the app isn't allowed to lose. Failure to comply with these regulations can result in sanctions and fines.

5.2.2   *Defining logging levels and using logging frameworks*

In this section, we discuss logging levels and properly implementing logging in an app using logging frameworks. We'll start by examining why logging levels are essential and then implement an example.

Logging levels, also called *severities*, are a way to classify log messages based on their importance to your investigation. An app usually produces a large number of log messages while running. However, you often don't need all the details in all the log messages. Some of the messages are more important to your investigation than others: some represent critical events that always require attention.

The most common log levels (severities) are as follows:

- *Error*—A critical issue. The app should always log such events. Usually, unhandled exceptions in Java apps are logged as errors.

- *Warn*—-An event that is potentially an error, but the application handles it. For example, if a connection to a third-party system initially fails but the app manages to send the call on a second try, the problem should be logged as a warning.
- *Info*—"Common" log messages. These messages represent the main app execution events that help you to understand the app's behavior in most situations.
- *Debug*—Fine-grained details that you should enable only when info messages are not enough

Note that different libraries may use more than, or different names for, these four severity levels. For example, in some cases, apps or frameworks may use the severity levels *fatal* (more critical than error) and *trace* (less critical than debug). In this chapter, I focus only on the most encountered severities and terminologies in real-world apps.

Classifying the log messages based on severity allows you to minimize the number of log messages your app stores. You should only allow your app to log the most relevant details and enable more logging only when you need more details.

Look at figure 5.10, which presents the log severity pyramid:

- An app logs a small number of critical issues, but these have high importance, so they always need to be logged.
- The closer you get to the bottom of the pyramid, the more log messages the app writes, but they become less critical and less frequently needed in investigations.

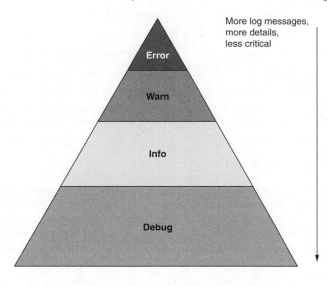

Figure 5.10   The log severity pyramid. On the top are the critical log messages that usually require immediate attention. The bottom represents the log messages that provide details you'll rarely need. From the top to the bottom, the log messages become less essential but greater in number. Usually, the debug-level messages are disabled by default, and the developer can choose to enable them if their investigation requires fine-grained details about the app's execution.

For most investigation cases, you won't need the messages classified as debug. Plus, because of their large number, they make your research more challenging. For this reason, debug messages are generally disabled, and you should enable them only when you face a problem for which you need more details.

When you started learning Java, you were taught how to print something in the console using `System.out` or `System.err`. Eventually, you learned to use `printStack-Trace()` to log an exception message, as I used in section 5.1.2. But these ways of working with logs in Java apps don't give enough flexibility for configuration. So, instead of using them in real-world apps, I recommend you use a logging framework.

Implementing the logging levels is simple. Today, the Java ecosystem offers various logging framework options such as Logback, Log4j, and the Java Logging API. These frameworks are similar, and using them is straightforward.

Let's take an example and implement logging with Log4j. This example is in project da-ch5-ex2. To implement the logging capabilities with Log4j, you first need to add the Log4j dependency. In our Maven project, you must change the pom.xml and add the Log4j dependency.

Listing 5.3   Dependencies you need to add in the pom.xml file to use Log4j

```
<dependencies>
    <dependency>
        <groupId>org.apache.logging.log4j</groupId>
        <artifactId>log4j-api</artifactId>
        <version>2.14.1</version>
    </dependency>
    <dependency>
        <groupId>org.apache.logging.log4j</groupId>
        <artifactId>log4j-core</artifactId>
        <version>2.14.1</version>
    </dependency>
</dependencies>
```

Once you have the dependency in the project, you can declare a `Logger` instance in any class where you want to write log messages. With Log4j, the simplest way to create a `Logger` instance is by using the `LogManager.getLogger()` method, as presented in listing 5.4. This method allows you to write log messages that are named the same as the severity of the event they represent. For example, if you want to log a message with the info severity level, you'll use the `info()` method. If you want to log a message with the debug severity level, you'll use the `debug()` method, and so on.

Listing 5.4   Writing the log messages with different severities

```
public class StringDigitExtractor {

    private static Logger log = LogManager.getLogger();    ⟵─┐ Declares a logger instance
                                                             │ for the current class to
    private final String input;                              │ write log messages

    public StringDigitExtractor(String input) {
```

```
      this.input = input;
   }

   public List<Integer> extractDigits() {
      log.info("Extracting digits for input {}", input);      ⟵  Writes a message
      List<Integer> list = new ArrayList<>();                     with the info severity
      for (int i = 0; i < input.length(); i++) {
         log.debug("Parsing character {} of input {}",       ⟵  Writes a message with
            input.charAt(i), input);                              the debug severity
         if (input.charAt(i) >= '0' && input.charAt(i) <= '9') {
            list.add(Integer.parseInt(String.valueOf(input.charAt(i))));
         }
      }

      log.info("Extract digits result for input {} is {}", input, list);
      return list;
   }
}
```

Once you've decided which messages to log and used the `Logger` instance to write them, you need to configure Log4j to tell the app how and where to write these messages. We'll use an XML file that we name log4j2.xml to configure Log4j. This XML file must be in the app's class path, so we'll add it to the resources folder of our Maven project. We need to define three things (figure 5.11):

- *A logger*—Tells Log4j which messages are to be written to which appender
- *An appender*—Tells Log4j where to write the log messages
- *A formatter*—Tells Log4j how to print the messages

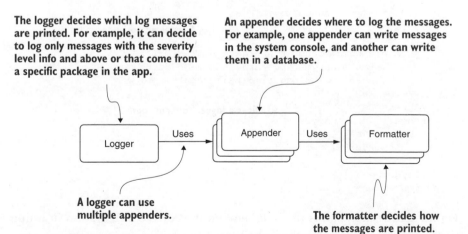

Figure 5.11   The relationship between the appender, logger, and formatter. A logger uses one or more appenders. The logger decides what to write (e.g., only log messages printed by objects in the package). The logger gives the messages to be written to one or more appenders. Each appender then implements a certain way to store the messages. The appender uses formatters to shape the messages before storing them.

The logger defines which messages the app logs. In this example, we use Root to write the messages from any part of the app. Its attribute level, which has the value info, means only the messages with a severity of info and higher are logged. The logger can also decide to log only messages from specific app parts. For example, when using a framework, you are rarely interested in the log messages the framework prints, but you are often interested in your app's log messages, so you can define a logger that excludes the framework's log messages and only prints those coming from your app. Remember that you want to write only essential log messages. Otherwise, an investigation can become unnecessarily more challenging since you must then filter out the nonessential log messages.

In a real-world app, you can define multiple appenders, which will most likely be configured to store the messages in different sources, like a database or files in the filesystem. In section 5.2.1, we discussed multiple ways apps can retain log messages. Appenders are simply implementations that take care of storing the log messages in a given way.

The appender also uses a formatter that defines the format of the message. For this example, the formatter specifies that the messages should include the timestamp and the severity level, so the app only needs to send the description.

Listing 5.5 shows the configuration that defines both an appender and a logger. In this example, we define just one appender, which tells Log4j to log the messages in the standard output stream of the system (the console).

Listing 5.5   Configuring the appender and the logger in the log4j2.xml file

```xml
<?xml version="1.0" encoding="UTF-8"?>
<Configuration status="WARN">                      Defines an appender
    <Appenders>                            ◁
        <Console name="Console" target="SYSTEM_OUT">
            <PatternLayout pattern="%d{yy-MM-dd HH:mm:ss.SSS} [%t]
              %-5level %logger{36} - %msg%n"/>
        </Console>
    </Appenders>                       Defines a logger configuration
    <Loggers>                    ◁
      <Root level="info">
        <AppenderRef ref="Console"/>
      </Root>
    </Loggers>
</Configuration>
```

Figure 5.12 visually shows the link between the XML configuration in listing 5.5 and the three components it defines: the logger, appender, and formatter.

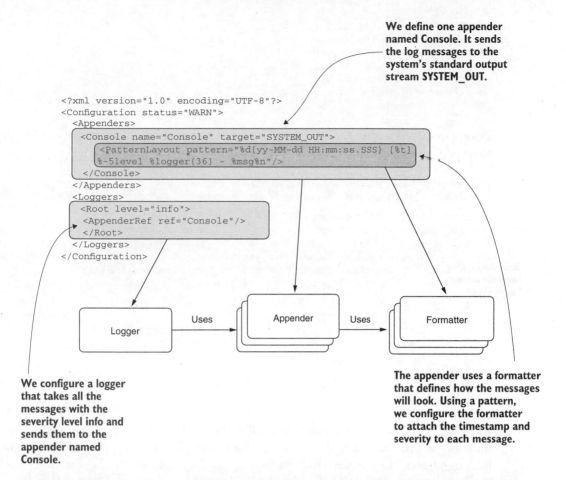

Figure 5.12 **The components in configuration. The logger** `Root` **takes all the log messages with severity level info that the app writes. The logger sends the messages to the appender named** `Console`**. The appender** `Console` **is configured to send the messages to the system terminal. It uses a formatter to attach the timestamp and the severity level to the message before writing it.**

The next snippet shows a section of the logs printed when the example runs. Note that debug messages aren't logged since they are lower in severity than info (line 10 in listing 5.5).

```
21-07-28 13:17:39.915 [main] INFO
  main.StringDigitExtractor
  Extracting digits for input ab1c
21-07-28 13:17:39.932 [main] INFO
  main.StringDigitExtractor
  Extract digits result for input ab1c is [1]
```

```
21-07-28 13:17:39.943 [main] INFO
➡ main.StringDigitExtractor
➡ Extracting digits for input a112c
21-07-28 13:17:39.944 [main] INFO
➡ main.StringDigitExtractor
➡ Extract digits result for input a112c is [1, 1, 2]
…
```

If we wanted the app to also log the messages with the debug severity, we would have to change the logger definition.

Listing 5.6   Using a different severity configuration

```
<?xml version="1.0" encoding="UTF-8"?>
<Configuration status="WARN">
    <Appenders>
        <Console name="Console" target="SYSTEM_OUT">
            <PatternLayout pattern="%d{yy-MM-dd HH:mm:ss.SSS} [%t]
            %-5level %logger{36} - %msg%n"/>
        </Console>
    </Appenders>

    <Loggers>
        <Root level="debug">
            <AppenderRef ref="Console"/>
        </Root>
    </Loggers>
</Configuration>
```

Sets the logging level for internal Log4j events → `<Configuration status="WARN">`

Changes the logging level to debug → `<Root level="debug">`

In listing 5.6, you can see a status and a logging level. This usually creates confusion. Most of the time, you care about the `level` attribute, which shows which messages will be logged according to severity. The `status` attribute in the `<Configuration>` tag is the severity of the Log4J events, the issues the library encounters. That is, the `status` attribute is the logging configuration of the logging library.

We can change the logger in listing 5.6 to also write the messages with the priority:

```
21-07-28 13:18:36.164 [main ] INFO
➡ main.StringDigitExtractor
➡ Extracting digits for input ab1c
21-07-28 13:18:36.175 [main] DEBUG
➡ main.StringDigitExtractor
➡ Parsing character a of input ab1c
21-07-28 13:18:36.176 [main] DEBUG
➡ main.StringDigitExtractor
➡ Parsing character b of input ab1c
21-07-28 13:18:36.176 [main] DEBUG
➡ main.StringDigitExtractor
➡ Parsing character 1 of input ab1c
21-07-28 13:18:36.176 [main] DEBUG
➡ main.StringDigitExtractor
➡ Parsing character c of input ab1c
```

```
21-07-28 13:18:36.177 [main] INFO
➥ main.StringDigitExtractor
➥ Extract digits result for input ab1c is [1]
21-07-28 13:18:36.181 [main] INFO
➥ main.StringDigitExtractor
➥ Extracting digits for input a112c
...
```

A logger library gives you the flexibility to log only what you need. Writing the minimum number of log messages necessary to investigate a certain issue is good practice as it can help you to understand the logs more easily and keep the app performing well and maintainable. A logging library also gives you the capability of configuring the logs without needing to recompile the app.

5.2.3 *Problems caused by logging and how to avoid them*

We store log messages so that we can use them to understand how an app behaved at a certain point in time or over time. Logs are necessary and extremely helpful in many cases, but they can also become malicious if mishandled. In this section, we discuss three main problems logs can cause and how to avoid them (figure 5.13):

- *Security and privacy issues*—Caused by log messages exposing private data
- *Performance issues*—Caused by the app storing too many or too-large log messages
- *Maintainability issues*—Caused by log instructions that make the source code more difficult to read

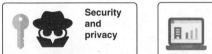 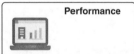 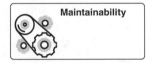

Figure 5.13 Small details can cause big problems. Developers sometimes consider an app's logging capability harmless by default and disregard the problems logging can introduce. Logging, however, like all the other software capabilities, deals with the data and, wrongly implemented, can affect the app's functionality and maintainability.

SECURITY AND PRIVACY ISSUES

Security is one of my favorite topics and one of the most important subjects a developer needs to consider when they implement an app. One of the books I wrote concerns security, and if you implement apps using the Spring Framework and want to learn more about securing them, I recommend you read it: *Spring Security in Action* (Manning, 2020).

Surprisingly, logs can sometimes cause vulnerabilities in applications, and in most cases, these issues happen because developers are not attentive to the details they expose. Remember that logs make specific details visible to anyone who can access them. You always need to think about whether the data you log should be visible to those who can access the logs (figure 5.14).

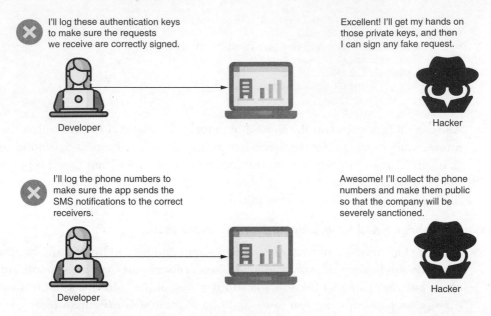

Figure 5.14   Log messages should not contain secret or private details. No one working on the app or the infrastructure where the app is deployed should access such data. Exposing sensitive details in logs can help a malicious person (hacker) to find easier ways to break the system or create security-related problems.

The following snippet shows some examples of log messages that expose sensitive details and cause vulnerabilities:

```
Successful login.
User bob logged in with password RwjBaWIs66

Failed authentication.
The token is unsigned.
The token should have a signature with IVL4KiKMfz.

A new notification was sent to
    the following phone number +1233…
```

What's wrong with the logs presented here? The first two log messages expose private details. You should never log passwords or private keys that are used to sign tokens, or any other exchanged information. A password is something only its owner should know. For this reason, no app should store any passwords in clear text (whether in a log or a database). Private keys and similar secret details should be stored in a secrets vault to protect them from being stolen. If someone gets the value of such a key, they can impersonate an application or a user.

The third log message example exposes a phone number. A phone number is considered a personal detail, and around the world, specific regulations restrict the use of such details. For example, the European Union implemented the General Data

Protection Regulation (GDPR) in May 2018. An application with users in any European Union state must comply with these regulations to avoid severe sanctions. The regulations allow any user to request all their personal data an app uses and to request immediate deletion of the data. Storing information such as phone numbers in logs exposes these private details and makes retrieving and deleting them more difficult.

PERFORMANCE ISSUES

Writing logs entails sending details (usually as strings) through an I/O stream somewhere outside the app. We can simply send this information to the app's console (terminal), or we can store it in files or even a database, as we discussed in section 5.2.1. Either way, you need to remember that logging a message is also an instruction that takes time; adding too many log messages can dramatically decrease an app's performance.

I remember an issue my team investigated some years ago. A customer in Asia reported a problem with the application we were implementing in factories for inventory purposes. The problem wasn't causing much trouble, but we found it challenging to get to the root cause, so we decided to add more log messages. After delivering a patch with the small change, the system became very slow, almost unresponsive sometimes, which ultimately caused a production standstill, and we had to quickly revert our change. We somehow managed to change a mosquito into an elephant.

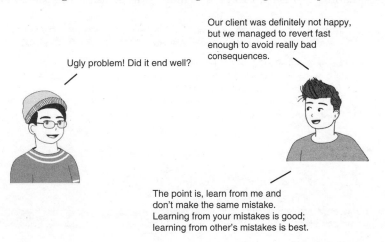

Our client was definitely not happy, but we managed to revert fast enough to avoid really bad consequences.

Ugly problem! Did it end well?

The point is, learn from me and don't make the same mistake. Learning from your mistakes is good; learning from other's mistakes is best.

But how could some simple log messages cause such big trouble? The logs were configured to send the messages to a separate server in the network, where they persisted. Not only was the network extremely slow in that factory, but also the log message added to a loop that was iterating over a significant number of items, making the app extremely slow.

In the end, we learned some things that helped us be more careful and avoid repeating the same mistake:

- Make sure you understand how the app logs the messages. Remember that even for the same app different deployments can have different configurations (see section 5.2.2).
- Avoid logging too many messages. Don't log messages in loops iterating over a large number of elements. Logging too many messages will also make reading the logs complicated. If you need to log messages in a large loop, use a condition to narrow the number of iterations for which the message is logged.
- Make sure that the app stores a given log message only when that's really needed. You limit the number of log messages you store by using logging levels, as we discussed in section 5.2.2.
- Implement the logging mechanism in such a way that you enable and disable it without needing to restart the service. This will allow you to change to a finer-grained logging level, get your needed details, and then make your logging less sensitive again.

MAINTAINABILITY

Log messages can also negatively affect an app's maintainability. If you add log messages too frequently, they can make the app's logic more difficult to understand. Let's look at an example: try reading listings 5.7 and 5.8. Which code is easier to understand?

Listing 5.7   A method implementing a simple piece of logic

```
public List<Integer> extractDigits() {
  List<Integer> list = new ArrayList<>();
  for (int i = 0; i < input.length(); i++) {
    if (input.charAt(i) >= '0' && input.charAt(i) <= '9') {
      list.add(Integer.parseInt(String.valueOf(input.charAt(i))));
    }
  }

  return list;
  }
```

Listing 5.8   A method implementing a simple piece of logic crowded with log messages

```
public List<Integer> extractDigits() {
  log.info("Creating a new list to store the result.");
  List<Integer> list = new ArrayList<>();
  log.info("Iterating through the input string " + input);
  for (int i = 0; i < input.length(); i++) {
    log.info("Processing character " + i + " of the string");
    if (input.charAt(i) >= '0' && input.charAt(i) <= '9') {
      log.info("Character " + i +
               " is digit. Character: " +
               input.charAt(i))
      log.info("Adding character" + input.charAt(i) + " to the list");
      list.add(Integer.parseInt(String.valueOf(input.charAt(i))));
    }
  }
```

```
    Log.info("Returning the result " + list);
    return list;
}
```

Both show the same piece of implemented logic. But in listing 5.8, I added numerous log messages, which make the method's logic more challenging to read.

How do we avoid affecting an app's maintainability?

- You don't necessarily need to add a log message for each instruction in the code. Identify those instructions that provide the most relevant details. Remember, you can add extra logging later if the existing log messages are not enough.
- Keep the methods small enough so that you only need to log the parameters' values and the value the method returned after the execution.
- Some frameworks allow you to decouple part of the code from the method. For example, in Spring, you can use custom aspects to log the result of a method's execution (including the parameters' values and the value the method returned after the execution).

5.3   Logs vs. remote debugging

In chapter 4, we discussed remote debugging, and you learned that you can connect the debugger to an app executing in an external environment. I start this discussion because my students often ask me why we need to use logs since we can connect and directly debug a given issue. But as I mentioned earlier in this chapter, and in previous ones, these debugging techniques don't exclude one another. Sometimes one is better than the other; in other cases, you need to use them together.

Let's analyze what we can and can't do with logs versus remote debugging to figure out how you can efficiently use these two techniques. Table 5.1 shows a side-by-side comparison of logs and remote debugging.

Table 5.1   Logs vs. remote debugging

Capability	Logs	Remote debugging
Can be used to understand a remotely executing app's behavior	✓	✓
Needs special network permissions or configurations	✗	✓
Persistently stores execution clues	✓	✗

Table 5.1   **Logs vs. remote debugging** *(continued)*

Capability	Logs	Remote debugging
Allows you to pause the execution on a given line of code to understand what the app does	✖	✔
Can be used to understand an app's behavior without interfering with the executed logic	±	✖
Is recommended for production environments	✔	✖

You can use both logs and remote debugging to understand the behavior of a remotely executing app. But both approaches have their own difficulties. Logging implies that the app writes the events and the data needed for the investigation. If that's not the case, you need to add those instructions and redeploy the app. This is what developers usually call "adding extra logs." Remote debugging allows your debugger to connect to the remotely executing app, but specific network configurations and permissions need to be granted.

A big difference is the philosophy each technique implies. Debugging is focused on the present. You pause the execution and observe the app's current state. Logging is more about the past. You get a bunch of log messages and analyze the execution, focusing on a timeline. It's common to use debugging and logging simultaneously to understand more complex issues, and I can tell you from experience that sometimes using logs versus debugging depends on the developer's preference. I sometimes see developers using a technique simply because they are more comfortable with one than another.

Summary

- Always check the app's logs when you start investigating any issue. The logs may indicate what's wrong or at least give you a starting point for your investigation.
- All log messages should include a timestamp. Remember that in most cases a system doesn't guarantee the order in which the logs are stored. The timestamp will help you to order the log messages chronologically.
- Avoid saving too many log messages. Not every detail is relevant or helpful in investigating a potential issue, and storing too many log messages can affect the app's performance and make the code more difficult to read.
- You should implement more logging only if needed. A running app should only log essential messages. If you require more details, you can always enable more logging for a short time.

- An exception in the logs is not necessarily the root of the problem. It could be a consequence of a problem. Research what caused the exception before treating it locally.

- You can use exception stack traces to figure out what called a given method. In large, messy, and difficult-to-understand codebases, this approach can be very helpful and save you time.

- Never write sensitive details (e.g., passwords, private keys, or personal details) in a log message. Logging passwords or private keys introduces security vulnerabilities since anyone with access to the logs can see and use them. Writing personal details such as names, addresses, or phone numbers also may not comply with various government regulations.

Part 2

Deep analysis of an app's execution

In part 2, we will discuss advanced techniques you can use to deeply investigate an app's execution. Most developers are exposed to debugging and logging (discussed in part 1), but not many know how to find all the "secrets" of an execution's process by using profiling techniques, investigating threads, and analyzing the memory consumption. Knowing these techniques is essential and sometimes is the only way to solve certain puzzles.

In chapter 6, you'll learn how to analyze CPU and memory consumption. In chapter 7, we'll discuss using a profiler to identify latency problems. In chapters 8 and 9, we'll do a deep dive into multithreaded architectures using profilers, and in chapter 10, we will discuss thread dumps. We end part 2 with chapter 11, where you'll learn how to identify memory consumption issues using heap dumps.

6
Identifying resource consumption problems using profiling techniques

This chapter covers
- Evaluating resource consumption
- Identifying issues with resource consumption

"And for you, Frodo Baggins, I give you the light of Eärendil, our most beloved star. May it be a light to you in dark places when all other lights go out."

—Galadriel (*Lord of the Rings*, by J.R.R. Tolkien)

In this chapter, we start with using a profiler. We'll continue the discussion in chapter 7. A profiler may not be as powerful as the light of Eärendil, but this tool is definitely a light in dark cases when all the other lights go out. A *profiler* is a powerful tool that has helped me to understand the root cause of an app's strange behavior in many difficult situations. I consider learning to use a profiler a must for all developers, as it can be a compass to guide you to the cause of a seemingly hopeless problem. As you'll learn in this chapter, the profiler intercepts the executing JVM processes and offers extremely useful details:

- How the app consumes resources such as the CPU and memory
- The threads in execution and their current status
- The code in execution and the resources spent by a given piece of code (e.g., the duration of each method's execution)

In section 6.1, we will analyze some scenarios so you can see how the details provided by a profiler can be useful and why they are so important. In section 6.2, we will discuss using a profiler to solve the scenarios in section 6.1. We'll start by installing and configuring a profiler in section 6.2.1. Then, in section 6.2.2., we'll analyze how an app consumes system resources, and in section 6.2.3, we'll learn how to identify when an app is having issues with managing the used memory. We'll continue our discussion about using a profiler in chapter 7, where you'll learn how to identify the code in execution and the performance problems related to it.

I use the VisualVM profiler for the examples in this chapter. VisualVM is a free profiler and an excellent tool I've successfully used for many years. You can download VisualVM here: https://visualvm.github.io/download.html. VisualVM is not the only profiling tool for Java apps. Some other well-known profiling tools are Java Mission Control (http://mng.bz/AVQE) and JProfiler (http://mng.bz/Zplj).

6.1   Where would a profiler be useful?

In this section, we analyze three scenarios in which a profiling tool can help you:

- Identifying abnormal usage of resources
- Finding which part of code executes
- Identifying slowness in an app's execution

6.1.1   Identifying abnormal usage of resources

A profiler is commonly used to determine how an app consumes CPU and memory, which helps you to understand the app's specific problems. Thus, it is the first step in investigating such issues. Observing how the app consumes resources will usually lead you to two categories of issues:

- *Thread-related issues*—Usually concurrency issues caused by a lack of or improper synchronization
- *Memory leaks*—Situations in which the app fails to remove unneeded data from memory, causing slowness in execution and potentially a complete failure of the app

I've encountered both types of issues in real-world apps more than I would have liked. The effects of resource usage issues are very diverse. In some cases, they just cause slowness in the app; in other cases, they may cause the app to fail entirely. My "favorite" thread-related issue I have had to solve using a profiler was causing battery problems on a mobile device. Slowness wasn't the biggest problem. Users complained that their device's battery was consumed unnaturally fast when they used this Android-based app. This behavior definitely required investigation. After spending some time observing the app's behavior, I discovered that one of the libraries the app used sometimes created threads that remained in execution and did nothing but consume the system's resources. In a mobile app, CPU resource use is often reflected in the battery's consumption.

Once you discover the potential problem, you can investigate it further with a thread dump, as you'll learn in chapter 10. Generally, the root cause of such problems is a faulty synchronization of the threads.

I also find memory leaks now and then in apps. In most cases, the final result of a memory leak is an `OutOfMemoryError` that leads to an app crash. So when I hear about an app crashing, I usually suspect a memory problem.

TIP Whenever you encounter an app that is randomly crashing, you should consider a memory leak.

The root cause of abnormal resource use is often an error in coding that allows object references to exist even after the objects are no longer needed. Remember that although the JVM has an automatic mechanism that releases unneeded data from memory (we call this mechanism the *garbage collector* [GC]), it's still the developer's responsibility to ensure that all references to unnecessary data are removed. If we implement code that retains references to objects, the GC doesn't know they are no longer used and won't remove them. We call this situation a *memory leak*. In section 6.2.3, you'll learn to use the profiler to identify when such a problem exists; then, in chapter 11, you'll learn to research its root cause using a heap dump.

6.1.2 Finding out what code executes

As a developer and consultant, I sometimes worked with large, complex, and dirty codebases. Several times I have been in a situation in which I had to investigate a particular app capability; I could reproduce the problem but had no idea which part of the code was involved. Some years ago, I investigated a problem with a legacy app running some processes. The company's management made the uninspired decision to let just one developer be responsible for the code. No one else had any idea what was there or how to work with it. When that developer departed, leaving behind no documentation or a friendly codebase, I was asked to help identify the cause of an issue.

The first look at the code scared me a bit: the app lacked a class design, and there was a combination of Java and Scala mixed with some Java reflection-driven code.

How do you figure out which code you need to investigate in such a case? Fortunately, a profiler has the capability of sampling the executing code. The tool intercepts the methods and visually displays what executes, giving you just enough to start an investigation. Once you find the code in execution, you can read it and, eventually, use a debugger, as discussed in chapters 2 to 4.

With a profiler, you can find what code executes behind the scenes without first looking into the code. This capability is called *sampling*, and it is particularly useful when the code is so muddy that you can't even understand what is being called.

6.1.3   Identifying slowness in an app's execution

In some cases, you have to deal with performance problems. The general question you want to answer for such cases is, "What is taking so long to execute?" Empirically, developers always first suspect the parts of the code related to I/O communication. Calling a web service, connecting to a database, or storing data in a file are examples of I/O actions that often cause latencies in apps. Still, an I/O call isn't always the cause of a slowness problem. And even then, unless you know the codebase by heart (which rarely happens), it is still difficult to spot where the problem comes from without some help.

Fortunately, the profiler is quite "magical" and has the ability to intercept code in execution and calculate the resources each piece of code consumes. We'll discuss these abilities in chapter 7.

6.2   Using a profiler

In this section, we examine how to use a profiler to solve problems such as those discussed in section 6.1. We begin (in section 6.2.1) with installing and configuring VisualVM. We'll then examine a profiler's investigative capabilities. I use an app to demonstrate each topic; the app is small enough to allow you to focus on the presented subject but complex enough to be relevant to our discussion.

In section 6.2.2, we will discuss system resource consumption and how to identify whether your app has any issues related to overconsumption. In section 6.2.3, you'll learn what kind of memory issues an app may encounter and how to spot them.

6.2.1   Installing and configuring VisualVM

In this section, you'll learn how to install and configure VisualVM. Before you use a profiler, you need to make sure you correctly install and configure this, or a similar, tool. Then, you can use the examples provided with the book to try out each of the capabilities we discuss in this chapter. If you work on a real-world project, I recommend using the techniques with the app you are implementing.

Installing VisualVM is straightforward. Once you download the version according to your operating system from the official site (https://visualvm.github.io/download .html), the only thing you need to do is make sure you correctly configure the location of the JDK you want VisualVM to use. In the configuration file, which you can find at the etc/visualvm.config location in the VisualVM folder, define the location of the JDK in your system. You need to assign the JDK path to the `visualvm_jdkhome` variable and uncomment the line (remove the # in front of it), as presented in the next snippet. VisualVM works with Java 8 or above:

```
visualvm_jdkhome="C:\Program Files\Java\openjdk-17\jdk-17"
```

Once you configure the JDK location, you can run VisualVM using the executable code in the bin folder where you installed the app. If you correctly configured the JDK location, the app will start, and you'll see an interface similar to the one presented in figure 6.1.

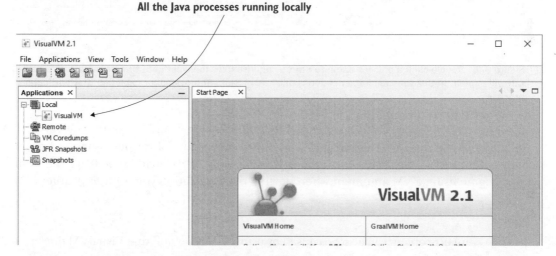

Figure 6.1   VisualVM welcome screen. Once you configure and start VisualVM, you find that the tool has a simple and easy-to-learn GUI. On the left of the welcome screen are the processes running locally that you can investigate with the tool.

Let's start a Java app. You can use the project da-ch6-ex1 provided with this book. Either use the IDE to start the app or start the app from the console directly. Profiling a Java process is not affected by the way the app is started.

Once you start the app, VisualVM displays the process on the left side. Usually, if you didn't explicitly give a particular name to the process, VisualVM uses the main class name, as presented in figure 6.2.

Once you start your app, you will also see
its process on the left side of the VisualVM frame.
Since we gave no particular name to our process,
VisualVM displays the main class name.

Double-click the process name, and
VisualVM displays the Details tab for
the process.

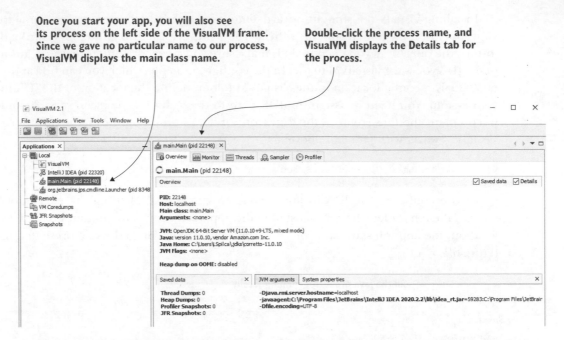

Figure 6.2   Double-click a process name to start using VisualVM to investigate that process, and a new tab will appear. In this tab are all the needed capabilities VisualVM provides for exploring that particular process.

Generally, starting the app should be enough. However, in some cases, VisualVM doesn't know how to connect to a local process because of various issues, as presented in figure 6.3. In such a case, the first thing to try is explicitly specifying the domain name using a VM argument when starting the application you want to profile:

```
-Djava.rmi.server.hostname=localhost
```

A similar problem can also be caused by using a JVM version that VisualVM doesn't support. If adding the `-Djava.rmi.server.hostname=localhost` argument doesn't solve your issue, check that the JVM distribution you configured is among those VisualVM supports (according to the download section on its website: https://visualvm.github.io/download.html).

You know something is incorrectly configured
if any of the tabs is missing (like in this case
with the Threads tab) or if VisualVM shows an
error message such as this one, which tells
you that the configured JVM isn't supported.

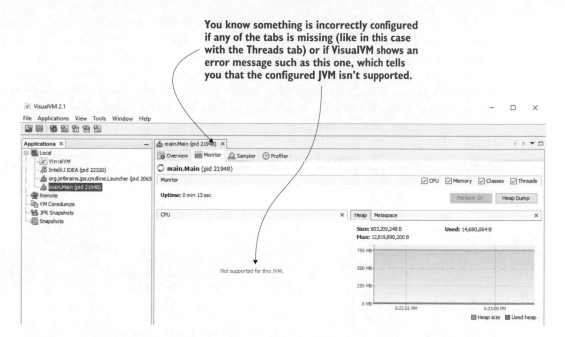

Figure 6.3 If the tool doesn't seem to be working properly, you need to check the way it is configured. Such problems can occur when the configured JVM distribution is not among those VisualVM supports. Sometimes the tool can't connect to the local process you want to investigate for some reason. In such cases, use a different JVM distribution that complies with the tool's requirements or review how the process you want to investigate was started.

6.2.2 Observing the CPU and memory usage

One of the simplest things you can do with a profiler is observe how your app consumes the system's resources. This way, you can spot problems such as memory leaks or zombie threads in your app.

DEFINITION   A memory leak is when your app doesn't deallocate unneeded data. Over time, there will be no more free memory. This is a problem.

As you'll learn in this section, you can use a profiler to visually confirm that your app isn't behaving correctly. For example, *zombie threads* are threads that remain in continuous execution, consuming the app's resources. You can easily observe such problems using VisualVM.

I prepared some projects to show you how to use a profiler to identify app issues that cause abnormal resource consumption. We'll run the apps provided with the book one by one, and we'll use VisualVM to observe the behavior and identify abnormalities.

Let's start with app da-ch6-ex1. The idea of the app is simple: two threads continuously add values to a list, while two other threads continuously remove (consume) the values from this list. We often call this implementation a *producer-consumer approach*, a multithreaded design pattern commonly encountered in apps.

Listing 6.1   The producer thread adding values to a list

```
public class Producer extends Thread {

  private Logger log = Logger.getLogger(Producer.class.getName());

  @Override
  public void run() {
    Random r = new Random();
    while (true) {
      if (Main.list.size() < 100) {          ⟵──┘ Sets a maximum number
        int x = r.nextInt();                          of values for the list
        Main.list.add(x);
        log.info("Producer " + Thread.currentThread().getName() +
                 " added value " + x);
      }
    }
  }

}
```

Adds a random value in the list ↳ `Main.list.add(x);`

Sets a maximum number of values for the list

The following code shows the implementation of the consumer thread.

Listing 6.2   The consumer thread removing values from the list

```
public class Consumer extends Thread {

  private Logger log = Logger.getLogger(Consumer.class.getName());

  @Override
  public void run() {
    while (true) {
      if (Main.list.size() > 0) {          ⟵──┘ Checks whether the list
        int x = Main.list.get(0);                  contains any value.
        Main.list.remove(0);
        log.info("Consumer " + Thread.currentThread().getName() +
                 " removed value " + x);
      }
    }
  }
}
```

If the list contains values, removes the first value from the list

Checks whether the list contains any value.

The Main class creates and starts two instances of the producer thread and two instances of the consumer thread.

Listing 6.3 The `Main` class creating and starting the producer and consumer threads

```
public class Main {

  public static List<Integer> list = new ArrayList<>();        ◁──── Creates a list
                                                                      to store the
  public static void main(String[] args) {                            random values
    new Producer().start();                                           the producer
    new Producer().start();                                           generates
    new Consumer().start();          Starts the consumer
    new Consumer().start();          and produces threads
  }
}
```

This application wrongly implements a multithreaded architecture. More precisely, multiple threads concurrently access and change a list of type `ArrayList`. Because `ArrayList` is not a concurrent collection implementation in Java, it doesn't manage the threads' access itself. Multiple threads accessing this collection potentially enter a *race condition*. A race condition happens when multiple threads compete to access the same resource. That is, they are in a race to access the same resource.

In project da-ch6-ex1, the implementation lacks thread synchronization. When you run the app, some of the threads stop after a short time because of exceptions caused by the race condition, while others remain forever alive, doing nothing (zombie threads). We'll use VisualVM to identify all these problems. Then, we'll run project da-ch6-ex2, which applies a correction to the app that synchronizes the threads that access the list. We'll compare the results displayed by VisualVM for the first example to the second example to understand the difference between a normal app and a problematic app.

The app will run quickly and then stop (potentially showing an exception stack trace in the console). The next code snippet shows what the log messages the app prints in the console look like:

```
Aug 26, 2021 5:22:42 PM main.Producer run
INFO: Producer Thread-0 added value -361561777
Aug 26, 2021 5:22:42 PM main.Producer run
INFO: Producer Thread-1 added value -500676534
Aug 26, 2021 5:22:42 PM main.Producer run
INFO: Producer Thread-0 added value 112520480
```

You may think that because this app only has three classes, you don't need a profiler to spot the problem—reading the code is enough here. Indeed, with only three classes, you may be able to spot the problem without using a separate tool. That's because the apps we use are simplified examples to allow you to focus on using the profiler. But in the real world, apps are more complex, and problems are much more challenging to spot without an appropriate tool (such as a profiler).

Even if the app looks like it's paused, you can see something interesting when you use VisualVM to investigate what is happening behind the scenes. To investigate this unexpected behavior, follow these steps:

1   Check the process CPU usage.
2   Check the process memory usage.
3   Visually investigate the executing threads.

The process is consuming a lot of CPU resources, so, somehow, it seems to still be alive. To observe its resource consumption, use the Monitor tab in VisualVM after double-clicking the process name in the left panel. One of the widgets you find on this tab shows you the CPU usage (figure 6.4).

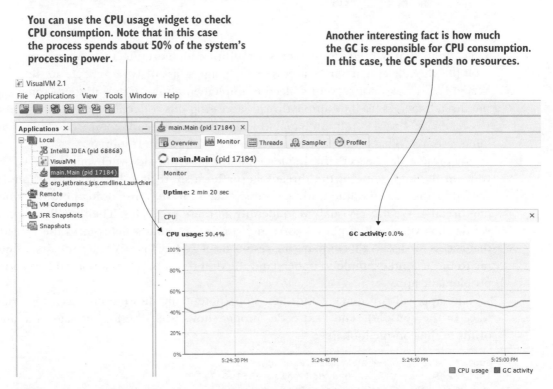

You can use the CPU usage widget to check CPU consumption. Note that in this case the process spends about 50% of the system's processing power.

Another interesting fact is how much the GC is responsible for CPU consumption. In this case, the GC spends no resources.

Figure 6.4   Using VisualVM to observe the use of CPU resources. The widget in the Monitor tab shows you how much CPU the process uses and how much of the usage is caused by the GC. This information helps you to understand whether the app has execution problems and is excellent guidance for the next steps in your investigation. In this particular example, the process spends about 50% CPU. The GC doesn't influence this value. These signs are often indicators of zombie threads that are usually generated by concurrency problems.

The consumer and producer threads seem to have entered a continuous running state where they consume the system's resources even if they don't correctly fulfill their tasks. In this case, the state is a consequence of race conditions because the threads are trying to access and change a nonconcurrent collection. But we already know there's something wrong with the app. We want to observe the symptoms such problems cause so that in other similar situations we will know our app encountered the same problem.

In this widget, you can also find the amount of CPU resources the GC uses. The GC is the JVM mechanism that deals with removing the data the app no longer needs from memory. The GC CPU usage is valuable information because it can indicate that the app has a problem with memory allocation. If the GC spends a lot of CPU resources, it can signify that the app has a memory leak issue.

In this case, the GC doesn't spend any CPU resources. This is not a good sign either. In other words, the app is spending a lot of processing power but isn't processing anything. These signs usually indicate zombie threads, which are generally a consequence of concurrency problems.

The next step is to look at the widget showing memory consumption. This widget is strategically placed near the one showing you the CPU consumption, as presented in figure 6.5. We'll discuss this widget in more detail in section 6.2.3, but for the moment, notice that the app spends almost no memory at all. This behavior is, again, not a good sign as it is equivalent to saying, "The app does nothing." Using just these two widgets, we can conclude that we are most likely facing a concurrency issue.

On the right side of the CPU usage widget, you find another widget that displays the memory consumption.

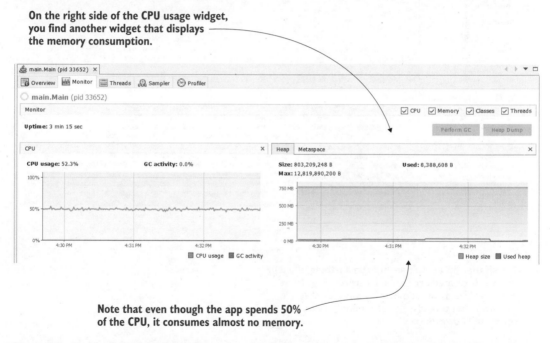

Note that even though the app spends 50% of the CPU, it consumes almost no memory.

Figure 6.5 On the right side of the CPU usage widget, you find the memory usage widget. In this example, the app uses almost no memory. This is also why the GC activity is zero. An app not consuming any memory means the app isn't doing anything.

We'll discuss using thread dumps in chapter 10. For now, we'll focus only on the high-level widgets the profile offers, and we'll compare the results these widgets provide for a healthy and an unhealthy app.

Before going into a detailed investigation of the threads in execution, I prefer to use VisualVM to visually observe how the threads execute. In most cases, doing so gives me some clues about which threads I need to pay attention to. Once I get this info, I use a thread dump to find the concurrency problem and learn how to fix it.

Figure 6.6 shows the Threads tab, which you find near the Monitor tab. The Threads tab offers a visual representation of the threads in execution and their states. In this example, all four threads the app started are executing and in a running state.

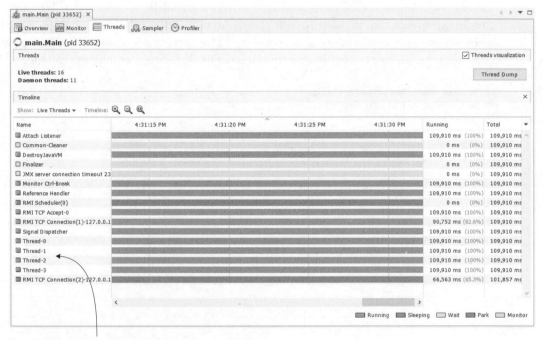

Even if the app doesn't seem to do anything, the four threads it created are continuously running. These running threads that do nothing but stay alive are called zombie threads. The only thing they do is consume CPU resources.

Figure 6.6   The Threads tab offers a visual representation of the threads that are alive and their status. The widget shows all the process threads, including those started by the JVM, which helps you to easily identify which threads you should pay attention to and eventually investigate deeper using a thread dump.

Concurrency problems can have different results. Not necessarily all the threads will remain alive, for example. Sometimes concurrent access can cause exceptions that interrupt some or all the threads entirely. The next snippet shows an example of such an exception that can occur during an app's execution:

```
Exception in thread "Thread-1"
   java.lang.ArrayIndexOutOfBoundsException:
   Index -1 out of bounds for length 109
      at java.base/java.util.ArrayList.add(ArrayList.java:487)
      at java.base/java.util.ArrayList.add(ArrayList.java:499)
      at main.Producer.run(Producer.java:16)
```

If such an exception happens, then some threads may be stopped, and the Threads tab won't display them. Figure 6.7 shows a case in which the app threw an exception and only one of the threads stayed alive.

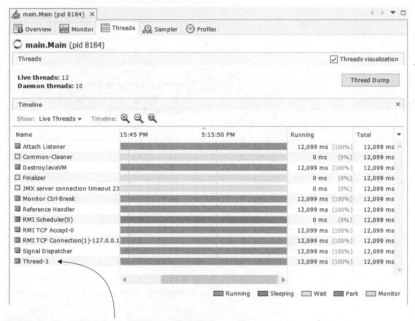

In this example, only one of the threads is alive and became a zombie thread. The other threads encountered exceptions caused by the race conditions and stopped.

Figure 6.7 If exceptions occur during an app's execution, some of the threads may be stopped. This figure shows a case in which the concurrent access caused exceptions in three of the threads and stopped them. Only one thread remained alive. Remember, concurrency problems in multithreaded apps can cause different unexpected results.

In this example, we focus only on discovering a resource consumption problem. The next step is to use a thread dump to figure out the exact cause of the concurrency problem. We'll discuss everything about thread dumps in chapter 7, but for now, let's remain focused on identifying resource consumption issues. We will run the same verifications on a healthy app and compare it to our unhealthy one. This way, you'll know how to immediately recognize correct and incorrect app behavior.

The example in project da-ch6-ex2 is the corrected version of the same app we just looked at. I added some synchronized blocks to avoid concurrent access for the threads and eliminate the race condition problems. I used the list instance as the thread monitor for the synchronized code blocks for both consumers and producers.

Listing 6.4 Synchronizing access for the consumer

```java
public class Consumer extends Thread {

  private Logger log = Logger.getLogger(Consumer.class.getName());

  public Consumer(String name) {
    super(name);
  }

  @Override
  public void run() {
    while (true) {
      synchronized (Main.list) {          ⟵  Synchronizes the access on
        if (Main.list.size() > 0) {            the list, using the list instance
          int x = Main.list.get(0);            as a thread monitor
          Main.list.remove(0);
          log.info("Consumer " +
              Thread.currentThread().getName() +
              " removed value " + x);
        }
      }
    }
  }
}
```

The following code shows the synchronization applied to the Producer class.

Listing 6.5 Synchronizing access for the producer

```java
public class Producer extends Thread {

  private Logger log = Logger.getLogger(Producer.class.getName());

  public Producer(String name) {
    super(name);
  }

  @Override
  public void run() {
    Random r = new Random();
    while (true) {                        ⟵  Synchronizes the access on
      synchronized (Main.list) {             the list, using the list instance
        if (Main.list.size() < 100) {         as a thread monitor
          int x = r.nextInt();
          Main.list.add(x);
          log.info("Producer " +
```

```
                    Thread.currentThread().getName() +
                    " added value " + x);
            }
        }
    }
}

}
```

I also gave custom names to each thread. I always recommend this approach. Did you spot the default names the JVM gave our threads in the previous example? Generally, Thread-0, Thread-1, Thread-2, and so on are not names you can easily use to identify a given thread. I prefer giving threads custom names whenever I can so that I can identify them quickly. Moreover, I give them names starting with an underline so it is easier to sort them. First, I defined the constructor in the Consumer and Producer classes (listings 6.4 and 6.5, respectively) and used the super() constructor to name the threads. I then gave them names, as presented in listing 6.6.

Listing 6.6 Setting custom names for the threads

```
public class Main {

  public static List<Integer> list = new ArrayList<>();

  public static void main(String[] args) {
    new Producer("_Producer 1").start();
    new Producer("_Producer 2").start();
    new Consumer("_Consumer 1").start();
    new Consumer("_Consumer 2").start();
  }
}
```

Notice that after starting this app, the console continuously shows logs. The app doesn't stop like it did with example da-ch6-ex1. Let's use VisualVM to observe resource consumption. In the CPU utilization widget, you can see that the app spends less CPU, while the memory usage widget shows that the app uses some of the allocated memory while running. Also, we can observe the activity of the GC. As you will learn later in this chapter, on the right side of the memory graph are valleys that are a result of the GC's activity.

The Threads tab shows that the monitor sometimes blocks the threads, which only allows one thread at a time through a synchronized block. The threads don't run continuously, which makes the app consume less CPU, as shown in figure 6.8. Figure 6.9 shows the threads' visualization in the Threads tab.

NOTE Even if we added synchronized blocks, some code still remains outside of these blocks. For this reason, the threads may still appear to run concurrently (as shown in figure 6.9).

An app that behaves correctly consumes less CPU resources.

The app consumes memory, which proves that the app actually does something.

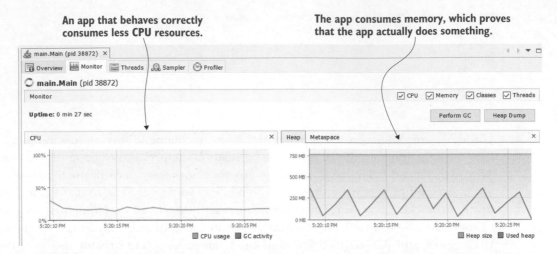

Figure 6.8 After correctly synchronizing the code, the resource consumption widgets look different. The CPU consumption is lower, and the app uses some memory.

The threads are no longer continuously running. The profiler shows you when the threads are blocked by a monitor, waiting, or sleeping.

Instructions left out of the synchronized blocks can still cause threads to run concurrently. Notice where the two producer threads appear shaded at the same time on the diagram.

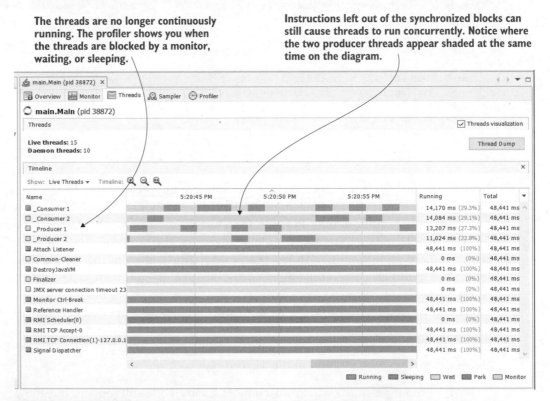

Figure 6.9 The Threads tab helps you to visualize the execution of the threads in your app. Since the threads' names start with an underline, you can simply sort them by name to see them grouped. Notice that their execution is interrupted from time to time by the monitor, which allows just one thread at a time through the synchronized blocks of code.

6.2.3 Identifying memory leaks

In this section, we discuss memory leaks and how to determine when your app is affected by them. A *memory leak* is when an app stores and keeps references to unused objects (figure 6.10). Because of these references, the GC (the mechanism responsible for removing unneeded data from the app's memory) cannot remove these objects. As the app continues to add more data, the memory fills up. When the app doesn't have enough space to add the new data, it throws an OutOfMemoryError and stops. We'll use a simple app that causes an OutOfMemoryError to demonstrate how to identify a memory leak using VisualVM.

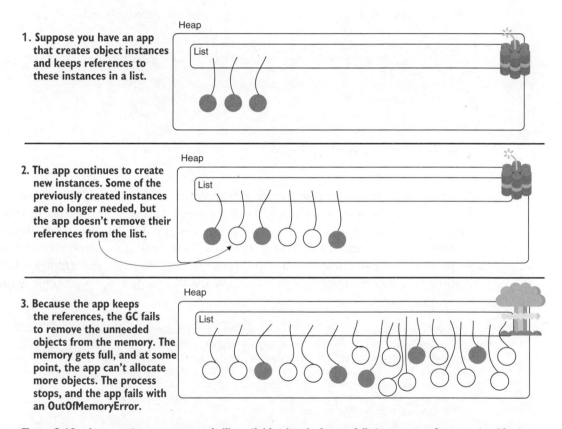

1. Suppose you have an app that creates object instances and keeps references to these instances in a list.

2. The app continues to create new instances. Some of the previously created instances are no longer needed, but the app doesn't remove their references from the list.

3. Because the app keeps the references, the GC fails to remove the unneeded objects from the memory. The memory gets full, and at some point, the app can't allocate more objects. The process stops, and the app fails with an OutOfMemoryError.

Figure 6.10 An OutOfMemoryError is like a ticking bomb. An app fails to remove references to objects it no longer uses. The GC can't remove these instances from the memory because the app keeps their references. While more objects are created, the memory gets full. At some point, there's no more space in the heap to allocate other objects, and the app fails with an OutOfMemoryError.

In the example provided with project da-ch6-ex3, you can find a simple app that stores random instances in a list but never removes their references. The following code provides an example of a simple implementation that produces an OutOfMemoryError.

Listing 6.7   Producing an `OutOfMemoryError`

```
public class Main {

  public static List<Cat> list = new ArrayList<>();

  public static void main(String[] args) {
    while(true) {
      list.add(new Cat(new Random().nextInt(10)));
    }
  }
}
```

Continuously adds new
instances to a list until the
JVM runs out of memory

The class `Cat` is a simple `java` object, as presented by the following code snippet:

```
public class Cat {

  private int age;

  public Cat(int age) {
    this.age = age;
  }

  // Omitted getters and setters
}
```

Let's run this app and observe resource usage with VisualVM. We're especially interested in the widget that shows memory usage. When a memory leak affects your app, this widget can confirm that the used memory grows continuously. The GC tries to deallocate unused data from memory, but it removes too few. In the end, the memory gets filled, the app cannot store the new data, and it throws an `OutOfMemoryError` (figure 6.11).

If you let the app run long enough, you'll eventually see the error stack trace in the app's console:

```
Exception in thread "main" java.lang.OutOfMemoryError: Java heap space
    at java.base/java.util.Arrays.copyOf(Arrays.java:3689)
    at java.base/java.util.ArrayList.grow(ArrayList.java:238)
    at java.base/java.util.ArrayList.grow(ArrayList.java:243)
    at java.base/java.util.ArrayList.add(ArrayList.java:486)
    at java.base/java.util.ArrayList.add(ArrayList.java:499)
    at main.Main.main(Main.java:13)
```

It's important to remember that an `OutOfMemoryError` stack trace doesn't necessarily indicate the place that causes the problem. Since an app has just one heap memory location, a certain thread can cause the problem, whereas another thread may be unlucky enough to be the last one trying to use the memory location and thus gets the error. The only sure way to identify the root cause is using a heap dump, which you'll learn in chapter 11.

Note how the used memory grows continuously. The GC attempts to free the memory, but it can't remove most of the instances because the app still keeps their references in memory.

When all the allocated memory is occupied, and the app can't store the new data, the app throws an **OutOfMemoryError.**

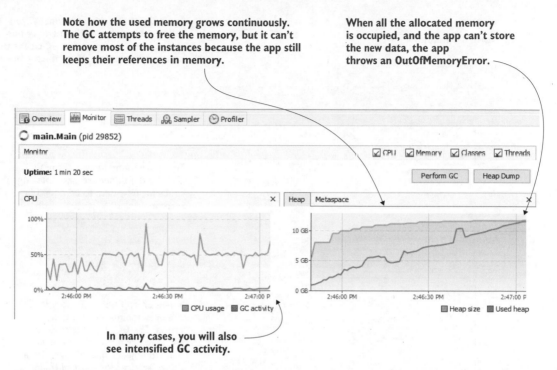

In many cases, you will also see intensified GC activity.

Figure 6.11   **When a memory leak affects your app, the used memory grows continuously. GC attempts to free the memory but cannot remove enough data. The used memory increases until the app can't allocate any more new data. At this point, the app throws an OutOfMemoryError and stops. In many cases, a memory leak also causes intensified GC activity, which can be seen in the CPU resource usage widget.**

Figure 6.12 compares normal behavior and the behavior of an app affected by a memory leak, as seen in VisualVM. For the app with a normal execution (not affected by a memory leak), notice that the graph has peaks and valleys. The app allocates memory that fills it up (the peaks), and from time to time, the GC removes the data that's no longer needed (the valleys). This ebb and flow is usually a good sign that the capability you are investigating is not affected by a memory leak.

However, if you see that the memory progressively fills and the GC doesn't clean it, your app may have a memory leak. Once you suspect a memory leak, you need to investigate further using a heap dump.

You can control the allocated heap size in a Java app. This way, you can enlarge the maximum limit the JVM allocates to your app. However, giving the app more memory is not a solution for a memory leak. But this approach can be a temporary solution to give you more time to solve the root cause of the problem. To set a maximum heap size for an app, use the JVM property -Xmx, followed by the amount you want to allocate (e.g., -Xmx1G will allocate a maximum heap size of 1 GB). You can similarly set a minimum initial heap size using the -Xms property (e.g., -Xms500m would allocate a minimum heap size of 500 MB).

Normal behavior

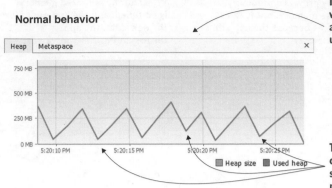

In an app that behaves normally, you will see this pattern. The memory fills, and at a certain point, the GC cleans the unneeded data, freeing up the memory.

These are moments when the GC cleaned the unneeded data, making space for new data to be added in memory.

Abnormal behavior

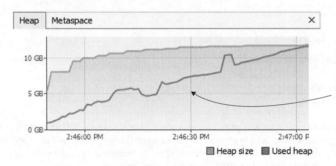

When an app has a memory leak, the used memory continuously grows. The GC attempts to free the memory but can't deallocate enough objects since the app holds the references for most of them.

Figure 6.12   A comparison between the memory usage for a healthy app versus an app suffering from a memory leak. The GC manages to free unneeded data from memory for a healthy app, and the allocated space never fills up. An app suffering from a memory leak doesn't allow the GC to remove enough data. At some point, the memory fills up completely, generating an `OutOfMemoryError`.

Aside from the normal heap space, any app also uses a *metaspace*: the memory location where the JVM stores the class metadata needed for the app's execution. In VisualVM you can observe the allocation of the metaspace in the memory allocation widget as well. To evaluate the metadata allocation, use the Metaspace tab of the widget, as presented in figure 6.13.

An `OutOfMemoryError` on the metadata space happens less often, but it's not impossible. I recently dealt with such a case in an app that was misusing a framework for data persistence. Generally, frameworks and libraries using Java reflection are the most likely to generate such problems if misused since they often rely on dynamic proxies and indirect calls.

In my situation, the app was misusing a framework named Hibernate. I would not be surprised if you have already heard about Hibernate since it's one of the most common solutions to manage persistent data in Java apps today. Hibernate is an excellent tool that helps to implement the most-used persistence capabilities of an app

The **Metaspace** tab of the memory usage widget
shows the size of the metaspace and
how much of it is used.

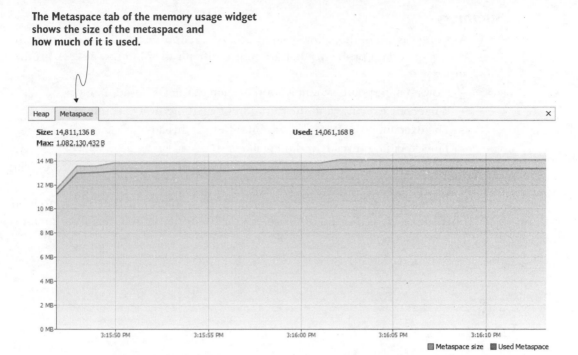

Figure 6.13   The metaspace is a part of the memory used to store class metadata. In particular cases, the metaspace can be overflowed. A VisualVM memory allocation widget also shows the usage of the metaspace.

while eliminating the need to write unneeded code. Hibernate manages a context of instances and maps the changes to this context to the database. But it's not recommended for a very large context. In other words, don't work with too many records from the database at once!

The app I had trouble with defined a scheduled process, loading many records from a database and processing them in a defined way. It seems that, at some point, the number of records this process was fetching was so large that the load operation itself caused the metaspace to fill; the problem was a misuse of the framework, not a bug in the framework. The developers should not have used Hibernate and instead used an alternate, more low-level solution like JDBC.

The problem was critical, and I had to find a short-term solution since a complete refactoring would have taken a long time. Just as for the heap, you can customize the metaspace size. Using the -XX:MaxMetaspaceSize property, you can enlarge the metaspace (e.g., -XX:MaxMetaspaceSize=100M), but remember that this is not a real solution to the problem. The long-term solution for such a case is to refactor the functionality to avoid loading so many records at once in the memory and eventually use an alternate persistence technology if needed.

Summary

- A profiler is a tool that allows you to observe an app's execution to identify the causes of certain problems that are more difficult to spot otherwise. A profiler shows you
  - How an app spends system resources such as the CPU and memory
  - What code executes and the duration of each method execution
  - The execution stack of methods on different threads
  - The executing threads and their status
- The profiler provides excellent visual widgets that help you to more quickly understand certain aspects.
- You can observe the GC's execution using the profiler, which helps you to identify issues such as the app not correctly deallocating unused data from memory (memory leaks).

Finding hidden issues using profiling techniques

This chapter covers

- Sampling an app's execution to find the currently executing methods
- Observing execution times
- Identifying SQL queries the app executes

In chapter 6, I said a profiler is a powerful tool that can show you a path when all the lights have gone out. But what we discussed was just a small part of the profiler's capabilities. A profiler offers powerful tools for investigating an app's execution, and learning to use these tools properly can help you in many scenarios.

In many cases, I have had to evaluate or investigate app executions for codebases I could barely read—old apps with poorly modeled code design, which some companies kept hidden in a wardrobe. In such cases, the profiler was the only efficient way to find what was executing when a specific capability was triggered. Now you can see why I compared a profiler with the light of Eärendil: as Galadriel says, it really was a light in many dark places where all the other lights were out.

In this chapter, we will analyze three investigation techniques through profiling, which I consider extremely valuable:

- Sampling for finding out what part of an app's code executes
- Profiling the execution (also called *instrumentation*) to identify wrong behavior and optimization
- Profiling the app to identify SQL queries it uses to communicate with a database management system (DBMS)

We'll continue our discussion in chapter 8 on advanced visualization techniques of an app's execution. When used appropriately, these techniques can save you a lot of time finding the causes of various issues. Unfortunately, even though these techniques are powerful, many developers are unfamiliar with them. Some developers know these techniques exist but tend to believe they are difficult to use (in this chapter I'll show you the opposite is true). Consequently, they try using other methods to solve problems that could be solved much more efficiently with a profiler (as presented in this chapter).

To make sure you properly understand how to use these techniques and what issues can be investigated, I created four small projects. We'll use these projects to apply the profiling techniques we discuss. Section 7.1 discusses sampling—a technique you use to identify what code executes at a given time. In section 7.2, you'll learn how a profiler can provide more details about the execution than sampling can offer. Section 7.3 discusses how to use a profiler to get details about SQL queries an app sends to a DBMS.

7.1   *Sampling to observe executing code*

What is sampling, and how can it benefit you? Sampling is an approach in which you use a profiler to identify what code the app executes. Sampling doesn't provide many details about the execution, but it draws the big picture of what happens, giving you valuable information on what you need to analyze further. For this reason, sampling should always be the first step when profiling an app, and, as you'll see, sampling may even be enough in many cases. For this section, I prepared project da-ch7-ex1. We'll use a profiler to sample this app and understand how we can use VisualVM to identify issues related to the execution time of a given capability.

The project we'll use to demonstrate sampling is a tiny app that exposes an endpoint, /demo. When someone calls this endpoint using cURL, Postman, or a similar tool, the app further calls an endpoint exposed by httpbin.org.

I like using httpbin.org for many examples and demonstrations. Httpbin.org is an open source web app and tool written in Python that exposes mock endpoints you can use to test different things you're implementing.

Here, we call an endpoint where httpbin.org responds with a given delay. We'll use a 5-second delay for this example to simulate a latency scenario in our app, and httpbin.org simulates the root cause of the problem.

With latency, we understand how an app reacts slower than expected.

The scenario is also visually represented in figure 7.1.

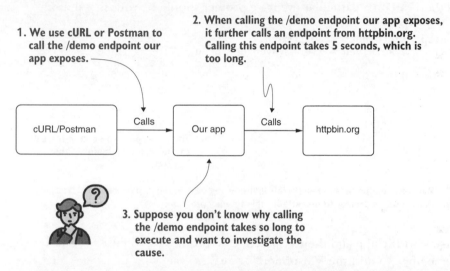

1. We use cURL or Postman to call the /demo endpoint our app exposes.

2. When calling the /demo endpoint our app exposes, it further calls an endpoint from httpbin.org. Calling this endpoint takes 5 seconds, which is too long.

3. Suppose you don't know why calling the /demo endpoint takes so long to execute and want to investigate the cause.

Figure 7.1 The app we are investigating exposes an endpoint: /demo. When you call this endpoint, you must wait for 5 seconds for the app to respond. We need to understand why it takes so long for the endpoint to respond. We know our app calls a mock endpoint from httpbin.org, which causes the delay, but we want to learn how to investigate this scenario with a profiler. This way, you'll know how to use similar techniques for real-world situations.

The profiling approach has two steps:

1 Sampling to find out what code executes and where you should go into more detail (the approach we discuss in this section).

2 Profiling (also called *instrumentation*) to get more details about the execution of specific pieces of code.

Sometimes step 1 (sampling) is enough to understand a problem, and you may not need to profile the app (step 2). As you'll learn in this chapter and chapters 8 to 10, profiling can provide more details about the execution if needed. But first you need to know what part of the code to profile, and for that, you use sampling.

How does the problem occur in our example? When calling the /demo endpoint, the execution takes 5 seconds (figure 7.2), which we consider too long. Ideally, we want the execution to take less than 1 second, so we need to understand why calling the /demo endpoint takes so long. What causes the latency? Is it our app, or something else?

When you investigate a slowness problem in an unknown codebase, using a profiler should be your first choice. The problem doesn't necessarily need to involve an endpoint. For this example, an endpoint was the easiest solution. But in any situation involving slowness—calling an endpoint, executing a process, or using a simple method call on a particular event—a profiler should be your first option.

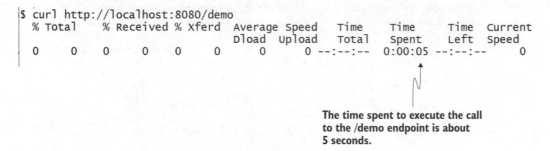

Figure 7.2   When the endpoint is called (in this figure, using cURL), the app takes about 5 seconds to respond. In our scenario, we use a profiler to investigate this latency problem.

First, start the app and then VisualVM (the profiler we will use for our investigations). Remember to add the VM option -Djava.rmi.server.hostname=localhost, as we discussed in chapter 6. This allows VisualVM to connect to the process. Select the process from the list on the left, and then select the Sampler tab, as presented in figure 7.3, to start sampling the execution.

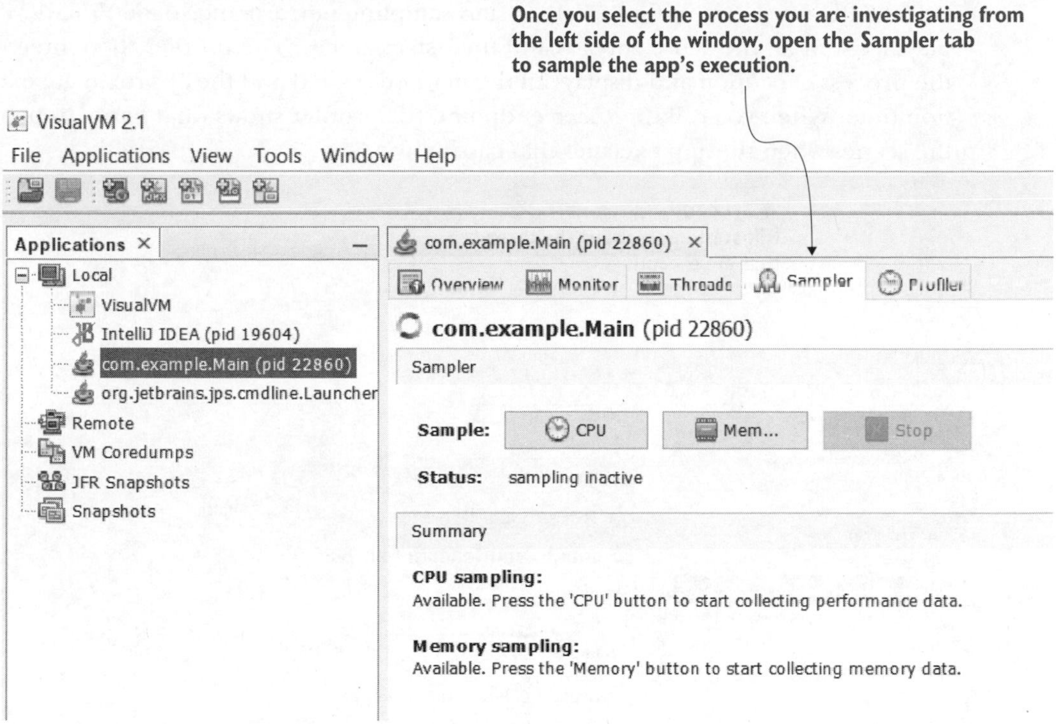

Once you select the process you are investigating from
the left side of the window, open the Sampler tab
to sample the app's execution.

Figure 7.3   To start sampling the execution, select the process from the list on the left side, and then select the Sampler tab.

Sampling the execution has three purposes:

- *To find out what code executes*—Sampling shows you what executes behind the scenes and is an excellent way to find the part of the app you need to investigate.
- *To identify CPU consumption*—We'll use this to investigate latency issues and understand which methods share execution time.
- *To identify memory consumption*—This allows us to analyze memory-related issues. We'll discuss sampling and profiling memory more in chapter 11.

Select CPU (as shown in figure 7.4) to start sampling performance data. VisualVM displays a list of all the active threads and their stack traces. The profiler then intercepts the process execution and displays all the methods called and the approximate execution time. When you call the /demo endpoint, the profiler shows what happens behind the scenes when the app executes that capability.

Select CPU, and VisualVM will start intercepting the threads that are executing.

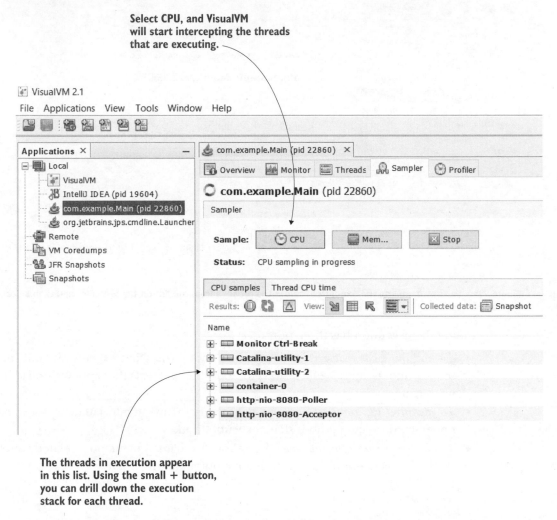

The threads in execution appear in this list. Using the small + button, you can drill down the execution stack for each thread.

Figure 7.4   The profiler shows all the active threads in a list. You can expand each item to see the execution stack and an approximate execution time. When the app executes, the newly created threads appear in the list, and you can analyze their execution.

We can now call the /demo endpoint and observe what happens. As shown in figure 7.5, some new threads appear in the list. The app started these threads when we called the `/demo` endpoint. When you open them, you should see precisely what the app does during its execution.

Before I discuss details such as the execution time, I want to highlight how vital this first step is. Many times when I've analyzed code, I used just sampling to figure out where to look for the problem. I may not have even been investigating a performance or latency issue but was simply looking for the point to start debugging. Remember our discussions in chapters 2 to 4: to debug something, you need to know where to add that breakpoint to pause the app's execution. If you have no clue where to add a breakpoint, you can't debug. Sampling can be a way to shed some light on a situation when you can't figure out where to start debugging (especially in cases like those I mentioned at the beginning of the chapter in which an app lacks clean code design).

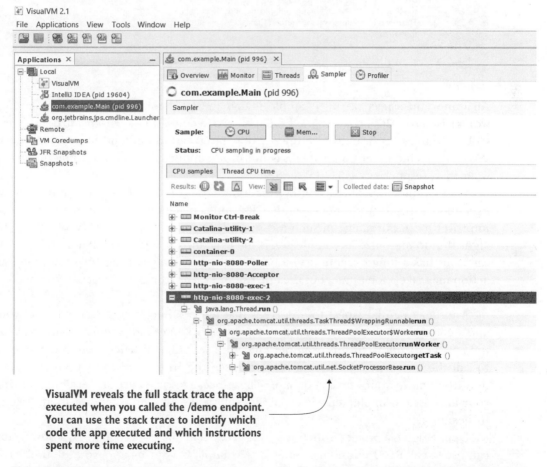

VisualVM reveals the full stack trace the app executed when you called the /demo endpoint. You can use the stack trace to identify which code the app executed and which instructions spent more time executing.

Figure 7.5   The stack trace shows what the app executes. You can see every method and each subsequent method that is called. This view helps you quickly find the code you want to focus on when investigating a certain capability.

Let's look at the execution stack to understand what the profiler shows us. When you want to figure out what code executes, you simply expand the stack trace up to the point where it displays the methods of the app you are interested in. When you are investigating a latency problem (as in this example), you can expand the stack trace to observe the maximum execution time, as shown in figure 7.6.

I expanded the execution stack by selecting the small (+) button in the last method. The profiler shows it took about 5 seconds to understand the execution and find which method causes the latency. In this particular case, we see that just one method causes the slowness: `getResponseCode()` of the `HttpURLConnection` class.

TIP   Remember that it's not always one method that spends all the execution time in real-world scenarios. You'll often find that the time spent is shared among multiple methods that execute. The rule is to first focus on the method that takes the longest time to execute.

An important aspect of this example is that the CPU time (how long the method works) is zero. Although the method spends 5 seconds in execution, it doesn't use CPU resources because it is waiting for the HTTP call to end and to get a response. We can conclude that the problem is not in the app; rather, it's slow only because it waits for a response to its HTTP request.

It's extremely valuable to differentiate between the total CPU time and the total execution time. If a method spends CPU time, it means the method "works." To improve the performance in such a case, you usually have to adjust (if possible) the algorithm to minimize its complexity. If the execution spends a small amount of CPU time but has a long execution time, the method is likely waiting for something: an action may take a long time, but the app doesn't do anything. In this case, you need to figure out what your app is waiting for.

Another essential aspect to observe is that the profiler doesn't just intercept your app's codebase. You can see that the dependencies' methods are also called during the app's execution. In this example, the app uses a dependency named OpenFeign to call the `httpbin.org` endpoint. You can see this in the stack trace packages that don't belong to your app's codebase. These packages are part of the dependencies your app uses to implement its capabilities. OpenFeign can be one of them, like in this example.

OpenFeign is a project from the Spring ecosystem of technologies that a Spring app can use to call REST endpoints. Since this example is a Spring app, you will find packages of Spring-related technologies in the stack trace. You don't have to understand what each part of the stack trace does. You won't know this in a real-world scenario either. In fact, this book is about understanding code that you don't yet know. If you

The profiler doesn't only intercept your app's codebase, but also code from frameworks and libraries the app uses.

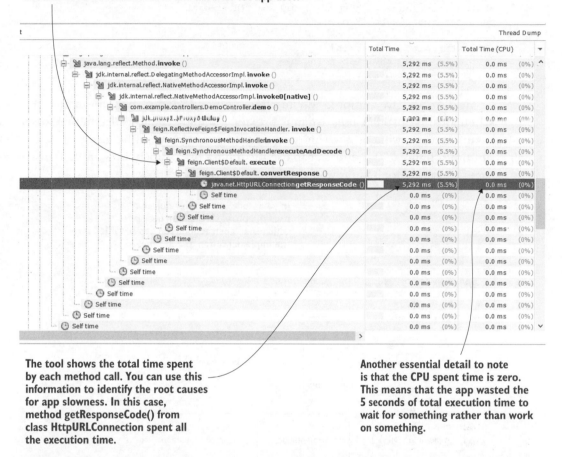

The tool shows the total time spent by each method call. You can use this information to identify the root causes for app slowness. In this case, method getResponseCode() from class HttpURLConnection spent all the execution time.

Another essential detail to note is that the CPU spent time is zero. This means that the app wasted the 5 seconds of total execution time to wait for something rather than work on something.

Figure 7.6   When you expand the execution stack, you find which methods execute and how much time they spend executing. You can also deduce how long they wait and how much they work. The profiler shows both the app's codebase methods and the methods called from specific dependencies (libraries or frameworks) the app uses.

want to learn Spring, I recommend starting with *Spring Start Here* (Manning, 2021), another book I wrote. You'll also find details about OpenFeign in *Spring Start Here*.

Why is observing dependencies' methods so important? Because, sometimes, it's almost impossible to figure out what executes from a given dependency using other means. Look at the code written in our app to call the httpbin.org endpoint (see listing 7.1). You can't see the actual implementation for sending the HTTP request. That's because, as happens in many Java frameworks today, the dependency uses dynamic proxies to decouple the implementation.

```
Listing 7.1   The HTTP client implementation using OpenFeign
```

```
@FeignClient(name = "httpBin", url = "${httpBinUrl}")
public interface DemoProxy {

  @PostMapping("/delay/{n}")
  void delay(@PathVariable int n);
}
```

Dynamic proxies give an app a way to choose a method implementation at run time. When an app capability uses dynamic proxies, it might actually call a method declared by an interface without knowing what implementation it will be given to execute at run time (figure 7.7). It is easier to use the framework's capabilities, but the disadvantage is that you don't know where to investigate an issue.

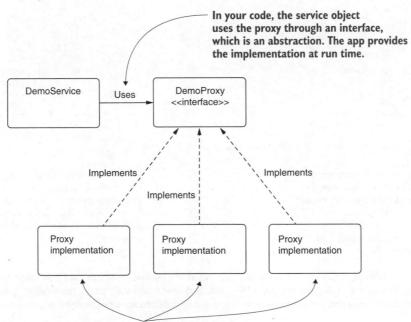

Figure 7.7   The framework keeps the implementations for an abstraction separate and provides them dynamically during execution. Because the implementation is decoupled and the app provides it during run time, it's more difficult to find it by reading the code.

One of my personal uses for sampling is when learning a new framework or library. Sampling helps me to understand what executes behind the scenes in a new functionality. I applied this approach when learning Hibernate and Spring Security, which have complex functionality, and it helped me quickly understand how to work with the given capabilities.

7.2 *Profiling to learn how many times a method executed*

Finding what code executes is essential, but sometimes it is not enough. Often, we need more details to precisely understand a given behavior. For example, sampling does not provide the number of method invocations. An app may take only 50 milliseconds to execute, but if it calls the method a thousand times, then it takes 50 seconds to execute when sampling. To demonstrate how to get details about the execution using a profiler and to identify situations where this is useful, we'll again use some projects provided with the book. We'll start with project da-ch7-ex1, which we also used in section 7.1, but this time we'll discuss profiling for details about the execution.

Start the app provided with project da-ch7-ex1. When you profile an app, you shouldn't investigate the entire codebase. Instead, you need to filter only on what's essential to your investigation. Profiling is a very resource-consuming operation, so unless you have a really powerful system, profile everything would take a ton of time. That's one more reason we always start with sampling—to identify what to profile further if needed.

TIP Never profile the app's entire codebase. You should always first decide, based on sampling, which part of the app you want to profile to get more details.

For this example, we'll ignore the app's codebase (without dependencies) and only take OpenFeign classes from the dependencies. Be aware that you can't refer to an app's entire code in a real-world app since that would likely be time- and resource-consumptive. For this small example, it won't be a problem, but for large apps, always restrict the intercepted code as much as possible when profiling.

In figure 7.8, you see how to apply these restrictions. On the right side of the Profiler tab, you can specify which part of the app to intercept. In this example, we use the following:

- `com.example.**`—The code in all the packages and subpackages of `com.example`
- `feign.**`—Code in all the packages and subpackages of `feign`

The syntax you can use to filter the packages and classes you want to profile has just a few simple rules:

- Write each rule on a separate line.
- Use one asterisk (*) to refer to a package; for example, we could use `com.example.*` if we wanted to profile all classes in the package `com.example`.
- Use two asterisks (**) to refer to a package and all its subpackages. In this case, by using `com.example.**`, we mean all classes in the package `com.example` as well as any of its subpackages.
- Write the full name of a class if you want to profile only that class; for example, we could use `com.example.controllers.DemoController` to profile only this class.

I chose these packages after sampling the execution, as discussed in section 7.1. Because I observed that the method call with the latency problem comes from classes of the `feign` package, I decided to add this package and its subpackages to the list to get more information.

Select CPU to start profiling the app.

Profiling helps us to get more information about the execution, but it's also more resource intensive. One of the first supplementary details you see here is the number of executions of a particular method.

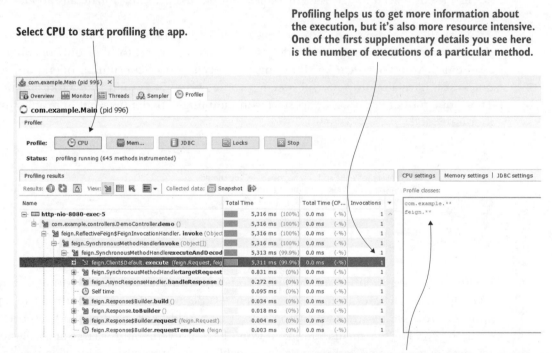

Always profile a small number of packages. Before starting to profile the execution, define the filters to tell the tool which classes need to be intercepted.

Figure 7.8   Profiling a part of the app during execution to get details about the times a given method was invoked. We can see that the method causing the 5 seconds of latency is invoked only once, meaning the number of invocations doesn't cause a problem here.

In this particular case, the number of invocations doesn't seem to cause issues: the method executes only once and takes about 5 seconds to finish its execution. A small number of method invocations implies that we don't have repeated unnecessary executions (which, as you'll learn later in this chapter, is a common problem in many apps).

In another scenario, you may have observed that the call to the given endpoint takes just 1 second, but the method is (because of some poor design) called 5 times. Then, the problem would have been in the app, and we would know how and where to solve it. In section 7.3, we'll analyze such a problem.

7.3 Using a profiler to identify SQL queries an app executes

In this section, you'll learn how to use a profiler to identify SQL queries an app sends to a DBMS. This subject is by far one of my favorites. Today, almost every app uses at least one relational database, and almost all scenarios encounter latencies caused by SQL queries from time to time. Moreover, today, apps use fancier ways to implement the persistence layer; in many cases, the SQL queries that the app sends are created dynamically by a framework or library. These dynamically generated queries are hard to identify, but a profiler can do some magic and greatly simplify your investigation.

We'll use a scenario implemented with project da-ch7-ex2 to learn how many times a method executes and intercepts a SQL query the app runs on a relational database. We'll then demonstrate that the executed SQL queries can be retrieved even when the app works with a framework and doesn't handle the queries directly. Finally, we'll discuss this subject further using a couple of examples.

7.3.1 Using a profiler to retrieve SQL queries not generated by a framework

This section uses an example to demonstrate how to use a profiler to obtain the SQL queries an app executes. We'll use a simple app that sends the queries directly to a DBMS directly without using a framework.

Let's start project da-ch7-ex2 and use the Profiler tab, as you learned in section 7.2. Project da-ch7-ex2 is also a small app. It configures an in-memory database with two tables (product and purchase) and populates the tables with a few records.

The app exposes all purchased products when calling the endpoint /products. By "purchased products," I mean products that have at least one purchase record in the purchase table. The purpose is to analyze the app's behavior when calling this endpoint without first analyzing the code. This way, we can see how much we can get just by using the profiler.

In figure 7.9, we use the Profiler tab since you already learned sampling in section 7.1, but remember that in any real-world scenario, you start with sampling. We start the app, and, using cURL or Postman, we call the /products endpoint. The profiler shows us precisely what happens:

1 A method `findPurchasedProductNames()` that belongs to the `Purchase-Controller` class was called.
2 This method delegated the call to the method `getProductNamesFor-Purchases()` in class `PurchaseService`.

3 The method getProductNamesForPurchases() in ProductService calls find-All() in PurchaseRepository.

4 The method getProductNamesForPurchases() in ProductService calls find-Product() in ProductRepository 10 times.

1. The execution starts with the findPurchasedProductNames() method in the PurchaseController class.

2. The getProductNamesForPurchases() method in PurchaseService is called.

3. The method in the PurchaseService class calls findAll() in PurchaseRepository.

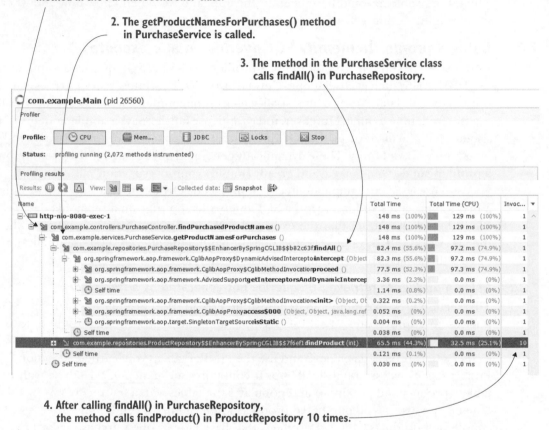

4. After calling findAll() in PurchaseRepository, the method calls findProduct() in ProductRepository 10 times.

Figure 7.9 When profiling the app, we observe that one of the methods is called 10 times. We now need to ask ourselves if this is a design issue. Since we now have a big picture of the entire algorithm and we know what code is executed, we can also debug the app if we can't figure out what happens.

Isn't this amazing? We didn't even look into the code, and we already know a lot of things about this execution. These details are fantastic, because now you know exactly where to go into the code and what you can expect to find. The profiler gave you class names, method names, and how they call each other. Let's now look into the code in listing 7.2 and figure out where all this happens. By using the profiler, we can see that most things happen in the getProductNamesForPurchases() method in the PurchaseService class, so that's most likely the place we need to analyze.

Listing 7.2   The algorithm's implementation in the `PurchaseService` class

```
@Service
public class PurchaseService {

  private final ProductRepository productRepository;
  private final PurchaseRepository purchaseRepository;

  public PurchaseService(ProductRepository productRepository,
                         PurchaseRepository purchaseRepository) {
    this.productRepository = productRepository;
    this.purchaseRepository = purchaseRepository;
  }

  public Set<String> getProductNamesForPurchases() {
    Set<String> productNames = new HashSet<>();
    List<Purchase> purchases = purchaseRepository.findAll();
    for (Purchase p : purchases) {
      Product product =
        productRepository.findProduct(p.getProduct());
      productNames.add(product.getName());
    }

    return productNames;
  }
}
```

Gets all the purchases from the database table

Iterates through each product

Gets the details about the purchased product

Adds the product into a set

Returns the set of products

Observe the implemented behavior: the app fetches some data in a list and then iterates over it to get more data from the database. Such an implementation typically indicates a design issue because you can usually reduce the execution of so many queries to one. Obviously, the fewer queries executed, the more efficient the app is.

In this example, it's effortless to retrieve the queries directly from the code. Since the profiler shows us exactly where they are, and the app is tiny, finding the queries isn't a problem. But real-world apps are not small, and in many cases, it's not easy to retrieve the queries directly from the code. But fear no more! You can use the profiler to retrieve all the SQL queries the app sends to a DBMS. You find this demonstrated in figure 7.10. Instead of selecting the CPU button, you select the JDBC button to start profiling for SQL queries.

What the tool does behind the scenes is pretty simple: a Java app sends the SQL queries to a DBMS through a JDBC driver. The profiler intercepts the driver and copies the queries before the driver sends them to the DBMS. Figure 7.11 shows this approach. The result is fantastic, as you can simply copy and paste the queries in your database client, where you can run them or investigate their plan.

The profiler also shows you how many times a query was sent. In this case, the app sent the first query 10 times. This design is faulty since it repeats the same query multiple times and thus spends unnecessary time and resources. The developer who implemented the code tried to obtain the purchases and then get the product details for each purchase. But a straightforward query with a join between the two tables

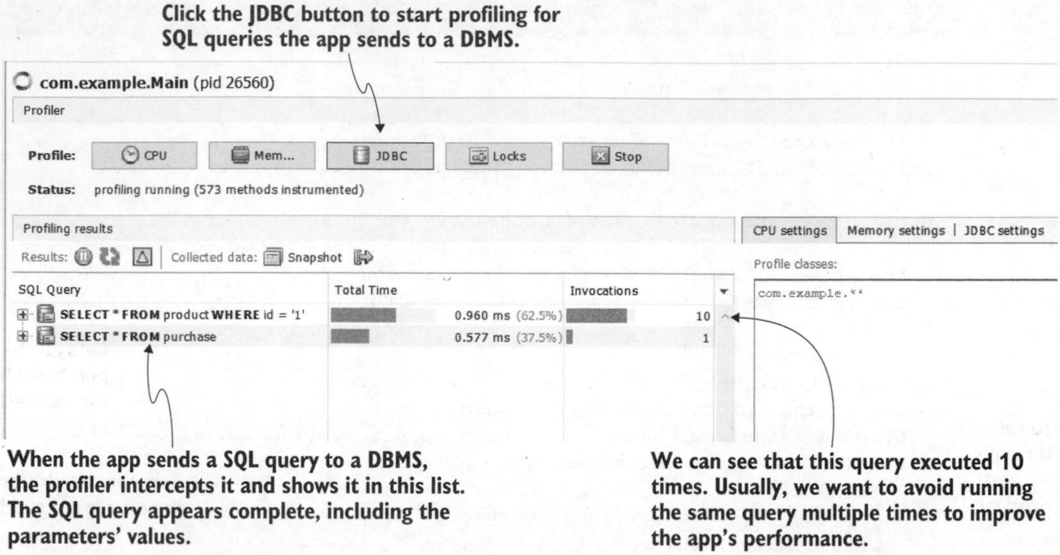

Click the JDBC button to start profiling for
SQL queries the app sends to a DBMS.

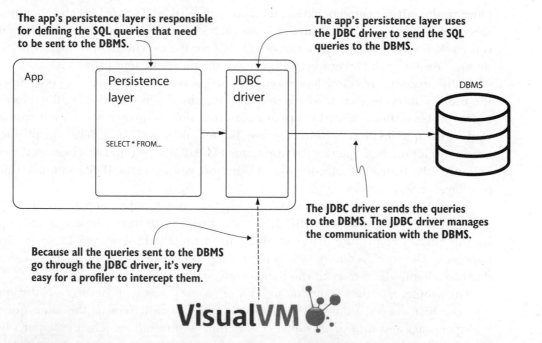

When the app sends a SQL query to a DBMS,
the profiler intercepts it and shows it in this list.
The SQL query appears complete, including the
parameters' values.

We can see that this query executed 10
times. Usually, we want to avoid running
the same query multiple times to improve
the app's performance.

Figure 7.10   The profiler intercepts the SQL queries the app sends to the DBMS through the JDBC driver. This gives you an easy way to get the queries, run them, observe what part of the codebase runs them, and know how many times a query is executed.

The app's persistence layer is responsible
for defining the SQL queries that need
to be sent to the DBMS.

The app's persistence layer uses
the JDBC driver to send the SQL
queries to the DBMS.

The JDBC driver sends the queries
to the DBMS. The JDBC driver manages
the communication with the DBMS.

Because all the queries sent to the DBMS
go through the JDBC driver, it's very
easy for a profiler to intercept them.

Figure 7.11   In a Java app, the communication with a relational DBMS is done through the JDBC driver. A profiler can intercept all method calls, including those of the JDBC driver, and retrieve the SQL queries the app sends to a DBMS. You can get the queries and use them in your investigations.

(product and purchase) would solve the problem in one step. Fortunately, using VisualVM, you identified the cause, and you know exactly what to change to improve this app.

Figure 7.12 shows you how to find the part of the codebase that sent the query. You can expand the execution stack and usually find the first method in the app's codebase.

Clicking the small + button shows the full stack trace that caused the execution of a certain SQL query.

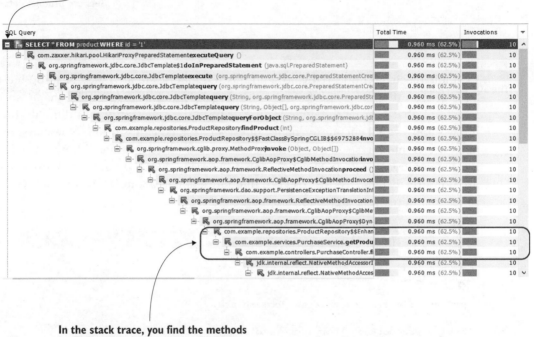

In the stack trace, you find the methods in the app's codebase that caused the execution of a certain query. This way, you identify where the problem is in your app.

Figure 7.12 For each query, the profiler also provides the execution stack trace. You can use the stack trace to identify which part of your app's codebase sent the query.

Listing 7.2 shows the code whose call we identified using the profiler. Once you identify where the problem comes from, it's time to read the code and find a way to optimize the implementation. In this example, everything could have been merged into one query. It may look like a silly mistake, but trust me, you'll find these types of cases, even in larger apps implemented by powerful organizations.

Listing 7.3   The algorithm's implementation in the `ProductService` class

```
@Service
public class PurchaseService {

  // Omitted code

  public Set<String> getProductNamesForPurchases() {
    Set<String> productNames = new HashSet<>();
    List<Purchase> purchases = purchaseRepository.findAll();
    for (Purchase p : purchases) {
      Product product = productRepository.findProduct(p.getProduct());
      productNames.add(product.getName());
    }
    return productNames;
  }
}
```

Iterates through each product

The app gets a list of all products.

Gets the product details

Example da-ch7-ex2 uses JDBC to send the SQL queries to a DBMS. The app has the SQL queries directly in the Java code (listing 7.3) and in their native shape, so you may think that copying the queries directly from the code is not that difficult. But in today's apps, you'll encounter native queries in the code less often. Nowadays, many apps use frameworks such as Hibernate (the most-used Java Persistence API [JPA] implementation) or Java Object Oriented Querying (JOOQ), and the native queries are not directly in the code. (You can find more details about JOOQ on their GitHub repository here: https://github.com/jOOQ/jOOQ).

Listing 7.4   A repository using native SQL queries

```
@Repository
public class ProductRepository {

  private final JdbcTemplate jdbcTemplate;

  public ProductRepository(JdbcTemplate jdbcTemplate) {
    this.jdbcTemplate = jdbcTemplate;
  }

  public Product findProduct(int id) {
    String sql = "SELECT * FROM product WHERE id = ?";
    return jdbcTemplate.queryForObject(sql, new ProductRowMapper(), id);
  }
}
```

A native SQL query the app sends to the DBMS

7.3.2   *Using the profiler to get the SQL queries generated by a framework*

Let's look at something even more extraordinary. To further prove the usefulness of a profiler in investigating SQL queries, let's review project da-ch7-ex3. From an algorithm point of view, this project does the same thing as the previous one: it returns the name of the purchased products. I intentionally kept the same logic to simplify the example and make it comparable.

The next code fragment shows the definition of a Spring Data JPA repository. The repository is a simple interface, and you don't see the SQL queries anywhere. With Spring Data JPA, the app generates the queries behind the scenes based on either the method's names or on a particular way of defining the queries, called Java Persistence Query Language (JPQL), which is based on the app's objects. Either way, there's no simple way to copy and paste the query from the code.

Some frameworks generate the SQL queries behind the scenes based on the code and configurations you write. In these cases, it's more challenging to get the executed queries. But a profiler can help you by extracting them from the JDBC driver before they are sent to the DBMS:

```
public interface ProductRepository
    extends JpaRepository<Product, Integer> {
}
```

The profiler comes to the rescue. Since the tool intercepts the queries before the app sends them to the DBMS, we can still use it to find exactly what queries the app uses. Start app da-ch7-ex3 and use VisualVM to profile the SQL queries like we did for the previous two projects.

Figure 7.13 shows you what the tool displays when profiling the /products end-point call. The app sent two SQL queries. Notice that the aliases in the query have strange names because the queries are framework generated. Also notice that even if the logic in the service is the same, and the app calls the repository method 10 times, the second query is executed only once because Hibernate optimizes the execution where it can. Now you can copy and investigate this query with a SQL development

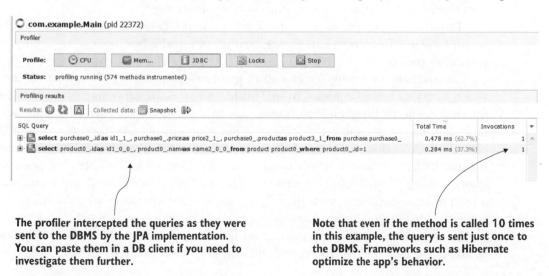

The profiler intercepted the queries as they were sent to the DBMS by the JPA implementation. You can paste them in a DB client if you need to investigate them further.

Note that even if the method is called 10 times in this example, the query is sent just once to the DBMS. Frameworks such as Hibernate optimize the app's behavior.

Figure 7.13   Even when working with a framework, the profiler can still intercept the SQL queries. This makes your investigation a lot easier because you can't copy the query directly from the code as you can when using JDBC and native queries.

client if needed. In many cases, investigating a slow query requires running it in a SQL client to observe which part of the query causes difficulty for the DBMS.

The query is executed only once even though the method is called 10 times. Do persistence frameworks usually do these kinds of tricks? Although they are smart, sometimes what they do behind the scenes can add complexity. Also, someone who does not properly understand the framework could write code that causes problems. This is another reason to use a profiler to check the queries the framework generates and make sure the app does what you expect.

The issues I mostly encounter with frameworks that require investigation are as follows:

- *Slow queries causing latencies*—Easy to spot using a profiler to examine the execution time
- *Multiple unneeded queries generated by the framework (usually caused by what developers call the N+1 query problem)*—Easy to spot using a profiler to determine the number of executions of a query
- *Long transaction commits generated by poor app design*—Easy to spot using CPU profiling

When a framework needs to get data from multiple tables, it usually knows to compose one query and get all the data in one call. However, if you don't correctly use the framework, it may take just part of the data with an initial query and then, for each record initially retrieved, run a separate query. So, instead of running just one query, the framework will send an initial query plus *N* others (one for each of the *N* records retrieved by the first); we call this an *N+1 query problem*, which usually creates significant latency by executing many queries instead of just one.

Most developers seem to be tempted to work with logs or a debugger to investigate such problems. But, in my experience, neither one is the best option to identify the problem's root cause.

The first issue with using logs for this type of case is that it's challenging to identify which query causes a problem. In real-world scenarios, the app may send dozens of queries—some of these multiple times, and in most cases, they are long and use a large number of parameters. With a profiler, which displays all the queries in a list with their execution time and the number of executions, you can almost instantaneously spot the problem. The second issue is that, even if you identify the potential query causing the problem (say, while monitoring logs, you observe that the app takes a long time to execute a given query), it's not straightforward to take the query and run it. In the log, you find parameters separated from the query.

You can configure your app to print the queries generated by Hibernate in the logs by adding some parameters to the application properties of the da-ch7-ex3 file:

```
spring.jpa.show-sql=true
spring.jpa.properties.hibernate.format_sql=true
logging.level.org.hibernate.type.descriptor.sql=trace
```

Beware that you'll have to use different ways to configure the logging depending on what technologies you use to implement the app. In the example provided with the book, we use Spring Boot and Hibernate. The next listing shows how the app prints the query in the logs.

Listing 7.5   Logs showing the native queries Hibernate sends

```
Hibernate:                        The query generated by the app
    Select        ◁
        product0_.id as id1_0_0_,
        product0_.name as name2_0_0_
    from
        product product0_
    where
        product0_.id=?                                   The first parameter's value

2021-10-16 13:57:26.566 TRACE 9512 --- [nio-8080-exec-2]
⇒ o.h.type.descriptor.sql.BasicBinder      : binding parameter [1] as
⇒ [INTEGER] - [1]
2021-10-16 13:57:26.568 TRACE 9512 --- [nio-8080-exec-2]
⇒ o.h.type.descriptor.sql.BasicExtractor   : extracted value ([name2_0_0_] :
⇒ [VARCHAR]) - [Chocolate]
```
The second parameter's value

The logs show us the query and give us both the input and the output of the query. But you need to bind the parameter values to the query if you want to run it separately. And, when multiple queries are logged, looking for what you need can be really frustrating. Logs also don't show you which part of the app runs the query, which can make your investigation even more challenging.

I recommend you always start with a profiler when investigating latency issues. Your first step should be sampling. When you suspect SQL query-related problems, continue profiling for JDBC. Then, problems will be easy understand, and you can use a debugger or the logs to confirm your speculations as needed.

7.3.3   *Using the profiler to get programmatically generated SQL queries*

For completeness, let's work on one more example that demonstrates how a profiler works when an app programmatically defines the queries. We'll investigate a performance problem with a query generated by Hibernate (the framework our example uses) in an app using *criteria queries*: a programmatic way of defining the app's persistence layer with Hibernate. You never write a query with this approach, either native or JPQL.

As you can see in listing 7.6, which presents the `ProductRepository` class reimplemented with a criteria query, this approach is more verbose. It's usually considered more difficult and leaves more room for mistakes. The implementation in project da-ch7-ex4 contains a mistake, which can cause significant performance problems in real-world apps. Let's see if we can find this issue and determine how the profiler can help us understand what's wrong.

Listing 7.6   The repository defined with a criteria query

```
public class ProductRepository {

  private final EntityManager entityManager;

  public ProductRepository(EntityManager entityManager) {
    this.entityManager = entityManager;
  }

  public Product findById(int id) {
    CriteriaBuilder cb = entityManager.getCriteriaBuilder();
    CriteriaQuery<Product> cq = cb.createQuery(Product.class);    ← Creates a new query

    Root<Product> product = cq.from(Product.class);    ← Specifies that the query selects products
    cq.select(product);    ← Selects the products

    Predicate idPredicate =
      cb.equal(cq.from(Product.class).get("id"), id);    ← Defines the condition that becomes part of the where clause on the next line
    cq.where(idPredicate);    ← Defines the where clause

    TypedQuery<Product> query = entityManager.createQuery(cq);
    return query.getSingleResult();    ← Runs the query and extracts the result
  }
}
```

We use JDBC profiling to intercept the queries the app sends to the DBMS. You can see that it contains a cross join between the product table and itself (figure 7.14). This is a huge problem! With the 10 records in our table, we don't observe anything suspicious here. But in a real-world app, where the table would have more records, this cross join would create huge latencies and eventually even wrong output (duplicated rows). Simply intercepting the query with VisualVM and reading it shows us the issue.

The next question is, "Why did the app generate the query this way?" I like the statement about JPA implementations, such as Hibernate: "The excellent thing is that they make the query generation transparent and minimize work. The bad thing is that they make the query generation transparent, making the app more prone to errors." When working with such frameworks. I generally recommend that developers profile the queries as part of the development process to discover such issues up front. Using a profiler is more for auditing purposes than finding issues, but doing so is a good safety measure.

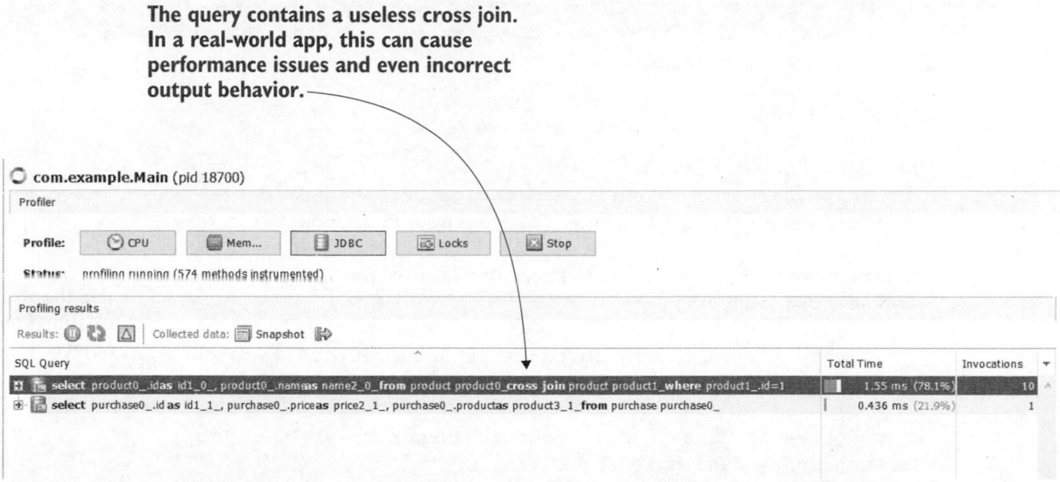

The query contains a useless cross join.
In a real-world app, this can cause
performance issues and even incorrect
output behavior.

Figure 7.14   The profiler can intercept any SQL query sent to the DBMS through the JDBC driver. Here, we spot an issue in the generated query—an unneeded cross join that causes performance problems.

In the following example, I intentionally introduced this tiny error with a significant impact. I called the `from()` method twice, instructing Hibernate to make a cross join.

Listing 7.7   The cause of the cross-join issue

```java
public class ProductRepository {

  // Omitted code

  public Product findById(int id) {
    CriteriaBuilder cb = entityManager.getCriteriaBuilder();
    CriteriaQuery<Product> cq = cb.createQuery(Product.class);

    Root<Product> product = cq.from(Product.class);     ⊲──┐ Calls the CriteriaQuery
    cq.select(product);                                      from() method once

    Predicate idPredicate = cb.equal(
      cq.from(Product.class).get("id"), id);            ⊲──┐ Calls the CriteriaQuery
    cq.where(idPredicate);                                    from() method again

    TypedQuery<Product> query = entityManager.createQuery(cq);
    return query.getSingleResult();
  }
}
```

Solving this problem is easy: use the product instance instead of calling the `Criteria-Query from()` method the second time, as in the following listing.

Listing 7.8   Correcting the cross-join issue

```java
public class ProductRepository {

  // Omitted code

  public Product findById(int id) {
    CriteriaBuilder cb = entityManager.getCriteriaBuilder();
    CriteriaQuery<Product> cq = cb.createQuery(Product.class);

    Root<Product> product = cq.from(Product.class);
    cq.select(product);

    Predicate idPredicate = cb.equal(product.get("id"), id);   ⟵ Use the already
    cq.where(idPredicate);                                          existing Root
                                                                   object.
    TypedQuery<Product> query = entityManager.createQuery(cq);
    return query.getSingleResult();
  }
}
```

Once you make this small change, the generated SQL query will no longer contain the unneeded cross join (figure 7.15). Still, the app runs the same query multiple times, which is not optimal. The algorithm the app runs should be refactored to get the data, preferably using only one query.

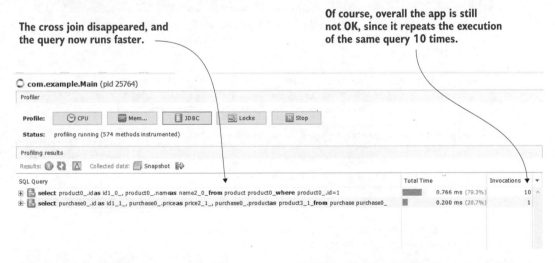

The cross join disappeared, and the query now runs faster.

Of course, overall the app is still not OK, since it repeats the execution of the same query 10 times.

Figure 7.15   By eliminating the supplementary `select()` method call, the cross join disappeared. However, the overall algorithm for this app should be revised, since it still runs the same query multiple times, which is not optimal.

Summary

- A profiler intercepts the app's execution and provides essential details about the code in execution, such as the execution stack trace for each thread, how long it takes for each method to execute, and how many times a certain method was called.

- When investigating latency problems, the first step to using a profiler is sampling—a way for the profiler to intercept the executing code without getting many details. Sampling is less resource consuming and allows you to observe the big picture of execution.

- Sampling gives you three essential details:
  - *What code executes*—When investigating an issue, you sometimes don't know what part of the code executes, and you can find this aspect by sampling.
  - *Total execution time of every method*—This detail helps you to identify what part of the code causes potential latency problems.
  - *Total CPU execution time*—This detail helps you to identify whether your code spends the execution time "working" or waiting for something.

- Sometimes sampling is enough to understand where a problem comes from. But in many cases, you need more details. You can get these details profiling the execution.

- Profiling is a resource-consuming process. With a real-world app, it's almost always impossible to profile the whole codebase. For this reason, when profiling for details, you should filter specific packages and classes on which you want to focus your investigation. You can usually determine what part of the app to focus on by sampling the execution first.

- An essential detail you get by profiling is the number of invocations of a method. When sampling, you know the total time a method spends executing, but not how often it was called. This aspect is important in identifying a method that is slow or wrongly used.

- You can use a profiler to get SQL queries the app sends to a DBMS. The profiler intercepts any queries, regardless of the technology used to implement the app's persistence layer. This is invaluable when investigating slow queries for apps that use frameworks (such as Hibernate) to work with a database.

Using advanced
visualization tools
for profiled data

This chapter covers

- Detecting problems with connections to relational databases
- Using call graphs to more quickly understand an app's design
- Using flame graphs to more easily visualize an app's execution
- Analyzing queries an app sends to a NoSQL database server

In this chapter, we discuss valuable techniques that can make life easier when investigating specific scenarios. We start the chapter by examining an approach for identifying connection problems between a Java app and a relational database server. We already discussed profiling SQL queries in chapter 7, but sometimes problems appear when an app establishes communication with a DBMS. Such situations can even lead to an app not responding at all, which makes finding the causes of such problems essential.

In section 8.2, I'll show you one of my favorite ways to understand the code behind a given execution scenario—a simple approach using call graphs, which are visual representations of the dependencies between an app's objects. I find call graphs helpful, especially when dealing with messy code I've never seen before. And since I'm sure most developers have to deal with messy codebases at some point in their careers, knowing this approach will be helpful.

Chapter 7 discussed one of the most used ways to visualize an app's execution—the execution stack. You learned how to generate an execution stack when sampling or profiling with VisualVM and how to use it to identify execution latencies. In section 8.3, we'll use a different representation of the execution stack: a flame graph. Flame graphs are a way to visualize an app's execution that focuses on both the executed code and the execution time. Viewing the same data from an additional perspective sometimes can help you to find what you're searching for more easily. As you'll learn in section 8.3, flame graphs offer you a different view of the app's execution, which helps you to identify potential latencies and performance problems. In section 8.4, we'll discuss techniques for analyzing how an app's persistence layer works when it doesn't use relational databases and instead uses different persistent approaches from what we call "the NoSQL family of technologies."

For the topics we discuss in this chapter, VisualVM is not enough. VisualVM is an excellent free tool that I use in more than 90% of the scenarios I investigate with a profiler, but it has its limitations.

To demonstrate the features we discuss in this chapter, we'll use JProfiler (http:// mng.bz/RvVn), a licensed profiler. JProfiler provides everything we discussed with VisualVM, but it also has capabilities VisualVM doesn't have (for a small price). You can use the trial period the software offers to try profiling the examples we use in this book and form your own opinion on the differences between VisualVM and JProfiler.

8.1 Detecting problems with JDBC connections

We discussed plenty of details about investigating problems with SQL queries in chapter 7. But what about the connection an app needs with a DBMS to send the queries? Negligence regarding connection management can cause problems, and in this section, we discuss these issues and how to find their root causes.

Some may argue that apps use frameworks and libraries that take care of connection management in most cases, and thus such problems no longer occur. However, experience tells me that these problems still happen, mainly because developers depend on many things to be automatic. Sometimes we should use less common and more low-level implementations, instead of depending on what the framework offers, which is where most of these types of problems occur.

Let me tell you a story of an issue I had to deal with recently. In a particular service (implemented with Spring), developers had to implement a less common capability: a way to cancel the execution of a stored procedure (a procedure running at the database level). The implementation wasn't complex, but it required directly accessing the connection object. In most cases, it was enough to allow Spring to use the connection behind the scenes. Spring is a robust framework and easy to customize, and you can easily access the connections it manages, but does it still manage these connections after you access them? The answer is sometimes. And this "sometimes" is what made things interesting (and also more challenging).

The developers found that in a standard method execution where Spring manages the transactions, the framework also closes the connections at the end. The procedure was cancelled with a batching approach, which was implemented from Spring Batch. In such cases, the framework doesn't close the connections; you must manage them. The developers used the same approach in both cases and didn't realize that the connections were not correctly closed in one of the cases, which could have caused a big problem. Fortunately, the development error was found in time and caused no harm.

This story shows why the technique you'll learn in this section is still relevant. The name of the frameworks you use doesn't matter, and you may never know everything that happens behind the scenes, so being prepared to investigate your app execution in any way will always be relevant.

We'll use project da-ch8-ex1 provided with the book. This project defines a simple app with a huge problem: one of its methods "forgets" to close the JDBC connections it opens. An app creates a JDBC connection to send SQL queries to the DBMS. The JDBC connections must always be closed once the app no longer needs them. All DBMSs offer clients (i.e., apps) the ability to get a limited number of connections (usually a small number, such as 100). When an app opens all these connections but doesn't close them, it cannot connect to the database server (figure 8.1).

The DBMS doesn't always offer precisely 100 connections. This number is configurable at the database level. When working with a database, it's best to find (usually by asking the database administrator) the maximum number of connections the app can open.

 **NOTE** To simplify our demonstration, we'll use a persistence layer that limits the number of connections to 10.

Let's start project da-ch8-ex1 and analyze the app's behavior. This project defines a simple application that stores details about products in a database. The app exposes an endpoint at the /products path. By calling the endpoint, the app returns details based on data it stores in its database. When you call the endpoint the first time, the app responds almost instantaneously. But when you send the second request to the

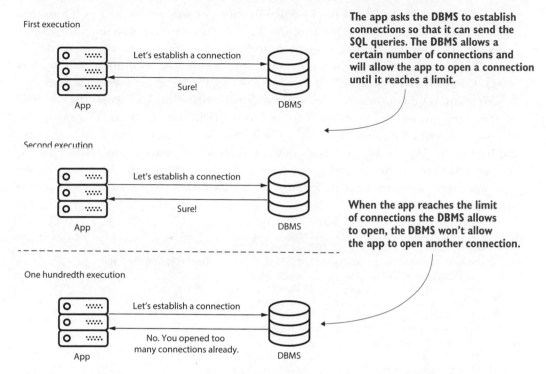

Figure 8.1 DBMS allows an app to open a finite and usually small number of connections. When the app reaches the limit of connections it can open, the DBMS doesn't allow the app to open other connections. In such a case, the app may become unable to execute its work.

same endpoint, the app responds after 30 seconds with an error message, as shown in figure 8.2.

When calling the endpoint the first time, the app responds immediately.

```
$ curl http://localhost:8080/products
  % Total    % Received % Xferd  Average Speed   Time    Time     Time  Current
                                 Dload  Upload   Total   Spent    Left  Speed
100    13    0    13    0     0    119       0 --:--:-- --:--:-- --:--:--   120["Chocolate"]
```

But when calling the endpoint the second time, the app throws an error after 30 seconds.

```
$ curl http://localhost:8080/products
  % Total    % Received % Xferd  Average Speed   Time    Time     Time  Current
                                 Dload  Upload   Total   Spent    Left  Speed
100   109    0   109    0     0     3       0 --:--:-- 0:00:30 --:--:--    28{"timestamp":"
07:55:09.272+00:00","status":500,"error":"Internal Server Error","path":"/products"}
```

Figure 8.2 When calling the /products endpoint the first time, the app responds instantaneously with a list containing the word "Chocolate." But when you try to call the endpoint a second time, the app appears to be stuck for about 30 seconds and then shows an error message.

What the app actually does is not essential for our demonstration, so I won't go into details about its functionality, but imagine that a friend working on a separate project calls you for your help and shows such a problem. They don't give you many details about how their app works (in a real-world app, it could be a complicated business case). Can you still help them? We start by analyzing the behavior they show us.

We want to find out what causes the problematic behavior. You access the logs and immediately suspect the problem is related to the JDBC connections. The exception message, shown in the following snippet, tells you that the app can't make a connection, most likely because the DBMS doesn't allow other connections to be opened. But let's assume we cannot always rely on logs. In the end, we can't know for certain that another framework or library that your app uses didn't generate the straightforward exception message:

```
java.sql.SQLTransientConnectionException:
   HikariPool-1 - Connection is not available,
   request timed out after 30014ms.          ⟵——— The exception message
      at com.zaxxer.hikari.pool.HikariPool
      .createTimeoutException(HikariPool.java:696) at
      com.zaxxer.hikari.pool.HikariPool
      .getConnection(HikariPool.java:197)
      at [CA]com.zaxxer.hikari.pool.HikariPool
      .getConnection(HikariPool.java:162)
      at [CA]com.zaxxer.hikari.HikariDataSource
      .getConnection(HikariDataSource.java:128)
      at [CA]com.example.repositories.PurchaseRepository
      .findAll(PurchaseRepository.java:31)
      at [CA]com.example.repositories.PurchaseRepository
   $$FastClassBySpringCGLIB$$d661c9a0.invoke(<generated>)
```

As I recommended in chapter 7, every profiling investigation should start with sampling, which gives you an overview of the execution and the details you need to continue your research. If you used VisualVM, the sampling result would look like figure 8.3.

After sampling and observing the exception stack trace in the logs, we know our app has a problem connecting to the DBMS. But what causes this problem? It could be one of two things:

- The communication between the app and the DBMS fails because of some infrastructure or networking problems.
- The DBMS doesn't want to provide a connection to our application:
  - Because of an authentication problem
  - Because the app already consumed all the connections the DBMS can offer

Since in our case the issue always happens the second time a request is sent (there is a defined pattern to reproduce it), we can exclude the communication problem. It must be that the DMBS doesn't provide a connection. But it can't be an authentication problem since the first call worked well. It's unlikely that something changed with the credentials, so the most plausible cause is that our app sometimes doesn't close

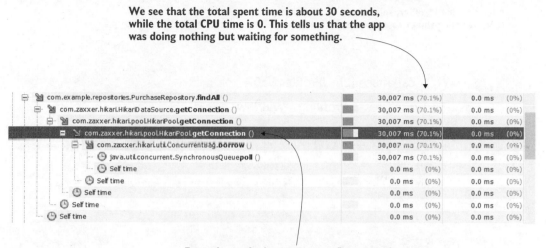

We see that the total spent time is about 30 seconds, while the total CPU time is 0. This tells us that the app was doing nothing but waiting for something.

From the method name, we can figure out that the app was waiting to establish a connection with the DBMS.

Figure 8.3   After sampling the execution, we have more reasons to suspect something is wrong with establishing a connection to the DBMS. In the execution stack, we see that the app waited for 30 seconds to get a connection.

the connections. Now we just have to find where this happens. Remember that the method that encountered the problem isn't necessarily the one causing it. It may be that this method is the "unlucky" one that tried to get a connection after someone else "ate" all the others.

But with VisualVM, you can't explicitly investigate JDBC connections, so we can't use it to identify which connection stays open. Instead, we'll continue our investigation using JProfiler. Attaching JProfiler to a running Java process is very similar to using VisualVM. Let's follow the approach step by step.

First, select Start Center in the upper-left corner of JProfiler's main window, as presented in figure 8.4.

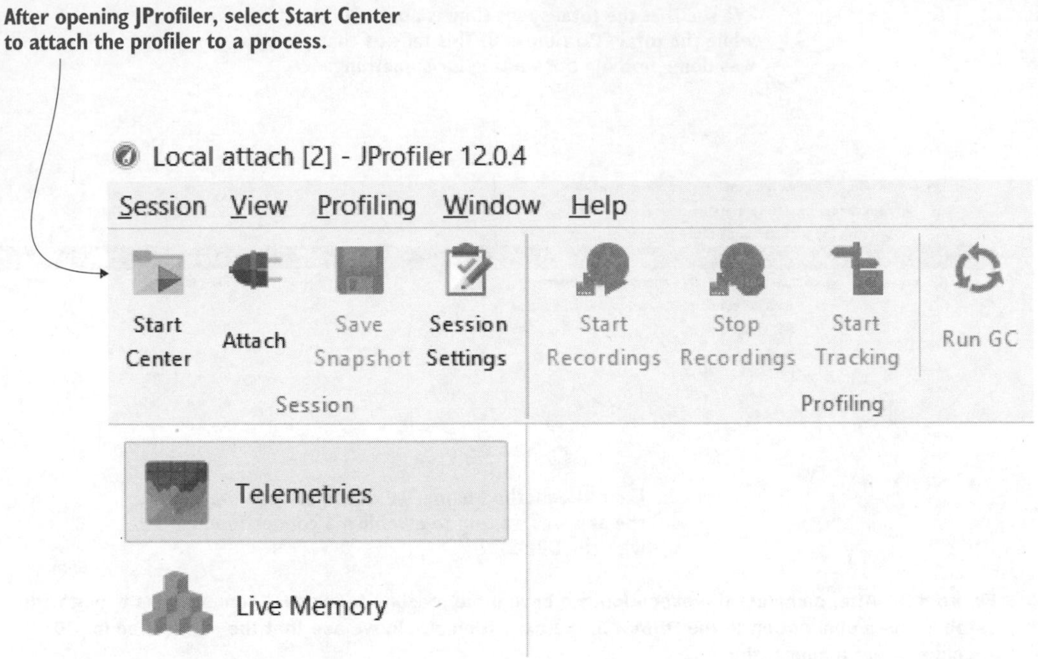

After opening JProfiler, select Start Center
to attach the profiler to a process.

Figure 8.4   Start a sampling or profiling session with JProfiler by selecting the Start Center menu in the upper-left corner of the JProfiler window.

A pop-up window appears (figure 8.5), and you can select Quick Attach on the left to get a list of all Java processes running locally. Choose the process you want to profile and then select Start. Just as with VisualVM, you identify the process by the name of the main class or the process ID (PID).

1. **Select Quick Attach on the left side of the Start Center window.**

2. **In the Start Center window, you find a list of all the Java processes running on the local system. Select the process you want to profile. You can identify the process using the Main class and main package names.**

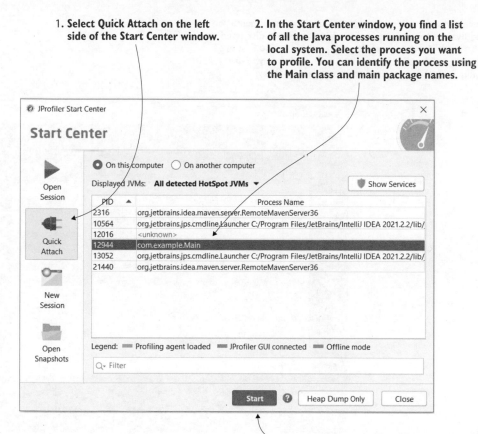

3. **After selecting the process you want to profile, click Start to begin the profiling session.**

Figure 8.5   In the pop-up window, select Quick Attach and, in the list, select the process you want to profile. Then select the Start button to begin the profiling session.

JProfiler will ask you if you want to use sampling or instrumentation (instrumentation is the equivalent to what we called profiling with VisualVM), as shown in figure 8.6. We select instrumentation since we are using the profiler to get details about the JDBC connections and thus want to analyze the execution in more depth.

We continue by selecting Instrumentation. Instrumentation is equivalent to profiling in VisualVM. Just as we discussed with VisualVM, when investigating a problem, you first use sampling to identify the problem area, and then you use profiling (instrumentation) to investigate further.

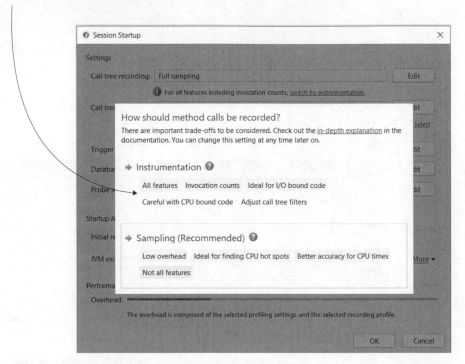

Figure 8.6   To analyze the execution in more depth, we need to select Instrumentation, the equivalent to what we call profiling in VisualVM.

Under Databases in the left menu, select JDBC. Then start the JDBC profiling as presented in figure 8.7.

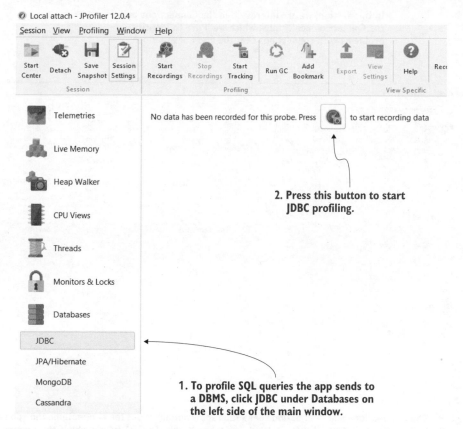

Figure 8.7 You can start JDBC profiling with JProfiler by first selecting JDBC in the left menu; then you begin the profiling process.

Once profiling begins, we are most interested in two tabs: Connections and Connection Leaks (figure 8.8). These tabs show us details about the connections to the DBMS the app opens, and we'll use them to identify the problem's root cause.

In this section, we are interested in the Connections and
the Connection Leaks tabs, which we'll use to identify
problems with connections that the app doesn't close.

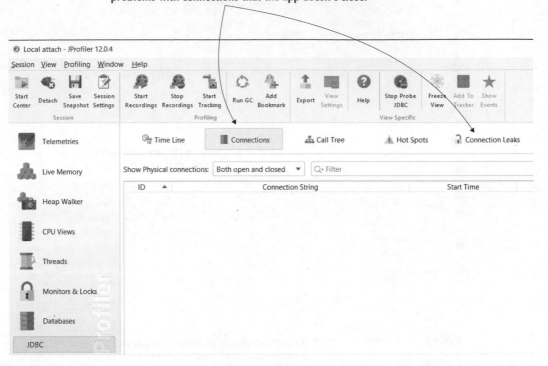

**Figure 8.8   The Connections and Connection Leaks tabs show details about the connections the app creates,
including potential problematic connections. We'll use these details to understand where the problem in our
app comes from.**

Now it's time to reproduce the problem and profile the execution. Send a request to
the /products endpoint, and let's see what happens. The Connections tab shows that
many connections are created, as presented in figure 8.9. Since we don't know what
the app does, many connections don't necessarily mean problems. But we expect that
the app closed these connections so that it can get other connections when needed.
What we need to figure out is if the app closed these connections correctly.

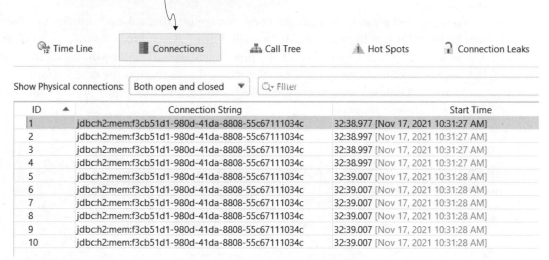

When sending a request to the /products endpoint, the app opens a large number of connections. We use the Connections tab in the profiler to see the connections when the app opens.

Figure 8.9 By sending a request to the `/products` endpoint, we see that the app creates many connections. We don't know exactly what the app does, but this can be alarming.

The Connection Leaks tab confirms our suspicion (figure 8.10); not only does the app open many connections, but the connections remain unclosed long after the endpoint responds. This is a clear sign of a connection leak. If we didn't explicitly start CPU profiling (I'll show you in a moment how to do that), you'd only see the name of the thread that created the connection. Sometimes the thread's name is enough, and in such a case, you wouldn't need to start CPU profiling at all. However, in situations such as this one, it doesn't tell us enough to identify the code that created the connection.

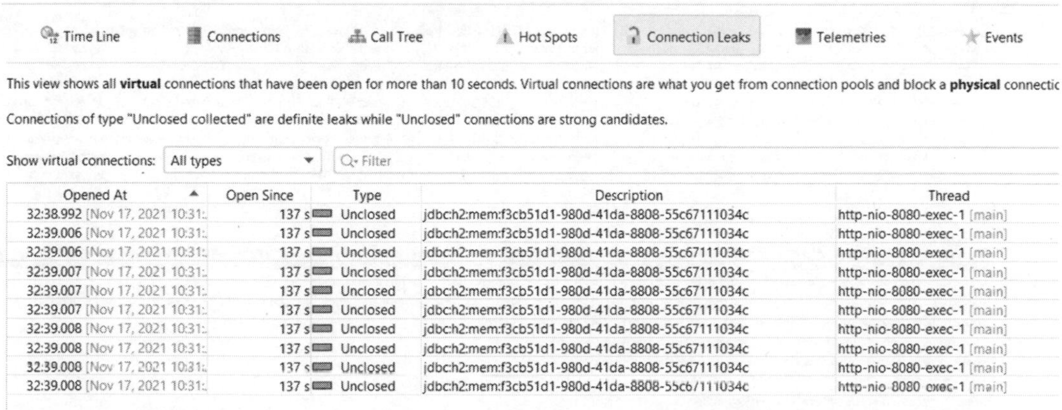

Figure 8.10 The Connection Leaks tab shows us the status of each connection. We are interested in the connections that close late or never. Here, the connections the app opened are still alive long after the endpoint sent a response back to the client, which strongly indicates a problem.

But that's not enough, is it? We had suspected that something was wrong with the app obtaining a connection to the DBMS. Now we need to use the profiler's CPU profiling capability to identify the part of the codebase that creates the connections and forgets to close them.

We still need a way to identify the code that creates the leaking connections. Fortunately, JProfiler can help us with this as well, but we'll need to redo the exercise after also enabling CPU profiling. With CPU profiling active, JProfiler will display, for each leaking connection, the stack trace to the method that created the connection.

Figure 8.11 shows how to enable CPU profiling and how you find the stack trace for each leaking connection.

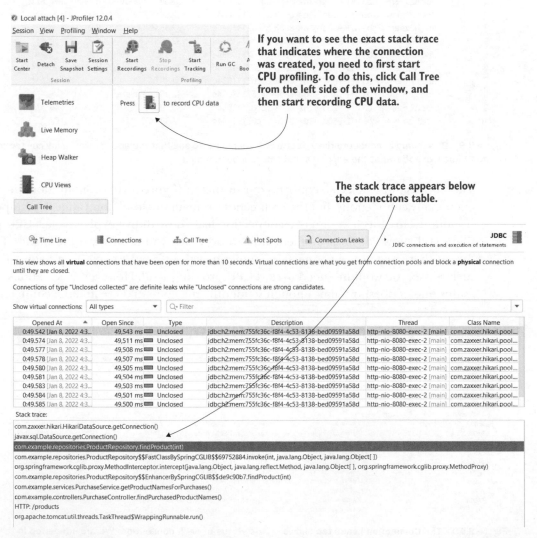

Figure 8.11   With CPU profiling enabled, JProfiler shows the stack trace, which helps you identify which part of the app's code creates the leaking connections.

Let's go straight to that code in our example da-ch8-ex1. We observe that the method indeed creates a connection that seems not to be closed anywhere. We found the root cause!

Listing 8.1   Identifying the problem root cause

```
public Product findProduct(int id) throws SQLException {
    String sql = "SELECT * FROM product WHERE id = ?";

    Connection con = dataSource.getConnection();
    try (PreparedStatement statement = con.prepareStatement(sql)) {
      statement.setInt(1, id);
      ResultSet result = statement.executeQuery();

      if (result.next()) {
        Product p = new Product();
        p.setId(result.getInt("id"));
        p.setName(result.getString("name"));
        return p;
      }
    }
    return null;
}
```

This line creates a connection that is never closed.

Project da-ch8-ex2 corrects the code. By adding the connection to the `try-with-resources` block, the app will close the connection at the end of the `try` block when the connection is no longer needed.

Listing 8.2   Solving the problem by closing the connection

```
public Product findProduct(int id) throws SQLException {
    String sql = "SELECT * FROM product WHERE id = ?";


    try (Connection con = dataSource.getConnection();
         PreparedStatement statement = con.prepareStatement(sql)) {
      statement.setInt(1, id);
      ResultSet result = statement.executeQuery();

      if (result.next()) {
        Product p = new Product();
        p.setId(result.getInt("id"));
        p.setName(result.getString("name"));
        return p;
      }
    }
    return null;
}
```

The connection is declared in the try-with-resources block, closing the connection at the end of the try block.

We can profile the app again after applying the correction. Now the Connection tab in JProfiler shows us that only one connection is created, and the Connection Leaks tab is empty, confirming that the problem was indeed solved (figure 8.12). When you test the app, you also see that you can send multiple requests to the /products endpoint.

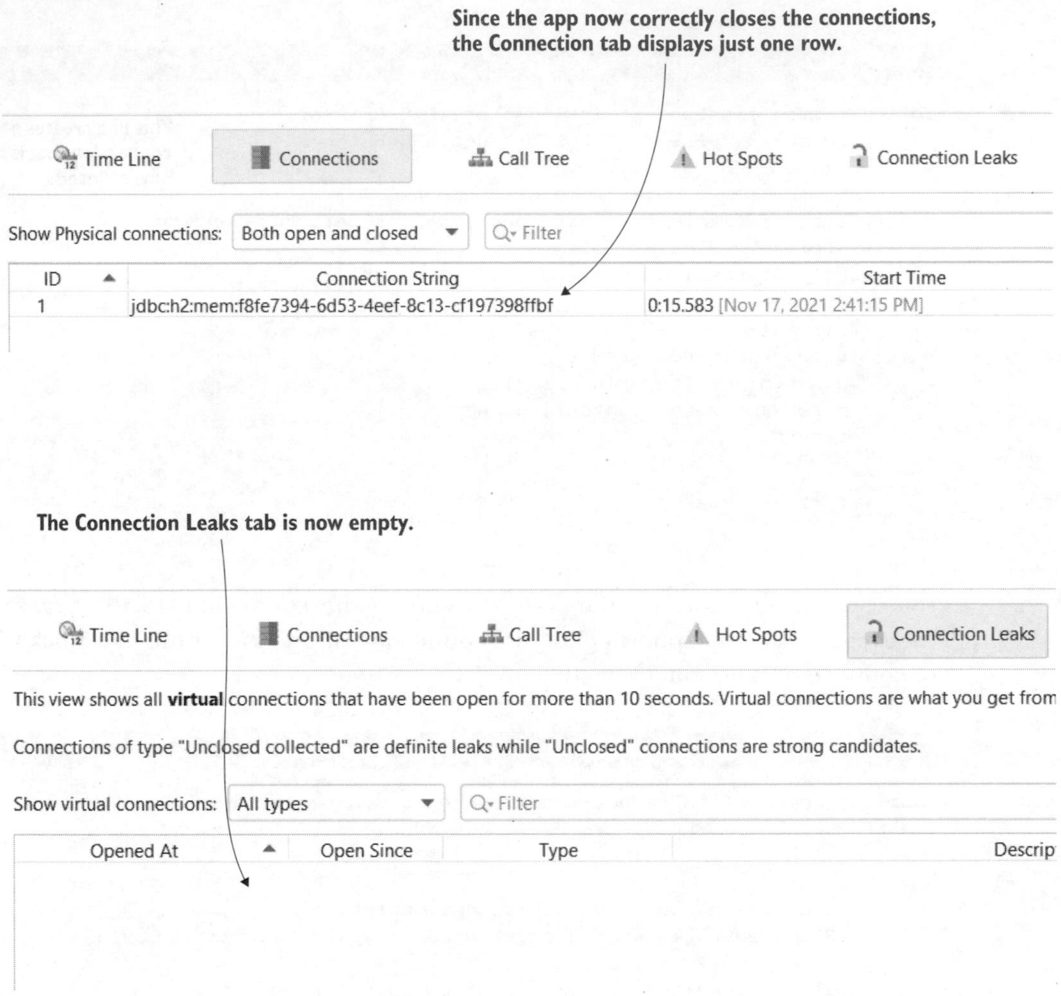

Since the app now correctly closes the connections, the Connection tab displays just one row.

| | ⏱ Time Line | 📊 Connections | 🔺 Call Tree | ⚠ Hot Spots | 🔌 Connection Leaks |

Show Physical connections: Both open and closed ▾   🔍 Filter

ID ▲	Connection String	Start Time
1	jdbc:h2:mem:f8fe7394-6d53-4eef-8c13-cf197398ffbf	0:15.583 [Nov 17, 2021 2:41:15 PM]

The Connection Leaks tab is now empty.

| | ⏱ Time Line | 📊 Connections | 🔺 Call Tree | ⚠ Hot Spots | 🔌 Connection Leaks |

This view shows all **virtual** connections that have been open for more than 10 seconds. Virtual connections are what you get from

Connections of type "Unclosed collected" are definite leaks while "Unclosed" connections are strong candidates.

Show virtual connections: All types ▾   🔍 Filter

Opened At ▲	Open Since	Type	Descrip

Figure 8.12   After fixing the error, we use JProfiler to confirm that no more connections are leaking. We observe that the app opens only one connection at a time and correctly closes the connection when it no longer needs it. The Connection Leaks tab doesn't show any other faulty connections.

Do you wonder if there is a best practice to avoid such problems in real-world scenarios? I recommend that developers take 10 minutes or so after each implementation or bug fix to test the capability they worked on with a profiler. This practice can help to identify latency issues caused by wrong queries or faulty connection management from the early phases of development.

8.2 Understanding the app's code design using call graphs

In this section, we discuss one of my favorite techniques to understand an app's class design: visualizing the execution as a call graph. This technique is especially helpful when dealing with messy code, an eventuality of working with a new app.

Thus far, we've used stack traces to understand execution. Execution stack traces are valuable tools, and we've already seen how many things we can do with them. They are helpful because of their straightforward way of representing as text, which allows them to be printed in logs (usually as exception stack traces). But from a visual point of view, they're not great at quickly identifying the relationship between objects and method calls. Call graphs are a different way to represent the data a profiler collects and focus more on the relationships between the objects and method calls.

To demonstrate how to obtain a call graph, we'll use example da-ch8-ex2 provided with the book to demonstrate how to use call graphs to quickly understand which objects and methods act behind an execution without analyzing the code. Of course, the idea isn't to avoid the code completely; you'll still end up digging through the code, but by using call graphs first, you'll have a better picture of what happens up front.

We will continue to use JProfiler for our demonstration. Since call graphs are a way to represent CPU profiler data, we first need to start CPU profiling. Figure 8.13 shows how to start CPU profiling, which results in a stack trace (referred to as a *call tree* in JProfiler). We'll investigate what happens when calling the /products endpoint the app exposes.

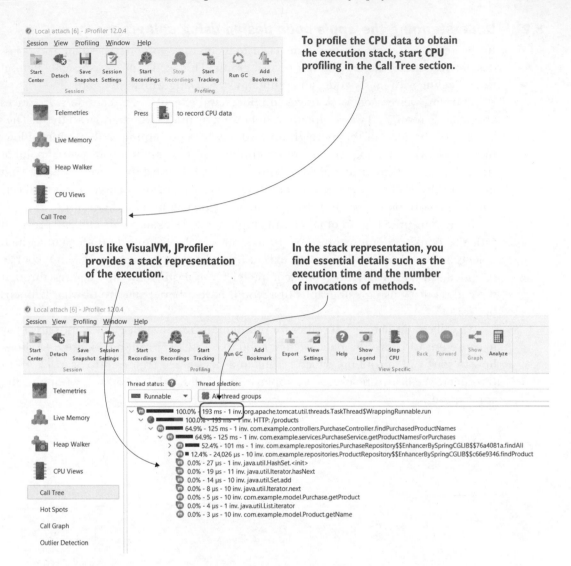

Figure 8.13   Select Call Tree from the left-hand menu to start profiling the CPU (recording CPU data). Send a request to the `/products` endpoint, and the profiler will initially show the recorded data as a stack trace, including details about the number of invocations and the execution time.

Right-click a line in the stack trace and select Show Call Graph to visualize the data collected about the execution as a call graph (figure 8.14).

JProfiler will generate a call graph representation, focusing on the method defined by the line you selected when generating the call graph. You'll initially only know where this method is called from and what this method calls. You can navigate further and observe the entire call chain (figure 8.15). The call graph also provides details about the execution time and the number of invocations, but its focus is mainly on the relationship between the objects and the method calls.

To obtain a call graph representation from the stack trace, right-click any method and select Show Call Graph.

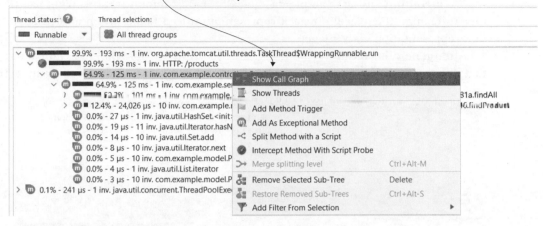

Figure 8.14 To get a call graph representation from an execution stack trace, right-click a line in the stack trace and select Show Call Graph.

Method findPurchasedProductNames() in the PurchaseController class is called directly from a thread created outside the app's codebase.

Method findPurchasedProductNames() calls getProductNamesForPurchases() in the PurchaseService class.

For each method, the profiler displays the CPU spent time and the number of invocations.

Select the small plus sign to extend the graph and see what methods are further called.

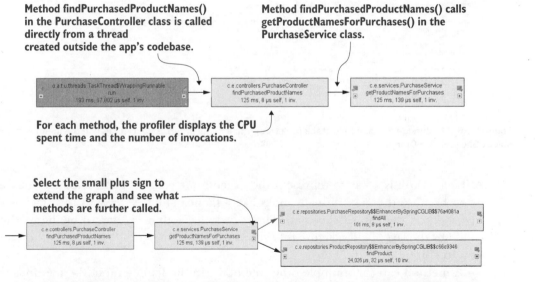

Figure 8.15 A call graph shows the execution, focusing mainly on the relationship between objects and method calls. You can linearly navigate the method execution chain to determine where each method is called from and what that method calls. The call graph also shows objects and methods that are part of the app's codebase and those of libraries and frameworks the app uses.

8.3 Using flame graphs to spot performance problems

Another way to visualize the profiled execution is using a *flame graph*. If call graphs focus on the relationship between objects and method calls, flame graphs are most helpful in identifying potential latencies. They are just a different way to see the same details a method execution stack provides, but, as mentioned in the chapter introduction, other representations of the same data may help to identify specific information.

We'll continue using example da-ch8-ex2 for this demonstration. We'll use JProfiler to change the execution stack representation to a flame graph and discuss the new representation's advantages.

After generating a call tree, as discussed in sections 8.1 and 8.2, you can change it to a flame graph using the Analyze item in the top menu bar, as shown in figure 8.16.

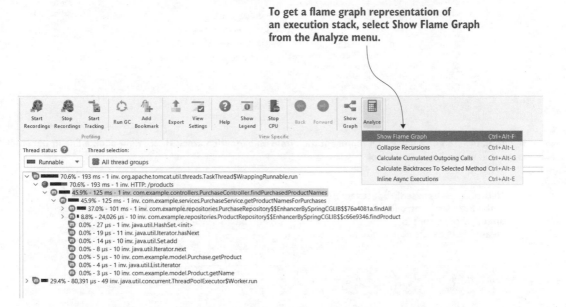

To get a flame graph representation of an execution stack, select Show Flame Graph from the Analyze menu.

Figure 8.16   To change an execution stack (call tree) into a flame graph, select Analyze in the menu and then select Show Flame Graph.

A flame graph is a way to represent the execution tree as a stack. The fancy name is given because the graph usually looks like a flame. The first level of this stack is the first method the thread executed. Then, every level above is shared by the methods called by the layer below. Figure 8.17 shows you the flame graph created for the execution tree in figure 8.16.

A method can call multiple other methods. In the flame graph, the methods that were called will appear on the same level. In such a case, the length of each is the time spent relative to the method calling it (the level below). In figure 8.17, you can see that method `findById()` in the `ProductRepository` class and method `findAll()` in the `PurchaseRepository` class were both called from `getProductNamesForPurchases()` in the `ProductService` class.

In figure 8.18, we observe that `getProductNamesForPurchases()` in the `ProductService` class is the bottom level for both method `findById()` in the `ProductRepository` class and method `findAll()` in the `PurchaseRepository` class. Moreover,

Each method is a level in the execution stack. The level below is what called that method; the levels above are what that method calls. For example, we see that method findPurchasedProductNames() in the PurchaseController class calls getProductNamesForPurchases() in the PurchaseService class. Further, the method in the PurchaseService class calls findAll() of PurchaseRepository.

We see the execution stack vertically.

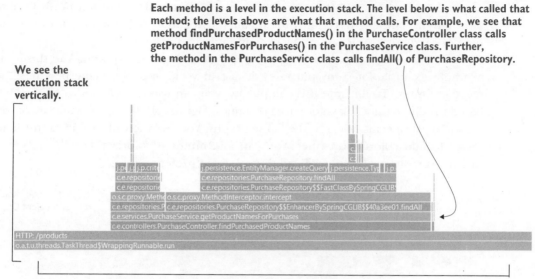

Horizontally, we have the execution time.

Figure 8.17   The flame graph is a stack representation of the execution trace. Each level shows the methods called by the level below. The first (bottom) level of the stack is the start of the thread. This way, we see the execution stack vertically, while the flame graph horizontally indicates the time spent by each level relative to the level below.

This is the findById() method in the ProductRepository class.

This is the findAll() method in the PurchaseRepository class.

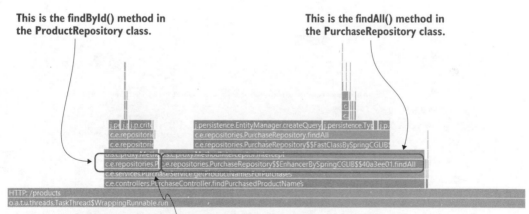

The length difference indicates the execution time relative to the level below. In this case, out of the total execution time spent by the getProductNamesForPurchases() method, a small part was spent executing findById(), and most of the time was spent executing findAll().

Figure 8.18   When multiple methods share the same level, they are all called by the method below them. The sum of the lengths of the representation equals the length of the method under them. Each method's length is a relative representation of the execution time from the total. In this case, findAll() took much longer to execute than findById().

findById() and findAll() share the same layer. But notice that they don't have the same length. The length is relative to the caller's execution, so in this case, the execution time of findById() is less than the execution time of findAll().

You may have already noticed that it's easy to get lost in this graph. And this is only a simple example for study purposes; in a real-world app, the flame may be much more complex. To mitigate this complexity, you can use JProfiler to color the layers based on the method, class, or package names. Figure 8.19 shows how to use colorization to mark specific layers in the flame graphs. You use the Colorize item in the top menu to add colorization rules. You can add multiple colorization rules to specify which layers should be colored and the color you prefer.

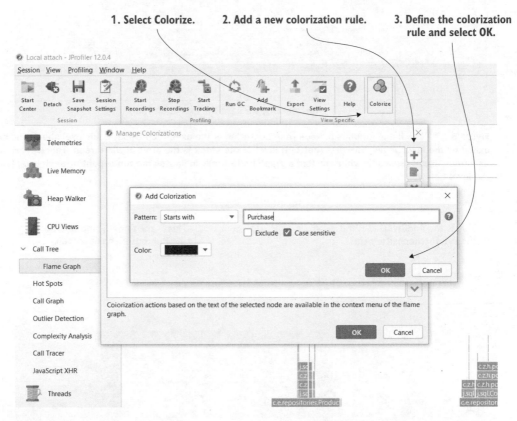

Figure 8.19   To color your flame graph and make it easier to read, add colorization rules using the Colorize item in the top menu. The rules define which layers in the flame graph should be colored and which color should be used.

In figure 8.20, you can see how I highlighted the levels for the methods containing the word "Purchase" in their names and had them colored blue (dark gray in the print version of this book).

You can independently color the levels based on the class and package names to more easily follow the graph. For example, in this case, I colored all the methods containing the word "Purchase" in their names in blue (dark gray in the print version of this book).

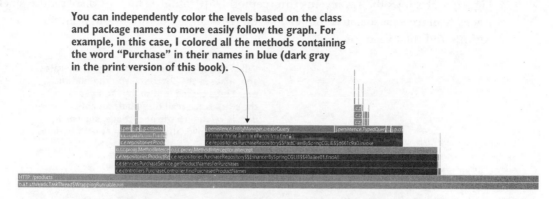

Figure 8.20   Colorizing levels helps highlight specific parts of the flame that you want to focus on. You can use multiple colors at the same time, which can help you to compare execution times.

8.4   Analyzing queries on NoSQL databases

Applications often use relational databases, but in many cases, certain implementations need different persistence technologies. We call these *NoSQL technologies*, and apps we implement can choose from a large variety of such implementations. Some of the best known examples are MongoDB, Cassandra, Redis, and Neo4J. Some profilers, such as JProfiler, can intercept queries the app sends to a specific NoSQL server to work with a database.

JProfiler can intercept events sent to MongoDB and Cassandra, and these details may help to save time when you are investigating the behavior of an app using such a persistence implementation. For this reason, in this section, we'll use a small app to demonstrate the use of JProfiler to observe an app's interaction with a MongoDB database.

Project da-ch8-ex3 works with MongoDB. The app implements a couple of endpoints: one that stores details of products in the database and another that returns a list of all previously added products. To make it simple, a product is only represented by a name and a unique ID.

To follow this section, you first need to locally install a MongoDB server to which project da-ch8-ex3 will connect. You can download and install MongoDB Community Server from the official page: https://www.mongodb.com/try/download/community.

Once you have installed the server, you can start project da-ch8-ex3. We will also attach JProfiler to the process. To begin monitoring MongoDB events, select the MongoDB section under Databases in the left menu and start recording. To observe how JProfiler presents the events, we will call the two endpoints the app exposes. You can call the two endpoints using the cURL commands (as in the following snippet) or a tool such as Postman:

```
curl -XPOST http://localhost:8080/product/Beer
```
Adds a product named "Beer" to the database

```
curl http://localhost:8080/product
```
Gets all the products in the database

Figure 8.21 shows the two events intercepted by JProfiler. The tool displays the stack traces (call trees) associated with each event. We get details about the number of invocations and the execution time.

When you trigger the endpoint that generates an update in the database, you can find the event intercepted in JProfiler. You get the stack trace (call tree) and valuable details related to the operations, such as the number of invocations and the execution time.

The second event you can observe is caused by a find query. In both cases, you can find the document to which the operation has been applied and the operation name.

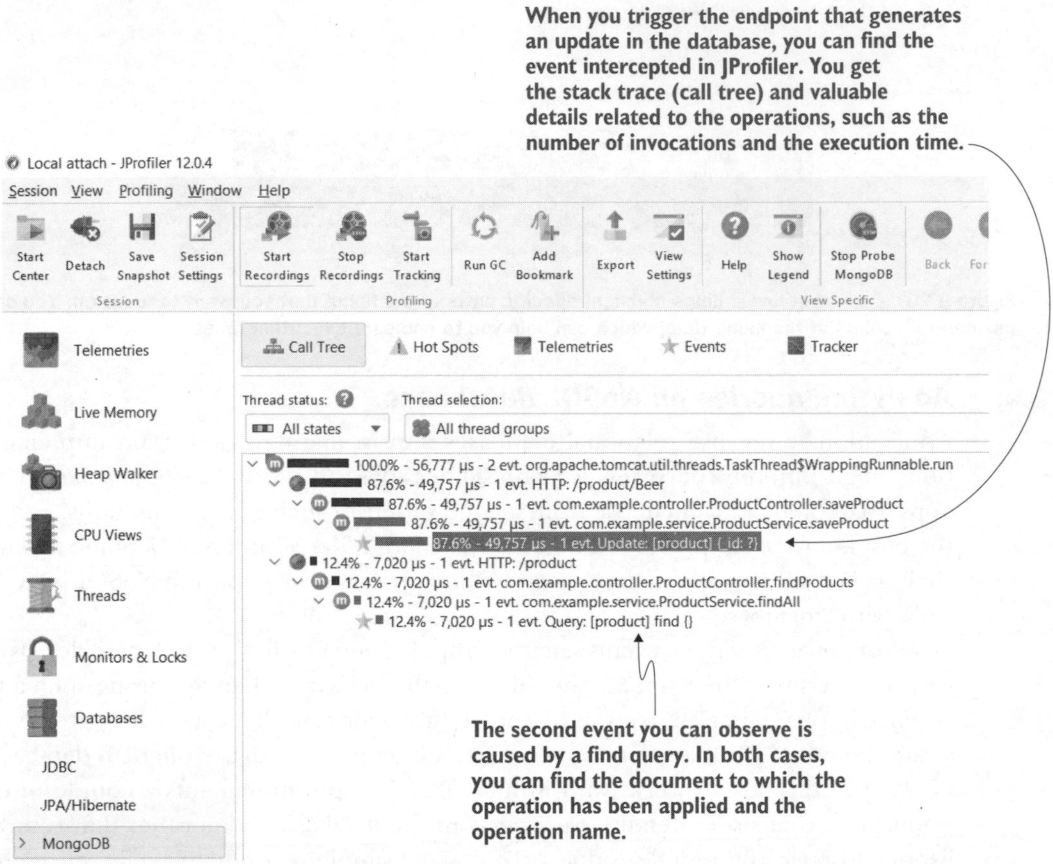

Figure 8.21   JProfiler can intercept the operations an app applies to a NoSQL database. In this example, JProfiler intercepts two events: an update and a read on a document named "product." This way, you can monitor the interaction between your app and a NoSQL database and consider the number of invocations for specific operations and the execution time. The profiler also gives you the complete stack trace for a particular operation so you can quickly find the code that caused a specific event.

Summary

- Free tools such as VisualVM offer plenty of widgets that can help with any investigation. But licensed tools such as JProfiler can make the investigations even more effective through different ways of representing the investigation data.
- Sometimes apps encounter issues when connecting to a DBMS. By using JProfiler, you can more easily investigate issues with a JDBC connection to a relational database server. You can evaluate whether connections remain open and identify the part of the code that "forgets" to close them.

- Call graphs are a different way to visualize the execution stack and focus mainly on the relationship between objects and method calls. For this reason, call graphs are an excellent tool you can use to more easily understand the class design behind the app's execution.

- Flame graphs offer a different perspective for visualizing profiled data. You can use flame graphs to more easily spot areas causing latencies in execution and long stack traces. You can color specific layers in a flame graph to better visualize the execution.

- Some licensed tools offer extended capabilities, such as investigating the communication between apps or between your app and a NoSQL database server.

Investigating locks in multithreaded architectures

This chapter covers
- Monitoring an application's threads
- Identifying thread locks and what causes them
- Analyzing threads that are waiting

In this chapter, we discuss approaches to investigating the execution of apps that leverage multithreaded architectures. Generally, developers find implementing multithreaded architectures one of the most challenging things in app development, and making the app performant brings another dimension of difficulty. The techniques we discuss in this chapter will give you visibility into the execution of such apps, allowing you to more easily identify problems and optimize the app execution.

To properly understand the content of this chapter, you need to know the basics of threading mechanisms in Java, including thread states and synchronization. For a refresher, read appendix D; it won't give you all the possible knowledge on threads and concurrency in Java (that would need its own bookshelf), but it will give you enough detail to understand this chapter's discussion.

9.1 *Monitoring threads for locks*

In this section, we discuss thread locks and how to analyze them to find eventual issues or opportunities to optimize an app's execution. *Thread locks* are caused by different thread synchronization approaches, usually implemented to control the flow of events in a multithreaded architecture. Examples include these:

- A thread wants to prevent other threads from accessing a resource while it's changing that resource.
- A thread needs to wait for another one to finish or reach a certain point in its execution before being able to continue its work.

Thread locks are necessary; they help an app control threads. But implementing thread synchronization leaves a lot of room for mistakes. Wrongly implemented locks may cause app freezes or performance issues. We need to use profilers to make sure our implementations are optimal and to make an app more efficient by minimizing the lock time.

In this section, we'll use a small application (project da-ch9-ex1) that implements a simple multithreaded architecture. We'll use a profiler to analyze the locks during the app's execution. We want to find out if the threads are locked and how they behave:

- Which thread locks another
- How many times a thread is locked
- The time at which a thread pauses instead of executing

These details allow us to understand whether the app execution is optimal and whether there are ways we can improve our app's execution. The app we use for our example implements two threads that run concurrently: the producer and the consumer. The producer generates random values and adds them to a list instance, and the consumer removes values from the same collection used by the producer (figure 9.1).

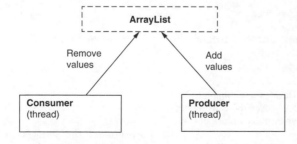

Figure 9.1 The app starts two threads that we refer to as "the producer" and "the consumer." Both threads use a common resource: they change a list instance of type ArrayList. The producer generates random values and adds them to the list, while the consumer concurrently removes the values added by the producer.

Let's follow the app implementation in listings 9.1, 9.2, and 9.3 to see what to expect when we investigate the execution. In listing 9.1, you find the Main class, which starts the two thread instances. I made the app wait for 10 seconds before starting the threads to allow us some time to start the profiler and observe the entire threads' timelines. The app names the threads _Producer and _Consumer to allow us to easily identify them when working with the profiler.

Listing 9.1   App's `Main` method that starts two threads

```
public class Main {

  private static Logger log = Logger.getLogger(Main.class.getName());

  public static List<Integer> list = new ArrayList<>();

  public static void main(String[] args) {
    try {
      Thread.sleep(10000);

      new Producer("_Producer").start();
      new Consumer("_Consumer").start();
    } catch (InterruptedException e) {
      log.severe(e.getMessage());
    }
  }
}
```

Starts a producer thread ⟶

Waits 10 seconds, in the beginning, to let the programmer start the profiling ⟶

Starts a consumer thread ⟵

In listing 9.2, you find the consumer thread's implementation. The thread iterates over a block of code one million times (this number should be enough for the app to run a few seconds and allow us to use the profiler to take some statistics). During every iteration, the thread uses a static list instance declared in the `Main` class. The consumer thread checks whether the list has values and removes the first value in the list. The whole block of code implementing the logic is synchronized, using the list instance itself as a monitor. The monitor won't allow multiple threads to enter at the same time in the synchronized blocks it protects.

Listing 9.2   The consumer thread's definition

```
public class Consumer extends Thread {

  private Logger log = Logger.getLogger(Consumer.class.getName());

  public Consumer(String name) {
    super(name);
  }

  @Override
  public void run() {
    for (int i = 0; i < 1_000_000; i++) {

      synchronized (Main.list) {
        if (Main.list.size() > 0) {
          int x = Main.list.get(0);
```

Iterates one million times over the consumer's synchronized block of code

Synchronizes the block of code using the static list defined in the Main class as a monitor

Tries to consume a value only if the list is not empty

```
                    Main.list.remove(0);          | Consumes the first value in the
                    log.info("Consumer " +        | list and removes that value
Logs the  ┌──▷
removed   │             Thread.currentThread().getName() +
value     │             " removed value " + x);
          │         }
                  }

              }
            }
          }
```

Logs the removed value — *Consumes the first value in the list and removes that value*

Listing 9.3 presents the producer's thread implementation, which is pretty similar to the consumer's. The producer also iterates one million times over a block of code. For each iteration, the producer generates a random value and adds it to a list statically declared in the `Main` class. This list is the same one from which the consumer removes the values. The producer adds new values only if the list size is smaller than 100.

Listing 9.3   The producer thread's definition

```
public class Producer extends Thread {

    private Logger log = Logger.getLogger(Producer.class.getName());

    public Producer(String name) {
        super(name);
    }

    @Override
    public void run() {
        Random r = new Random();
        for (int i = 0; i < 1_000_000; i++) {       ◁
            synchronized (Main.list) {              ◁
                if (Main.list.size() < 100) {
                    int x = r.nextInt();
                    Main.list.add(x);
                    log.info("Producer " +
                        Thread.currentThread().getName() +
                        " added value " + x);
                }
            }
        }
    }
}
```

Iterates one million times over the producer's synchronized block of code

Synchronizes the block of code using the static list defined in the Main class as a monitor

Adds a value only if the list has under 100 elements

Generates a new random value and adds it to the list

Logs the value added to the list

The producer's logic is also synchronized using the list as a monitor. This way, only one of the threads, the producer or the consumer, can change this list at a time. The monitor (the list instance) allows one of the threads to enter its logic and keeps the other thread waiting at the beginning of its block of code until the other thread finishes the execution of the synchronized block (figure 9.2).

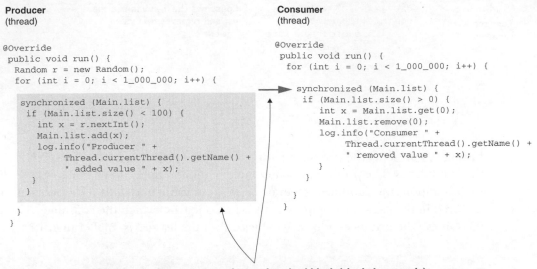

Producer
(thread)

```
@Override
 public void run() {
  Random r = new Random();
  for (int i = 0; i < 1_000_000; i++) {

    synchronized (Main.list) {
      if (Main.list.size() < 100) {
        int x = r.nextInt();
        Main.list.add(x);
        log.info("Producer " +
            Thread.currentThread().getName() +
            " added value " + x);
      }
    }

  }
 }
```

Consumer
(thread)

```
@Override
 public void run() {
    for (int i = 0; i < 1_000_000; i++) {

      synchronized (Main.list) {
        if (Main.list.size() > 0) {
          int x = Main.list.get(0);
          Main.list.remove(0);
          log.info("Consumer " +
              Thread.currentThread().getName() +
              " removed value " + x);
        }
      }

    }
 }
```

**While the producer executes the synchronized block (shaded rectangle),
the consumer cannot access its synchronized block. The consumer waits
for the monitor (list) to allow it to enter its synchronized block.**

**Figure 9.2   Only one thread at a time can be in the synchronized block. Either the producer executes the logic
defined in its `run()` method or the consumer executes its logic.**

Can we find this app behavior and other details about the execution using a profiler?
In a real-world app, the code may be much more complicated, so understanding what
the app does just by reading the code would, in most cases, not be enough.

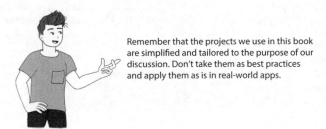

Remember that the projects we use in this book
are simplified and tailored to the purpose of our
discussion. Don't take them as best practices
and apply them as is in real-world apps.

Let's use VisualVM to see what this looks like in the Threads monitoring tab (figure
9.3). Notice that the colors (shading) alternate since most of the code for each thread
is synchronized. In most cases, either the producer is running and the consumer waits
or the consumer is running and the producer waits.

These two threads may rarely execute code simultaneously. Since there are instructions outside the synchronized block, the two threads can run simultaneously to execute the code. An example of such code is the `for` loop, which in both cases is defined
outside the synchronized block.

A thread can be blocked by a synchronized block of code, it can be waiting for
another thread to finish its execution (joining), or it can be controlled by a blocking

You can see the two threads (consumer and producer) executing on the timeline.

The timelines show alternate colors to indicate when the thread is running and when it's waiting.

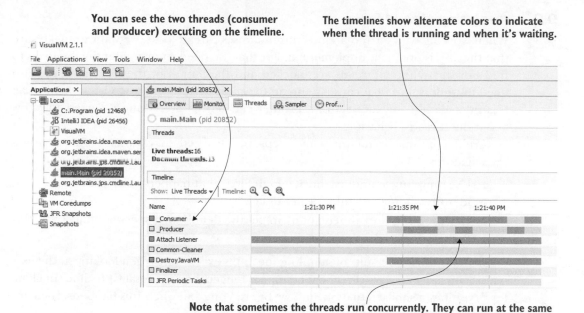

Note that sometimes the threads run concurrently. They can run at the same time when they execute instructions that are outside the synchronized blocks.

Figure 9.3   In most cases, the threads will sequentially lock each other and execute their synchronized blocks of code. The two threads can still concurrently execute the instructions, which are outside the synchronized block.

object. In cases where the thread is blocked and it can't continue its execution, we say the thread is *locked*. In figure 9.4 you can see the same information presented in JProfiler, which works with the approaches we used.

The executing threads are displayed on a timeline with alternate colors to mark when they are running and when they are blocked.

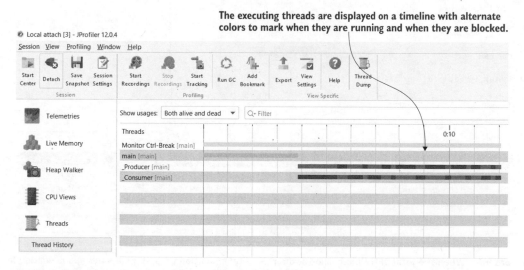

Figure 9.4   You can use other profilers instead of VisualVM. Here, you see the way thread timelines are displayed in JProfiler.

9.2   *Analyzing thread locks*

When working with an app architecture that uses thread locks, we want to make sure that the app is optimally implemented. For that, we need a way to identify the locks to find how many times threads are blocked and the length of the lock time. We also need to understand what causes a thread to wait in given scenarios. Can we collect all this information somehow? Yes, a profiler can tell us everything we need to know about the thread's behavior.

We'll continue using the same steps you learned in chapter 7 for profiling investigations:

1 Use sampling to understand at a high level what happens during execution and identify where to go into further detail.

2 Use profiling (instrumentation) to get the details on a specific subject we want to investigate.

Figure 9.5 shows the results of sampling the app's execution. When looking at the execution times, we observe that the total time is longer than the total CPU time. In chapter 7, you saw a similar situation, and we figured out that when this happens, it means the app waits for something.

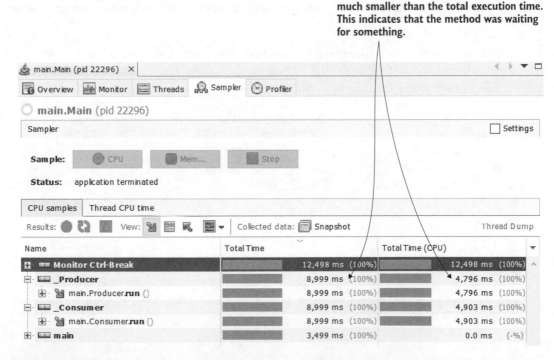

For both threads, the total CPU time is much smaller than the total execution time. This indicates that the method was waiting for something.

Figure 9.5   When the total CPU time is shorter than the total execution time, it means the app is waiting for something. We want to figure out what the app waits for and if this time can be optimized.

In figure 9.6, we can see something interesting: the method waits, but, as shown in the sampling data, it doesn't wait for something else. It simply seems to wait on itself. The row marked as "Self time" tells us how much time it took the method to execute. Notice that the method spent only about 700 ms CPU time as self time but a much larger value of 4903 ms as total execution self time.

In chapter 7, we worked on an example in which the app was waiting for an external service to respond. The app was sending a call and then waiting for the other service to reply. In that case, why the app was waiting made sense, but here the situation looks peculiar. What could cause such behavior?

You may wonder, "How can a method be waiting for itself? Is it too lazy to run?" When we observe such behavior, in which a method is waiting but not for something external, its thread has likely been locked. To get more details about what locks the thread, we need to engage in further analysis by profiling the execution.

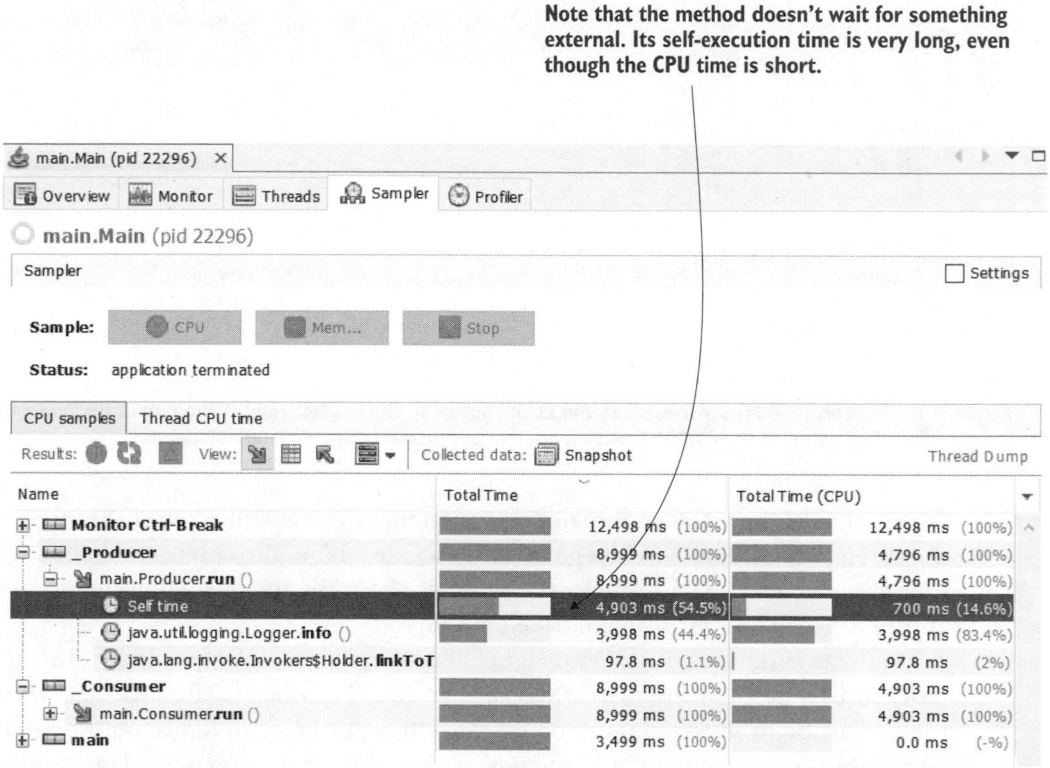

Note that the method doesn't wait for something external. Its self-execution time is very long, even though the CPU time is short.

Figure 9.6 The method doesn't wait for something, but instead it waits for itself. We observe that its self-execution time is longer than the total CPU time, which usually means that the thread is locked. The thread could have been blocked by another thread.

Sampling didn't answer all our questions. We can see the methods are waiting, but we don't know what they are waiting for. We need to continue with profiling (instrumentation) to get more information. In VisualVM, we use the Profiler tab to start lock monitoring. To start profiling for locks, use the Locks button, as presented in figure 9.7, which shows the profiling result. The button appears disabled in the figure because the process was already stopped at the end of the profiling session.

To start profiling for data about locks, use the Locks button. Once the session ends, the button becomes disabled.

We can see that the threads have been blocked a large number of times. Each thread indicates over 3,600 locks during the execution.

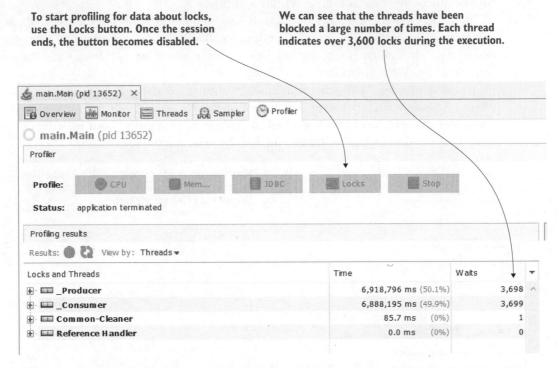

Figure 9.7   To start profiling for locks, use the Locks button in the Profiler tab. At the end of the profiling session, we observe more than 3,600 locks on each of our producer and consumer threads.

For each thread, we can go into detail by selecting the small plus sign (+) to the left of the thread name. Now, you can get details about each monitor object that affected the thread's execution. The profiler shows details about the threads that were blocked by another thread as well as what blocked the thread.

You can find these details in figure 9.8. We see that the producer thread was blocked by a monitor instance of type `ArrayList`. The object reference (4476199c in the figure) helps us to uniquely identify the object instance to figure out whether the same monitor affected multiple threads. It also allows us to precisely identify the relationship between the threads and the monitor.

What we find in figure 9.8 can be read this way:

- The thread named `_Producer` was blocked by a monitor instance with reference 4476199c—an instance of type `ArrayList`.

- The _Consumer thread blocked the _Producer thread 3,698 times by acquiring the monitor 4476199c.
- The producer thread also held (owned) the monitor with reference 4476199c for 3,699 times, or the thread _Producer blocked the thread _Consumer 3,699 times.

Here, we find the objects (monitors) that
caused the thread to be blocked as well as
the monitors that the thread acquired.

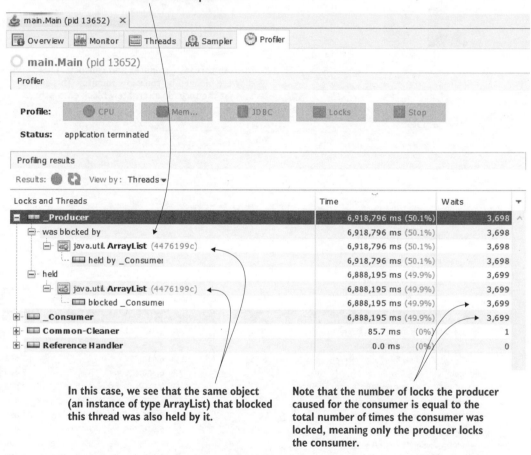

In this case, we see that the same object
(an instance of type ArrayList) that blocked
this thread was also held by it.

Note that the number of locks the producer
caused for the consumer is equal to the
total number of times the consumer was
locked, meaning only the producer locks
the consumer.

Figure 9.8   The profiling results give us a good understanding of what creates locks and what is affected by them. We see that there's only one monitor the producer thread works with. Also, the producer thread was blocked by the consumer thread 3,698 times using the monitor. Using the same monitor instance, the producer blocked the consumer for a similar number of times: 3,699.

Figure 9.9 extends the perspective to the consumer thread. You find that all data correlates. Throughout the whole execution, only one monitor instance, an instance of type ArrayList, locks one of the threads or another. The consumer thread ends up being locked 3,699 times while the producer thread executed a block synchronized by the `ArrayList` object. The producer thread is blocked 3,698 times while the consumer thread executed a block synchronized with the `ArrayList` monitor.

Remember that you won't necessarily get the same numbers when you execute the app on your computer. In fact, it's very likely you won't, even when you repeat the execution on the same computer. Although you may get different values, overall, you can make similar observations.

Both threads (producer and consumer) held and were blocked by the same monitor. This shows that the threads alternately block each other.

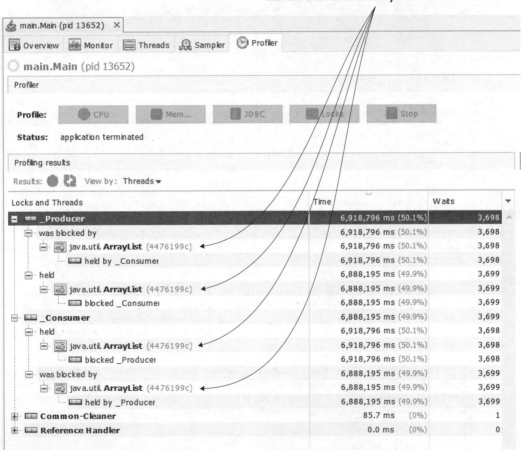

Figure 9.9   Both threads use the same monitor to block each other. While one thread executes the synchronized block with an `ArrayList` instance monitor, the other waits. This way, one thread is locked for 3,698 times and the other for 3,699.

For this demonstration, I used VisualVM because it's free and I'm comfortable with it. But you can use the same approach with other tools as well, such as JProfiler.

After attaching JProfiler to a process (as discussed in chapter 8), make sure you set the JVM exit action to Keep the VA Alive for Profiling, as presented in figure 9.10.

When you attach JProfiler to a process, configure the JVM exit action to keep the VM alive so that you can still see the statistics after the profiled app ends its execution.

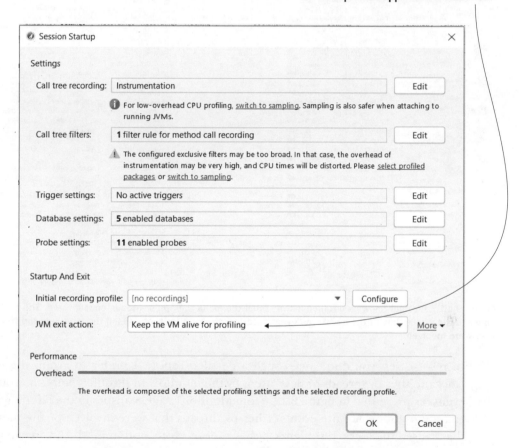

Figure 9.10   When starting the profiling session with JProfiler, remember to set the JVM action to Keep the VM Alive for Profiling so that you can see the profiling results after the app finishes its execution.

JProfiler offers multiple perspectives for visualizing the same details we obtained with VisualVM, but the results are the same. Figure 9.11 shows the Monitor History view report for locks.

To access the lock history in JProfiler, select Monitor History under Monitors & Locks in the left menu.

JProfiler shows a complete history of the lock events: the lock duration, the monitor used, the thread that acquired the lock (owning thread), the thread that was blocked (waiting thread), and the exact time of the event.

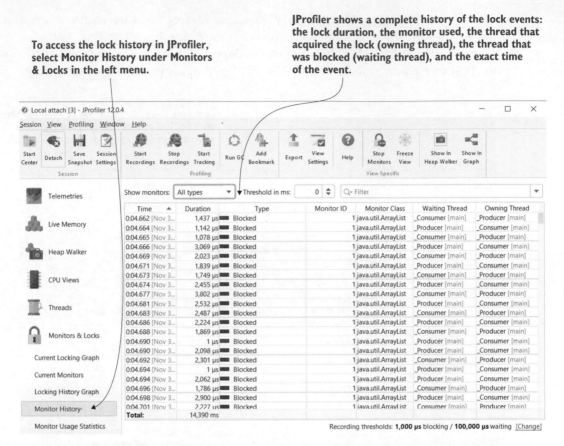

Figure 9.11   JProfiler shows a detailed history of all the locks the app's threads encountered. The tool displays the exact time of the event, the event duration, the monitor that caused the lock, and the threads that were involved.

In most cases, you don't need such a detailed report. I prefer to group the events (locks) either by threads or, less often, by the monitor. In JProfiler, you can group the events as presented in figure 9.12. From Monitor Usage Statistics in the left menu, you can choose to group the events either by threads that were involved or the monitors that caused the locks. JProfiler even has a more exotic option in which you can group the locks by the monitor objects' classes.

In JProfiler, you can use the Monitor Usage Statistics section to get information about locks grouped by affected threads or by the monitor that caused the lock.

To get statistics of all the intercepted lock events grouped by affected threads, select Group by Threads and then click OK.

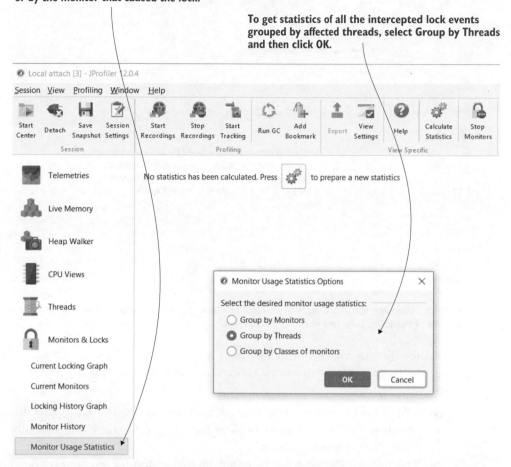

Figure 9.12 You can group the lock events by threads involved or by monitors using the Monitor Usage Statistics section. You can use the aggregated view to understand which threads are more affected and what affects them or which monitor causes the threads to stop more often.

If you group the lock events by involved threads, you get a statistic similar to the one VisualVM provided. Each thread is locked over 3,600 times during the app's execution (figure 9.13).

Is the execution optimal? To answer this question, we need to know the app's purpose. In our case, the app is a simple, demonstrative example, and because it doesn't have a real purpose, it's difficult to fully analyze whether the results indicate the app can be enhanced.

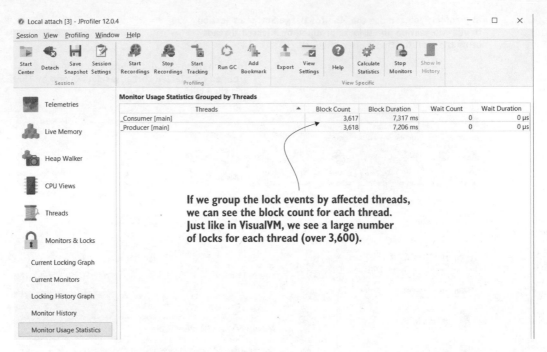

Figure 9.13   Grouping the lock events by threads provides you with an aggregated view showing how many times each of the threads locked during its execution.

But since the app uses two threads that use a common resource (the list), if we consider the fact that they can't work at the same time with the shared resource, then we expect the following:

- The total execution time should be the sum of the CPU execution times (because the threads can't work at the same time, they will mutually exclude each other), approximately.

- The threads should have a similar time allocated for execution and should be locked approximately the same number of times. If one of the threads is preferred, the other can end up in *starvation*: the situation in which a thread is blocked in an "unfair" way and doesn't get to execute.

If you look again at the thread analysis, you can see that the two threads are fairly treated. They indeed get locked a similar number of times, and they mutually exclude each other but have a similar active (CPU time) execution. This is optimal, and there's not much we can do to enhance it. But remember that it depends on what the app does and our expectations about how should it execute.

Here's an example of a different scenario in which the app would not necessarily be considered optimal. Suppose that you had an app that was actually processing values. Say that the producer needed more time to add each value to the list than the consumer needed to process the value afterward. In a real-world app, something like this can happen: the threads don't need to have equivalent difficult "work" to do.

In such a case, you can enhance the app:

- Minimize the number of locks for the consumer and make it wait to allow the producer to work more.
- Define more producer threads or make the consumer thread read and process the values in batches (multiple at a time).

Everything depends on what the app does, but understanding what you can do to make it better starts with analyzing the execution. Because you never have one approach you can apply to all apps, I always recommend developers use a profiler and analyze the changes in app execution when they implement a multithreaded app.

9.3 Analyzing waiting threads

In this section, we analyze threads that are waiting to be notified. Waiting threads are different than locked threads. A monitor locks a thread for the execution of a synchronized block of code. In this case, we don't expect the monitor to execute a specific action to "tell" the blocked thread to continue its execution. But a monitor can make the thread wait for an indefinite amount of time and later decide when to allow that thread to continue its execution. Once a monitor makes a thread wait, the thread will return to execution only after being notified by the same monitor. The ability to make a thread wait until being notified gives great flexibility in controlling threads, but it can also cause issues when not used correctly.

To visualize the difference between locked and waiting threads, look at figure 9.14. Imagine the synchronized block is a restricted area managed by a police officer. The threads are cars. The police officer allows just one car to run at a time in the restricted area (the synchronized block). The cars that are blocked we say are *locked*. The police officer can also manage the cars running in the restricted area. The police officer can order a car running inside this area to wait until they are explicitly ordered to continue; we say they are *waiting*.

We'll use the same application we analyzed earlier in this chapter and consider the following scenario: one of the developers working on the app thought about an improvement to our producer-consumer architecture. Now, the consumer thread can't do anything when the list is empty, so it just iterates multiple times over a false condition until the JVM makes it wait to allow a producer thread to run and to add values to the list. The same thing happens when the producer adds 100 values to the list. The producer thread runs over a false condition until the JVM allows a consumer to remove some of the values from the list.

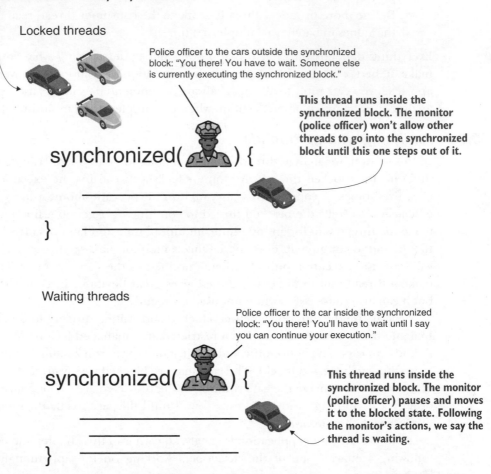

These threads are in a blocked state. They cannot continue execution while another thread is running inside the synchronized block. We say they are locked.

Locked threads

Police officer to the cars outside the synchronized block: "You there! You have to wait. Someone else is currently executing the synchronized block."

This thread runs inside the synchronized block. The monitor (police officer) won't allow other threads to go into the synchronized block until this one steps out of it.

synchronized( ) {

}

Waiting threads

Police officer to the car inside the synchronized block: "You there! You'll have to wait until I say you can continue your execution."

This thread runs inside the synchronized block. The monitor (police officer) pauses and moves it to the blocked state. Following the monitor's actions, we say the thread is waiting.

synchronized( ) {

}

Figure 9.14   Locked threads versus waiting threads. A locked thread is blocked at the entrance of a synchronized block. The monitor won't allow a thread to enter a synchronized block while another thread actively runs inside the block. A waiting thread is a thread that the monitor has explicitly set to the blocked state. The monitor can make any thread inside the synchronized block it manages wait. The waiting thread can continue its execution only after the monitor explicitly tells it that it can proceed with its execution.

Can we do something to make the consumer wait when it has no value to consume and make it run only when we know the list contains at least one value (figure 9.15)? Similarly, can we make the producer wait when there are already too many values in the list and allow it to run only when it makes sense to add other values? Would this approach make our app more efficient?

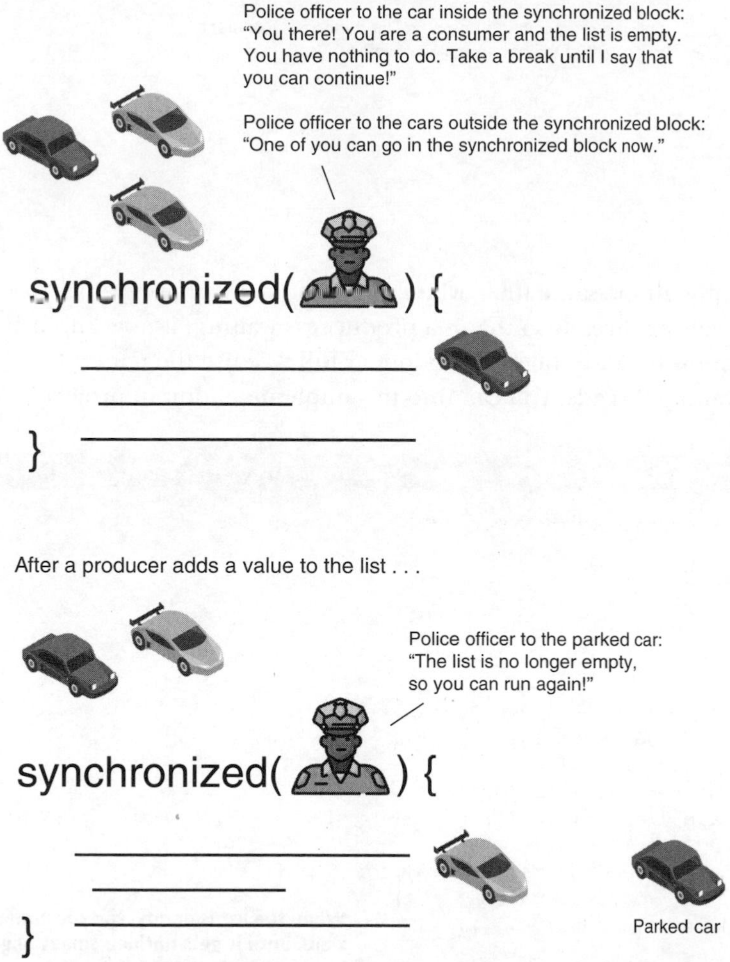

Police officer to the car inside the synchronized block:
"You there! You are a consumer and the list is empty.
You have nothing to do. Take a break until I say that
you can continue!"

Police officer to the cars outside the synchronized block:
"One of you can go in the synchronized block now."

synchronized( ) {

_____

_____

} _____

After a producer adds a value to the list . . .

Police officer to the parked car:
"The list is no longer empty,
so you can run again!"

synchronized( ) {

_____

_____

} _____   Parked car

**Figure 9.15   Some of the cars are consumer threads, and others are producer threads. The
police officer orders a consumer to wait if the list doesn't have values that can be consumed,
allowing producers to work and add values. Once the list contains at least a value that can
be consumed, the officer orders the waiting consumer to continue its execution.**

We'll change the application to implement this new behavior, but we'll also demonstrate that, for our scenario, the app isn't more efficient. On the contrary, the execution is less optimal.

It might look like a good idea to make the threads wait when they can't work with the shared resource (the list). But, upon analysis, you can see that it badly affects the performance instead of helping the app run faster.

Listing 9.4 shows the new implementation of the consumer thread. The consumer thread waits when the list is empty since it has nothing to consume. The monitor makes the consumer thread wait and will notify it to continue its execution only after a producer adds something to the list. We use the wait() method to tell the consumer to wait

I always recommend using a profiler during development to prove that the app executes optimally.

if the list is empty. At the same time, when the consumer removes values from the list, it notifies the waiting threads so that if a producer is waiting, it now knows it can continue its execution because the list is no longer full. We use the `notifyAll()` method to notify the waiting threads. You can find this implementation in project da-ch9-ex2.

Listing 9.4   Making the consumer thread wait when the list is empty

```java
public class Consumer extends Thread {

  // Omitted code

  @Override
  public void run() {
    try {
      for (int i = 0; i < 1_000_000; i++) {
        synchronized (Main.list) {
          if (Main.list.size() > 0) {
            int x = Main.list.get(0);
            Main.list.remove(0);
            log.info("Consumer " +
                Thread.currentThread().getName() +
                " removed value " + x);
            Main.list.notifyAll();
          } else {
            Main.list.wait();
          }
        }
      }
    } catch (InterruptedException e) {
      log.severe(e.getMessage());
    }
  }
}
```

After consuming an element from the list, the consumer notifies the waiting threads a change has been made in the list contents.

When the list is empty, the consumer waits until it gets notified something has been added to the list.

The following code shows the producer thread implementation. Similar to the consumer thread, the producer thread waits if there are too many values in the list. A consumer will eventually notify the producer and allow it to run again when it consumes a value from the list.

Listing 9.5 Making the producer thread wait if the list is already full

```
public class Producer extends Thread {

  // Omitted code

  @Override
  public void run() {
    try {
      Random r = new Random();
      for (int i = 0; i < 1_000_000; i++) {
        synchronized (Main.list) {
          if (Main.list.size() < 100) {
            int x = r.nextInt();
            Main.list.add(x);
            log.info("Producer " +
                    Thread.currentThread().getName() +
                    " added value " + x);
            Main.list.notifyAll();
          } else {
            Main.list.wait();
          }
        }
      }
    } catch (InterruptedException e) {
      log.severe(e.getMessage());
    }
  }
}
```

After adding an element to the list, the producer notifies the waiting threads a change has been made in the list contents.

When the list has 100 elements, the producer waits until it gets notified something has been removed from the list.

As you know, we start our investigations by sampling the execution. We already see something suspicious: the execution seems to take much longer (figure 9.16). If you go back to the previous observations we made in section 9.1, you'll see that the whole execution was only about 9 seconds. Now, the execution takes about 50 seconds—a huge difference.

Sample details (figure 9.17) show us that the wait() method we added caused most of the thread waiting time. The thread is not locked for long since the self execution time is very close to the CPU execution time. Still, our purpose is to make our app more efficient overall, but it seems we only shifted the waiting from one side to the other, and we made the app slower in the process.

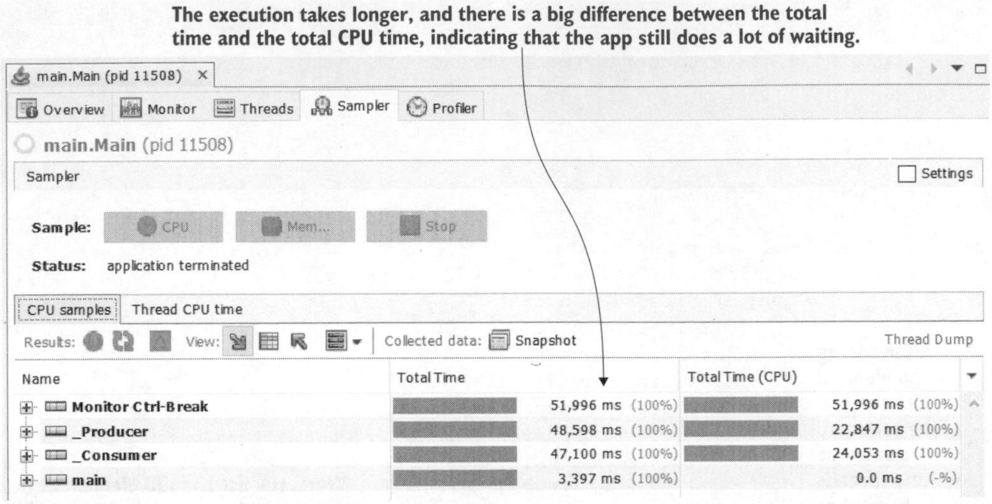

The execution takes longer, and there is a big difference between the total
time and the total CPU time, indicating that the app still does a lot of waiting.

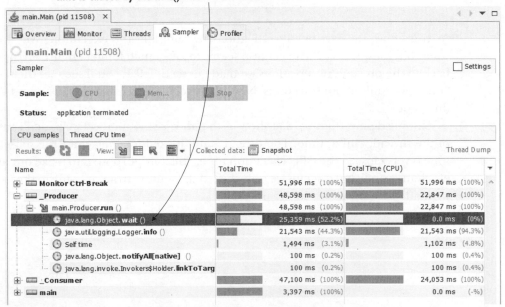

**Figure 9.16   By sampling the execution, we see that the execution time is slower than before we made
threads wait.**

The execution details indicate that most of the waiting
time is caused by the wait() method the monitor invokes.

**Figure 9.17   By analyzing the details, we can see that the self execution time is not that long, but the
thread is blocked and thus waits for a longer time.**

We continue by profiling for more detail (figure 9.18). Indeed, the profiling results show fewer locks, but that doesn't help much, since the execution is much slower.

**Note that the number of locks decreased.
Even so, the total execution time increased.**

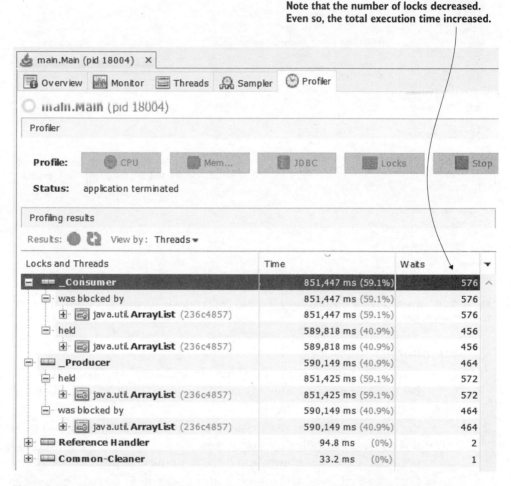

Figure 9.18 The lock pattern is similar to our previous results, but the threads are locked less frequently.

Figure 9.19 shows you the same investigation details obtained using JProfiler. In JProfiler, once we group the lock events by threads, we get both the number of locks and the waiting time. In the previous exercise, the waiting time was zero, but we had many more locks. Now we have fewer locks but a longer waiting time. This tells us that the JVM changes more slowly between threads when using a wait/notify approach than when allowing the threads to get naturally locked and unlocked by the monitor of a synchronized block.

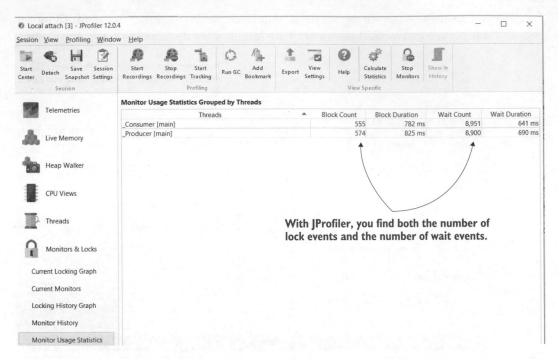

Figure 9.19   We get the same details using JProfiler. Fewer threads are locked, but now they are blocked for a much longer time.

Summary

- A thread can be locked and forced to wait by a synchronized block of code. Locks appear when threads are synchronized to avoid changing shared resources at the same time.

- Locks are needed to avoid race conditions, but sometimes apps use faulty thread synchronization approaches, which can lead to undesired results such as performance issues or even app freezes (in the case of deadlocks).

- Locks caused by synchronized code blocks slow down the app's execution because they force threads to wait instead of letting them work. Locks may be needed in certain implementations, but it's better to find ways to minimize the time an app's threads are locked.

- We can use a profiler to identify when locks slow down an app, how many locks the app encounters during execution, and how much they slow down performance.

- When using a profiler, always sample the execution first to figure out if the app's execution is affected by locks. You'll usually identify locks when sampling by observing that a method is waiting on itself.

- If you find by sampling that locks may be affecting the app's execution, you can continue investigating using lock profiling (instrumentation), which will show the threads affected, the number of locks, the monitors involved, and the relationship between locked threads and threads that cause the locks. These details help you decide if the app's execution is optimal or if you can find ways to enhance it.

- Each app has a different purpose, so there's no unique formula for understanding thread locks. In general, we want to minimize the time threads are locked or waiting and make sure threads are not unfairly excluded from execution (starving threads).

Investigating deadlocks with thread dumps

This chapter covers

- Getting thread dumps using a profiler
- Getting thread dumps using the command line
- Reading thread dumps to investigate issues

In this chapter, we'll discuss using thread dumps to analyze thread execution at a given moment in time. Often, we use thread dumps in situations in which the application becomes unresponsive, such as in the case of a deadlock. A deadlock occurs when multiple threads pause their execution and wait for each other to fulfill a given condition. If hypothetical thread A waits for thread B to do something, and thread B waits for thread A, neither can continue their execution. In such a case, the app, or at least a part of it, will freeze. We need to know how to analyze this issue to find its root cause and eventually solve the problem.

Because a deadlock may cause a process to completely freeze, you usually can't use sampling or profiling (instrumentation), like we did in chapter 9. Instead, you can get a statistic of all the threads and their states for a given JVM process. This statistic is called a *thread dump*.

10.1 Getting a thread dump

In this section, we'll analyze ways to obtain a thread dump. We'll use a small application that implements a problem that creates deadlocks on purpose. You can find this app in project da-ch10-ex1. We'll run this app and wait for it to freeze (this should happen in a few seconds), and then we'll discuss multiple ways to get thread dumps. Once we know how to obtain the thread dumps, we discuss how to read them (section 10.2).

Let's look at how the app we'll use is implemented and why its execution causes deadlocks. The app uses two threads to change two shared resources (two list instances). A thread named the "producer" adds values to one list or another during execution. Another thread named the "consumer" removes values from these lists. If you read chapter 9, you may recall we worked on a similar app. But since the app's logic is irrelevant for our example, I've omitted it from the listings and kept only the part that is important to our demonstration—the synchronized blocks.

The example is simplified to allow you to focus on the investigation techniques we discuss. In a real-world app, things usually get more complicated. Also, wrongly used synchronized blocks are not the only way to get into deadlocks. Faulty use of blocking objects such as semaphores, latches, or barriers can also cause such problems. But the steps you'll learn to investigate the issues are the same.

In listings 10.1 and 10.2, notice that the two threads use nested synchronized blocks with two different monitors: listA and listB. The problem is that one of the threads uses monitor listA for the outer synchronized block, while listB is used for the inner. The other thread uses them the other way around. Such a code design leaves room for deadlocks as are shown visually in figure 10.1.

> **Listing 10.1 Using nested synchronized blocks for the consumer thread**

```
public class Consumer extends Thread {

  // Omitted code

  @Override
  public void run() {
    while (true) {
      synchronized (Main.listA) {          ⊲┐ The outer synchronized block
                                              uses the listA monitor.
        synchronized (Main.listB) {        ⊲   The inner synchronized block
          work();                              uses the listB monitor.
        }
      }
    }
  }

  // Omitted code
}
```

In listing 10.1, the consumer thread uses `listA` as the monitor for the outer synchronized block. In listing 10.2, the producer thread uses the same monitor for the inner block, while the `listB` monitor is also swapped between the two threads.

Listing 10.2   Using nested synchronized blocks for the producer thread

```java
public class Producer extends Thread {

  // Omitted code

  @Override
  public void run() {
    Random r = new Random();
    while (true) {
      synchronized (Main.listB) {          ◁── The listB monitor is used by
                                               the outer synchronized block.
        synchronized (Main.listA) {        ◁── The listA monitor is used by
          work(r);                             the inner synchronized block.
        }
      }
    }
  }

  // Omitted code
}
```

Figure 10.1 shows how the two threads can run into a deadlock.

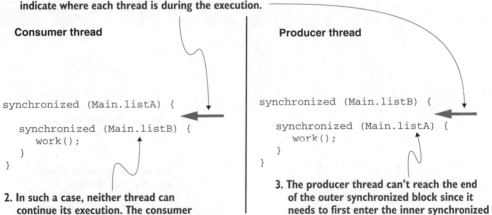

1. Suppose that, while running, two threads enter the outer synchronized block but don't go into the inner synchronized block. The arrows indicate where each thread is during the execution.

Consumer thread

```java
synchronized (Main.listA) {

  synchronized (Main.listB) {
    work();
  }
}
```

Producer thread

```java
synchronized (Main.listB) {

  synchronized (Main.listA) {
    work();
  }
}
```

2. In such a case, neither thread can continue its execution. The consumer cannot continue into the inner synchronized block since monitor "listB" is acquired by the producer thread. Monitor "listB" should be released first, meaning that the producer thread should reach the end of the block.

3. The producer thread can't reach the end of the outer synchronized block since it needs to first enter the inner synchronized block, but it cannot because monitor "listA" is acquired by the consumer.

Figure 10.1   If both threads enter the outer synchronized block, but not the inner one, they remain stuck and wait for each other. We say that they went into a deadlock.

10.1.1 Getting a thread dump using a profiler

What do we do when we have a frozen app and we want to identify the problem's root cause? Using a profiler to analyze the locks most likely won't work in a scenario in which the app, or part of it, is frozen. Instead of analyzing the locks during execution, as we did in chapter 9, we'll take a snapshot just of the app's thread states. We'll read this snapshot (i.e., thread dump) and find out which threads are affecting each other and causing the app to freeze.

You can obtain a thread dump either by using a profiler tool (e.g., VisualVM, JProfiler) or by directly calling a tool provided by the JDK using the command line. In this section, we'll discuss how to obtain a thread dump using a profiler, and in section 10.1.2, we'll learn how to get the same information using the command line.

We'll start our application (project da-ch10-ex1) and wait a few seconds for it to enter a deadlock. You'll know the app gets into a deadlock when it no longer writes messages in the console (it gets stuck).

Getting the thread dump using a profiler is a simple approach. It's no more than the click of a button. Let's use VisualVM to get a thread dump. Figure 10.2 shows the

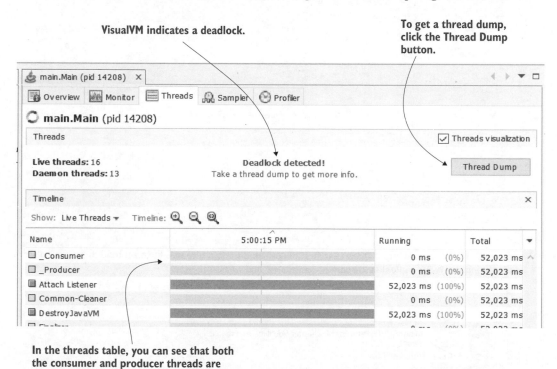

Figure 10.2 When some of the app's threads get into a deadlock, VisualVM indicates the situation with a message in the Threads tab. Notice that both the _Consumer and _Producer threads are locked on the graphic timeline. To get a thread dump, you simply select the Thread Dump button in the window's upper-right corner.

Visual VM interface. You can see that VisualVM is smart and figured out that some of the threads of our process ran into a deadlock. This is indicated in the Threads tab.

After the thread dump is collected, the interface looks like figure 10.3. The thread dump is represented as plain text that describes the app threads and provides details about them (e.g., their state in the life cycle, who blocks them, etc.).

The thread dump shows information about each active thread. You find the producer and consumer threads in the generated thread dump.

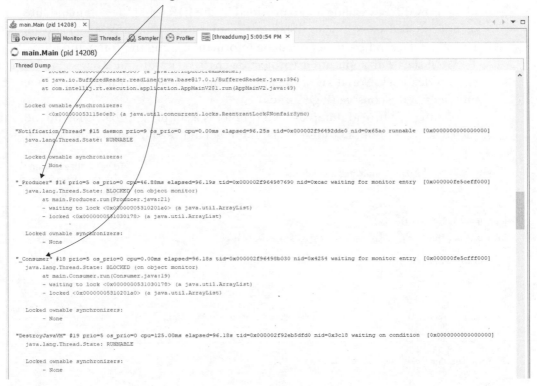

Figure 10.3   A thread dump in plain text that describes an app's threads. In the thread dump we collected, we can find the two deadlocked threads `_Consumer` and `_Producer`.

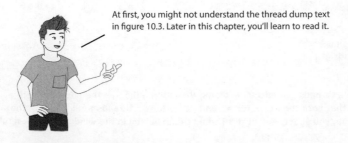

At first, you might not understand the thread dump text in figure 10.3. Later in this chapter, you'll learn to read it.

10.1.2 *Generating a thread dump from the command line*

A thread dump can also be obtained using the command line. This approach is particularly useful when you need to get a thread dump from a remote environment. Most of the time, you won't be able to remote profile an app installed in an environment (and remember, remote profiling and remote debugging aren't recommended in a production environment, as discussed in chapter 4). Since in most cases you can only access a remote environment using the command line, you need to know how to get a thread dump this way too.

Fortunately, getting a thread dump using the command line is quite easy (figure 10.4):

1 Find the process ID for which you want a thread dump.
2 Get the thread dump as text data (raw data) and save it in a file.
3 Load the saved thread dump to make it easier to read in a profiler tool.

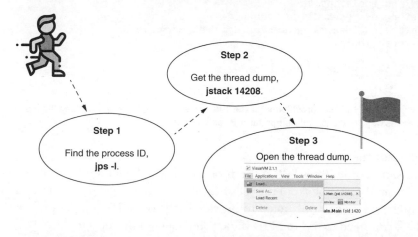

**Figure 10.4   Follow three simple steps to get a thread dump using the command line.
First, find the process ID for which you want the thread dump. Second, use a JDK tool to
get the thread dump. Finally, open the thread dump in a profiler tool to read it.**

STEP 1: FIND THE PROCESS ID FOR THE PROCESS UNDER INVESTIGATION

Thus far, we have identified the process we want to profile using its name (represented as the main class's name). But when getting a thread dump using the command line, you need to identify the process using its ID. How do you get a process ID (PID) for a running Java app? The simplest way is using the `jps` tool provided with the JDK. The next snippet shows the command you need to run. We use the `-l` (lowercase "L") option to get the main class names associated with the PIDs. This way, we can identify the processes the same way we did in chapters 6 to 9 where we learned to profile an app's execution:

```
jps -l
```

Figure 10.5 shows the result of running the command. The numeric values in the output's first column are the PIDs. The second column associates the main class name to each PID. This way, we get the PID that we'll use in step 2 to obtain the thread dump.

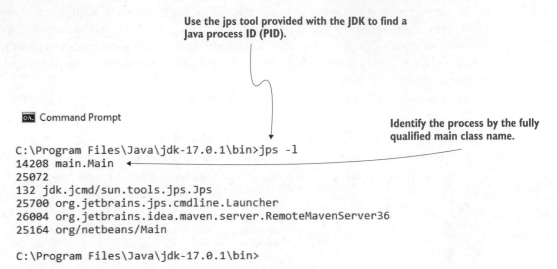

Figure 10.5   By using the `jps` tool provided with the JDK, we get the PIDs of the running Java processes. These PIDs are necessary to get thread dumps for a given process.

STEP 2: COLLECT THE THREAD DUMP

Once you can identify (by its PID) the process for which you want to collect a thread dump, you can use another tool the JDK provides, `jstack`, to generate a thread dump. When using `jstack`, you only need to provide the process ID as a parameter (instead of <<PID>>, you need to use the PID value you collected in step 1):

```
jstack <<PID>>
```

An example of such a command execution is

```
jstack 14208
```

Figure 10.6 shows you the result of running the `jstack` command followed by a PID. The thread dump is provided as plain text that you can save in a file to move or load into a tool for investigation.

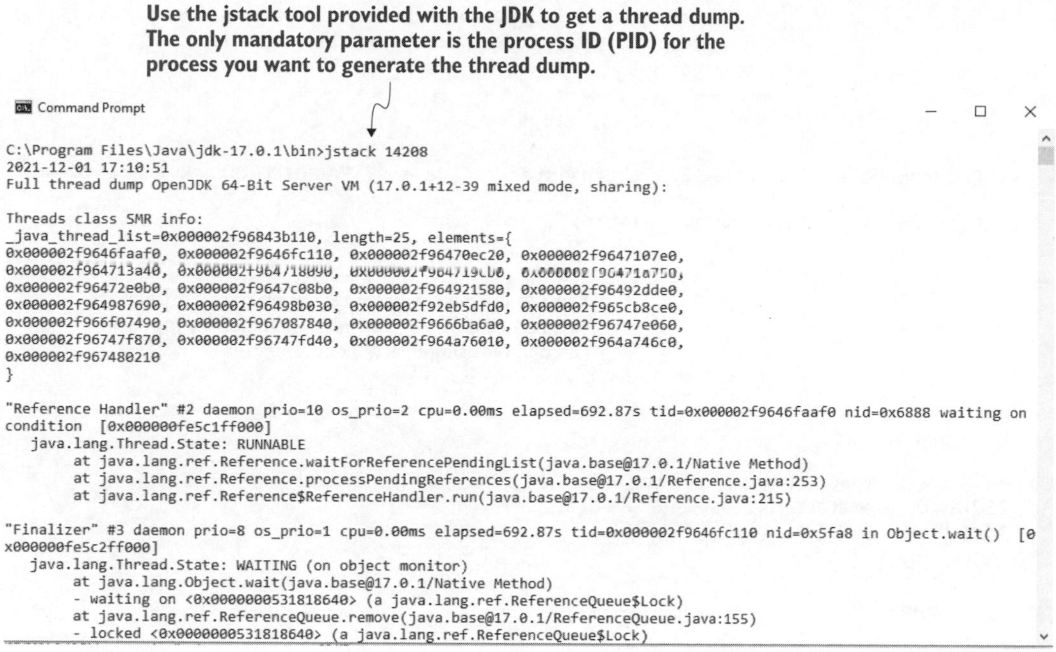

Use the jstack tool provided with the JDK to get a thread dump.
The only mandatory parameter is the process ID (PID) for the
process you want to generate the thread dump.

```
Command Prompt                                                          —  □  ✕

C:\Program Files\Java\jdk-17.0.1\bin>jstack 14208
2021-12-01 17:10:51
Full thread dump OpenJDK 64-Bit Server VM (17.0.1+12-39 mixed mode, sharing):

Threads class SMR info:
_java_thread_list=0x000002f96843b110, length=25, elements={
0x000002f9646faaf0, 0x000002f9646fc110, 0x000002f96470ec20, 0x000002f9647107e0,
0x000002f964713a40, 0x000002f964718090, 0x000002f96471acb0, 0x000002f96471a750,
0x000002f96472e0b0, 0x000002f9647c08b0, 0x000002f964921580, 0x000002f96492dde0,
0x000002f964987690, 0x000002f96498b030, 0x000002f92eb5dfd0, 0x000002f965cb8ce0,
0x000002f966f07490, 0x000002f967087840, 0x000002f9666ba6a0, 0x000002f96747e060,
0x000002f96747f870, 0x000002f96747fd40, 0x000002f964a76010, 0x000002f964a746c0,
0x000002f967480210
}

"Reference Handler" #2 daemon prio=10 os_prio=2 cpu=0.00ms elapsed=692.87s tid=0x000002f9646faaf0 nid=0x6888 waiting on
condition  [0x000000fe5c1ff000]
   java.lang.Thread.State: RUNNABLE
      at java.lang.ref.Reference.waitForReferencePendingList(java.base@17.0.1/Native Method)
      at java.lang.ref.Reference.processPendingReferences(java.base@17.0.1/Reference.java:253)
      at java.lang.ref.Reference$ReferenceHandler.run(java.base@17.0.1/Reference.java:215)

"Finalizer" #3 daemon prio=8 os_prio=1 cpu=0.00ms elapsed=692.87s tid=0x000002f9646fc110 nid=0x5fa8 in Object.wait()  [0
x000000fe5c2ff000]
   java.lang.Thread.State: WAITING (on object monitor)
      at java.lang.Object.wait(java.base@17.0.1/Native Method)
      - waiting on <0x0000000531818640> (a java.lang.ref.ReferenceQueue$Lock)
      at java.lang.ref.ReferenceQueue.remove(java.base@17.0.1/ReferenceQueue.java:155)
      - locked <0x0000000531818640> (a java.lang.ref.ReferenceQueue$Lock)
```

Figure 10.6   The `jstack` command followed by a PID will generate a thread dump for the given process. The thread dump is shown as plain text (also called a raw thread dump). You can collect the text in a file to import it and investigate it later.

STEP 3: IMPORT THE COLLECTED THREAD DUMP INTO A PROFILER TO MAKE IT EASIER TO READ

Usually, you save the output of the jstack command, the thread dump, into a file. Storing the thread dump in a file allows you to move it, store it, or import it into tools that help you investigate its details.

Figure 10.7 shows you how you can put the output of the jstack command in a file in the command line. Once you have the file, you can load it in VisualVM using the File > Load menu.

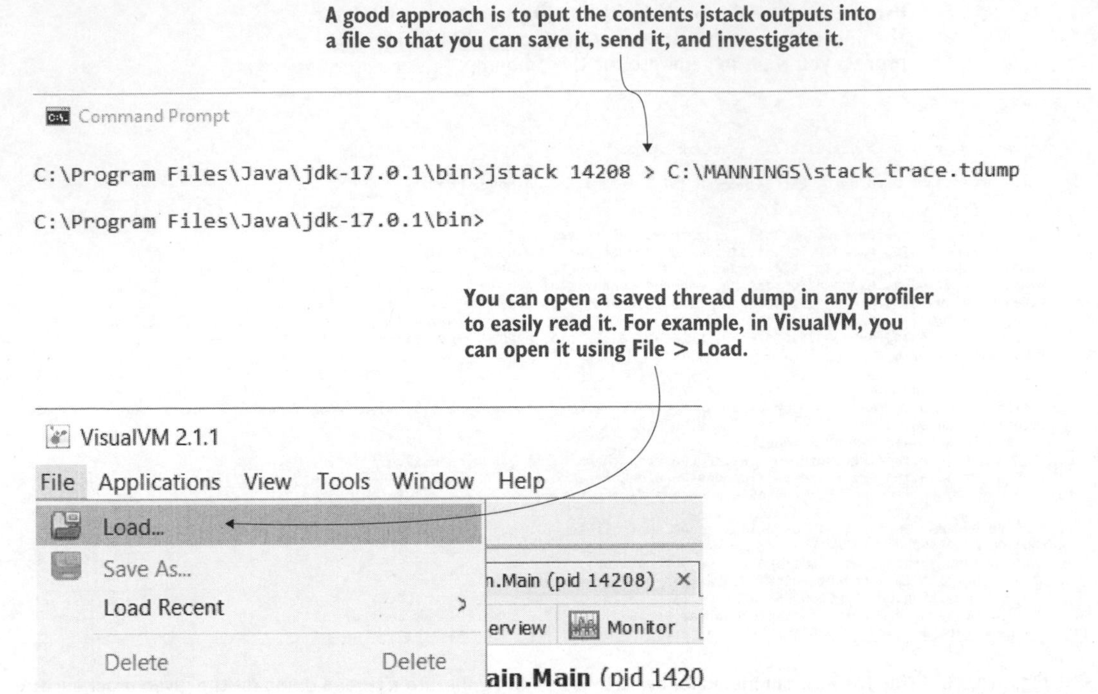

**A good approach is to put the contents jstack outputs into
a file so that you can save it, send it, and investigate it.**

Command Prompt

```
C:\Program Files\Java\jdk-17.0.1\bin>jstack 14208 > C:\MANNINGS\stack_trace.tdump

C:\Program Files\Java\jdk-17.0.1\bin>
```

**You can open a saved thread dump in any profiler
to easily read it. For example, in VisualVM, you
can open it using File > Load.**

VisualVM 2.1.1

File   Applications   View   Tools   Window   Help

Load...

Save As...   n.Main (pid 14208)   ✕

Load Recent   >   erview   Monitor

Delete   Delete   ain.Main (pid 1420

Figure 10.7   Once you save the thread dump into a file, you can open it in various tools to investigate it. For example, to open it in VisualVM, you select File > Load.

10.2   Reading thread dumps

In this section, we'll discuss reading thread dumps. Once you collect a thread dump, you need to know how to read it and how to efficiently use it to identify issues. We'll start by discussing how to read plain-text thread dumps in section 10.2.1—meaning you'll learn to read raw data as provided by jstack (see section 10.1.2). Then, in section 10.2.2, we'll use a tool named fastThread (https://fastthread.io/), which provides a simpler way to visualize the data in a thread dump.

Both approaches (reading plain-text thread dumps and using advanced visualization) are useful. Of course, we always prefer advanced visualization, but if you can't obtain it, you need to know how to rely on raw data.

10.2.1   Reading plain-text thread dumps

When you collect a thread dump, you get a description of the threads in plain-text format (i.e., raw data). Although we have tools you can use to easily visualize the data (as we'll discuss in section 10.2.2), I've always considered it important for a developer to understand the raw representation as well. You may get into a situation in which you can't remove the raw thread dump from the environment in which you generated it. Say you connect to a container remotely and can only use the command line to dig into the logs and investigate what happens with the running app. You suspect a thread-related problem, so you want to generate a thread dump. If you can read the thread dump as text, you need nothing more than the console itself.

Let's look at listing 10.3, which shows one of the threads in the thread dump. It is nothing more than similarly displayed details for each thread active in the app when the dump was taken. Here are the details you get for a thread:

- Thread name
- Thread ID
- Native thread ID
- Priority of the thread at the operating system level
- Total and CPU time the thread consumed
- State description
- State name
- Stack trace
- Who's blocking the thread
- What locks the thread acquires

The first thing displayed is the *thread name*—in our case, `"_Producer"`. The thread name is essential since it's one of the ways you identify the thread in the thread dump later if you need it. The JVM also associates the thread with a *thread ID* (in listing 10.3, `tid=0x000002f964987690`). Since the developer gives the name, there's a small chance some threads will get the same name. If this unlucky situation happens, you can still identify a thread in the dump by its ID (which is always unique).

In a JVM app, a thread is a wrapper over a system thread, which means you can always identify the operating system (OS) thread running behind the scenes. If you ever need to do that, look for the *native thread ID* (in listing 10.3, `nid=0xcac`).

Once you have identified a thread, you identify the details you are interested in. The first three pieces of information you get in a thread dump are the *thread's priority*, the *CPU execution time*, and the *total execution time*. Every OS associates a priority to each of its running threads. I don't often use this value in a thread dump. But if you see that a thread isn't as active as you think it should be, and you see that the OS designates it as a lower priority, then this may be the cause. In this situation, the total execution time would also be much higher than the CPU execution time. Remember from chapter 7 that the total execution time is how long the thread was alive, while the CPU execution time is how well it worked.

State description is a valuable detail. It tells you in plain English what happens to the thread. In our case, the thread is "waiting for monitor entry," meaning it is blocked at the entrance to a synchronized block. The thread could have been "timed waiting on a monitor," which would mean it's sleeping for a defined time or is running. A *state name* (Running, Waiting, Blocked, etc.) is associated with the state description. Appendix D offers a good refresher on thread life cycle and thread states in case you need it.

The thread dump provides a *stack trace* for every thread, which shows exactly what part of the code the thread was executing when the dump was taken. The stack trace is valuable since it shows you exactly what the thread was working on. You can use the stack trace to find a specific piece of code you want to further debug, or, in the case of a slow thread, to determine exactly what delays or blocks that thread.

Finally, for threads that acquire locks or are locked, we can find *which locks they acquire* and *which locks are they waiting for.* You'll use these details every time you investigate a deadlock. They can also give you optimization hints. For example, if you see that a thread acquires many locks, you may wonder why and how you can change its behavior so that it doesn't block so many other executions.

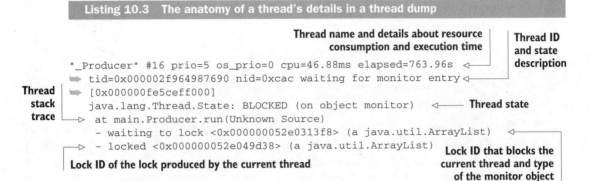

Listing 10.3   The anatomy of a thread's details in a thread dump

An important thing to remember about thread dumps is that they give you almost as many details as a normal lock profiling (discussed in chapter 9). Lock profiling offers an advantage over a thread dump: it shows the dynamics of the execution. Just like the difference between a picture and a movie, the thread dump is just a snapshot at a given time (here, during the execution), while profiling shows you how parameters change during the execution. But in many situations, a picture is enough and much easier to obtain.

Sometimes it is enough to use a thread dump instead of a profiler.

If the only thing you need to know is what code executes at a given time, a thread dump is sufficient. You have learned to use sampling for this purpose, but it's good to know a thread dump can do this too. Say you don't have access to remotely profile an app, but you need to find out what code executes behind the scenes. You can get a thread dump.

Let's now focus on how can you find the relationship between threads with a thread dump. How can we analyze the way in which threads interact with one another? We are particularly interested in threads locking each other. In listing 10.4, I added the details from the thread dump for the two threads that we know are in a deadlock. But the question is, "How would we find they are in a deadlock if we didn't know this detail up front?"

If you suspect a deadlock, you should focus your investigation on the locks the threads cause (figure 10.8):

1 Filter out all threads that are not blocked so that you can focus on the threads that can cause the deadlock.
2 Start with the first candidate thread (a thread you didn't filter in step 1), and search the lock ID that causes it to be blocked.
3 Find the thread causing that lock, and check what blocks that thread. If at some point you return to the thread you started with, all the threads you parsed are in a deadlock.

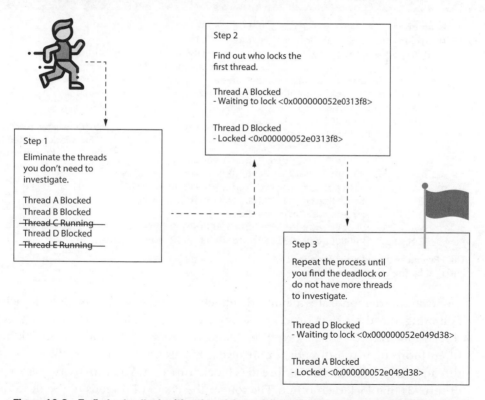

Figure 10.8   To find a deadlock with a thread dump, follow these three easy steps. First, remove all threads that are not blocked. Then, start with one of the blocked threads and find what is blocking it using the lock ID. Continue this process for each thread. If you return to a thread you already investigated, it means you found a deadlock.

STEP 1: FILTER OUT THREADS THAT ARE NOT LOCKED

First, filter out all the threads that are not locked so that you can focus only on the threads that are potential candidates for the situation you are investigating—the deadlock. A thread dump can describe dozens of threads. You want to eliminate the noise and focus only on the threads that are blocked.

STEP 2: TAKE THE FIRST CANDIDATE THREAD AND FIND WHAT BLOCKS IT

After eliminating the unnecessary thread details, start with the first candidate thread and search by the lock ID that causes a thread to wait. The lock ID is the one between angle brackets (in listing 10.4, "_Producer" waits for a lock with ID 0x000000052e0313f8).

STEP 3: FIND WHAT BLOCKS THE NEXT THREAD

Repeat the process. If at some point you get to a thread that was already investigated, you've found a deadlock; please see the following listing.

Listing 10.4 Finding threads that lock each other

```
"_Producer" #16 prio=5 os_prio=0 cpu=46.88ms
  elapsed=763.96s tid=0x000002f964987690
  nid=0xcac waiting for monitor entry  [0x000000fe5ceff000]
   java.lang.Thread.State: BLOCKED (on object monitor)
    at main.Producer.run(Unknown Source)
     - waiting to lock <0x000000052e0313f8>
  (a java.util.ArrayList)
     - locked <0x000000052e049d38>
  (a java.util.ArrayList)

"_Consumer" #18 prio=5 os_prio=0 cpu=0.00ms
  elapsed=763.96s tid=0x000002f96498b030
  nid=0x4254 waiting for monitor entry  [0x000000fe5cfff000]
   java.lang.Thread.State: BLOCKED (on object monitor)
    at main.Consumer.run(Unknown Source)
     - waiting to lock <0x000000052e049d38> (a java.util.ArrayList)
     - locked <0x000000052e0313f8> (a java.util.ArrayList)
```

> The _Consumer thread waits for a lock initiated by the _Producer thread.

> The _Producer thread waits for a lock initiated by the _Consumer thread.

Our example demonstrates a simple deadlock that assumes two threads lock each other. Following the three-step process discussed earlier, you'll see that the "_Producer" thread blocks the "_Consumer" thread, and vice versa. A complex deadlock happens when more than two threads are involved. For example, thread A blocks thread B, thread B blocks thread C, and thread C blocks thread A. You can discover a long chain of threads that lock each other. The longer the chain of threads in the deadlock, the more difficult the deadlock is to find, understand, and solve. Figure 10.9 shows the difference between a complex deadlock and a simple one.

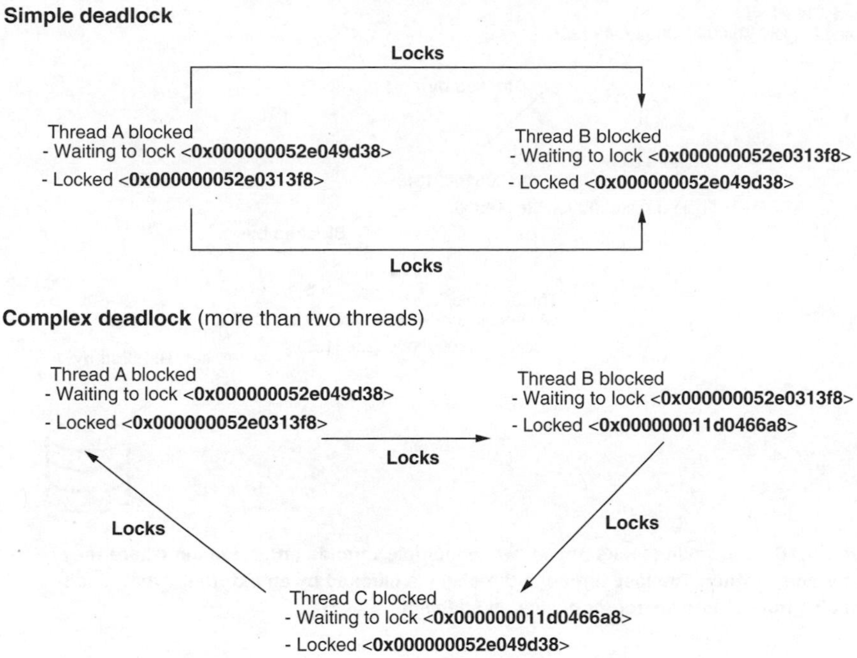

Simple deadlock

Locks

Thread A blocked
- Waiting to lock <**0x000000052e049d38**>
- Locked <**0x000000052e0313f8**>

Thread B blocked
- Waiting to lock <**0x000000052e0313f8**>
- Locked <**0x000000052e049d38**>

Locks

Complex deadlock (more than two threads)

Thread A blocked
- Waiting to lock <**0x000000052e049d38**>
- Locked <**0x000000052e0313f8**>

Thread B blocked
- Waiting to lock <**0x000000052e0313f8**>
- Locked <**0x000000011d0466a8**>

Locks

Locks

Locks

Thread C blocked
- Waiting to lock <**0x000000011d0466a8**>
- Locked <**0x000000052e049d38**>

**Figure 10.9   When only two threads block each other, it's called a simple deadlock, but
a deadlock can be caused by multiple threads that block each other. More threads means
more complexity. Thus, when more than two threads are involved, it's called a complex
deadlock.**

Sometimes a complex deadlock can be confused with cascading blocked threads (figure 10.10). *Cascading blocked threads* (also known as *cascading locks*) are a different issue
you can spot using a thread dump. To find cascading threads, follow the same steps as
when investigating a deadlock. But instead of finding that one of the threads is
blocked by another in the chain (as in the case of a deadlock), in a cascade of locks,
you'll see that one of the threads is waiting for an external event, causing all others to
also wait.

Cascading blocked threads usually signal a bad design in the multithreaded architecture. When we design an app with multiple threads, we implement threading to
allow the app to process things concurrently. Having threads waiting for one another
defeats the purpose of a multithreaded architecture. Although sometimes you need to
make threads wait for one another, you shouldn't expect long chains of threads with
cascading locks.

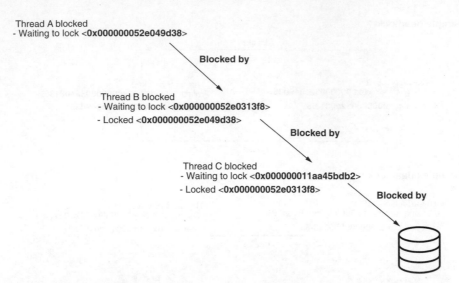

Thread A blocked
- Waiting to lock <**0x000000052e049d38**>

Blocked by

Thread B blocked
- Waiting to lock <**0x000000052e0313f8**>
- Locked <**0x000000052e049d38**>

Blocked by

Thread C blocked
- Waiting to lock <**0x000000011aa45bdb2**>
- Locked <**0x000000052e0313f8**>

Blocked by

Figure 10.10   Cascading locks appear when multiple threads enter a chain where they wait for one another. The last thread in the chain is blocked by an external event, such as reading from a data source or calling an endpoint.

10.2.2 *Using tools to better grasp thread dumps*

Reading the plain-text raw representation of a thread dump is useful but sometimes can be quite difficult. Most prefer a simpler way to visualize the data in a thread dump, if possible. Today we can use tools to help us to more easily understand a thread dump. Whenever possible, I remove the thread dump from the environment where I collect it. I usually prefer using fastThread (fastthread.io) to investigate the dump instead of dealing with the raw data.

fastThread is a web tool designed to help you read thread dumps. It offers both free and paid plans, but the free plan has always been enough for my needs. Simply upload a file containing the thread dump raw data and wait for the tool to extract the details you need and put them in a shape easier to grasp. Figure 10.11 shows you the starting page, where you choose the file containing the thread dump raw data from your system and upload it for analysis.

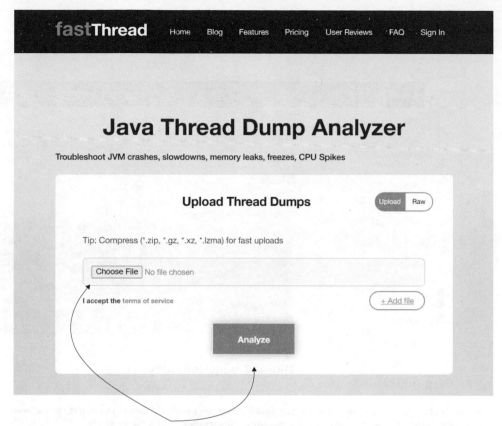

To analyze a thread dump, upload the file with
the raw data and then click Analyze.

Figure 10.11   To analyze a thread dump, upload a file containing the thread dump raw data to fastThread.io and wait for the tool to present the details in a simple-to-understand shape.

The fastThread analysis shows various details from the thread dump, including deadlock detection, dependency graphs, stack traces, resource consumption, and even a flame graph (figure 10.12).

**After analyzing the thread dump, the tool presents multiple
visualization widgets, such as identifying deadlocks, CPU consumption
per thread, and even a flame graph representation of the process.**

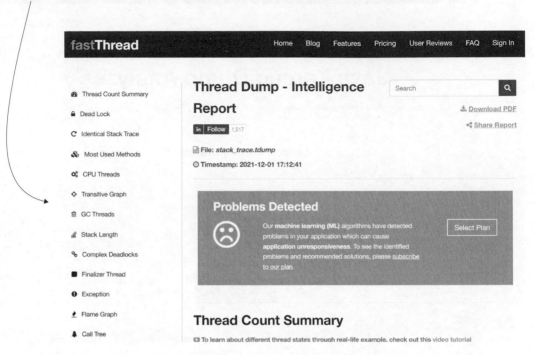

**Figure 10.12   fastThread provides various details in an easy-to-read format. These details include
deadlock detection, dependency graphs, resource consumption, and a flame graph.**

Figure 10.13 shows how fastThread identified the deadlock in our thread dump.

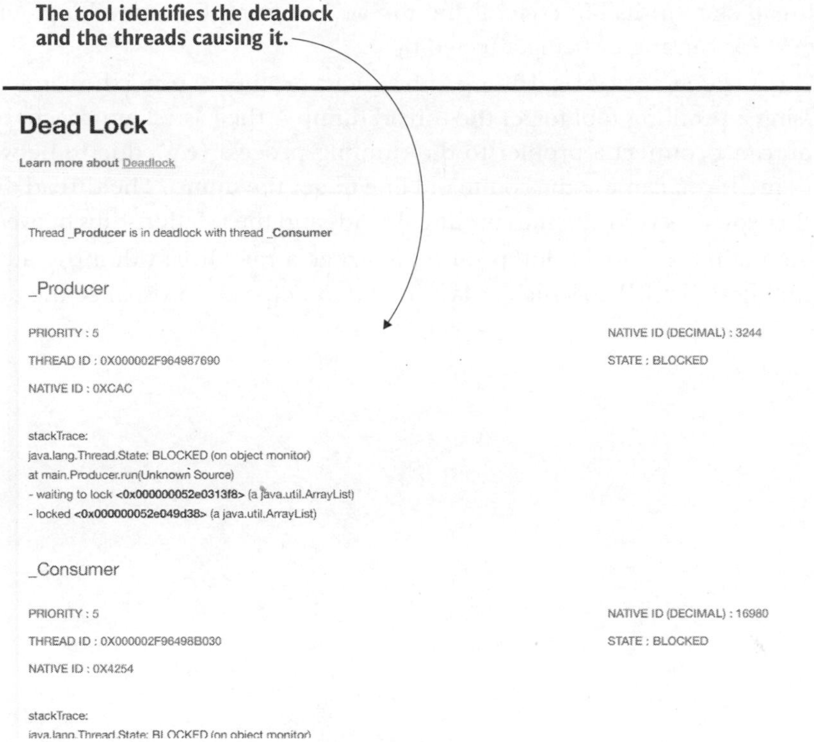

The tool identifies the deadlock
and the threads causing it.

Dead Lock

Learn more about Deadlock

Thread _**Producer** is in deadlock with thread _**Consumer**

_Producer

PRIORITY : 5

NATIVE ID (DECIMAL) : 3244

THREAD ID : 0X000002F964987690

STATE : BLOCKED

NATIVE ID : 0XCAC

stackTrace:
java.lang.Thread.State: BLOCKED (on object monitor)
at main.Producer.run(Unknown Source)
- waiting to lock <0x000000052e0313f8> (a java.util.ArrayList)
- locked <0x000000052e049d38> (a java.util.ArrayList)

_Consumer

PRIORITY : 5

NATIVE ID (DECIMAL) : 16980

THREAD ID : 0X000002F96498B030

STATE : BLOCKED

NATIVE ID : 0X4254

stackTrace:
java.lang.Thread.State: BLOCKED (on object monitor)

Figure 10.13 After analyzing the thread dump raw data, fastThread identifies and provides details about the deadlock caused by the `_Consumer` and `_Producer` threads.

Summary

- When two or more threads get blocked while waiting for each other, they are in a deadlock. When an app gets into a deadlock, it usually freezes and can't continue its execution.
- You can identify the root cause of a deadlock using thread dumps, which show the status of all threads of an app at the time the thread dump was generated. This information allows you to find which thread is waiting for another.
- A thread dump also shows details such as resource consumption and stack traces for each thread. If these details are sufficient, you can use a thread dump instead of instrumentation for your investigation. Imagine the difference between a thread dump and profiling as the difference between a picture and a movie. With a thread dump, you only have a still image, so you miss the execution dynamics, but you can still get a lot of relevant and helpful details.
- The thread dump provides information about the threads that were executing in the app when the dump was taken. The thread dump shows essential details about the threads in a plain-text format, including resource consumption,

thread state in its life cycle, if the thread is waiting for something, and which locks it's causing or being affected by.

- You can generate a thread dump with either a profiler or using the command line. Using a profiling tool to get the thread dump is the easiest approach, but when you can't connect a profiler to the running process (e.g., due to network constraints), you can use the command line to get the dump. The thread dump will allow you to investigate the running threads and the relationships between them.

- The plain-text thread dump (also known as a raw thread dump) can be challenging to read. Tools such as fastThread.io help you to visualize the details.

Finding memory-related issues in an app's execution

This chapter covers

- Sampling an execution to find memory allocation issues
- Profiling a part of the code to identify the root causes of memory allocation problems
- Obtaining and reading heap dumps

Every app processes data, and to do this, the app needs to store that data somewhere while working with it. The app allocates part of the system's memory to work with the data, but the memory isn't an infinite resource. All the apps running on a system share a finite amount of memory space that the system provides. If an app doesn't wisely manage its allocated memory, it can run out of it, making it impossible to continue its work. Even if the app doesn't run out of memory, using too much can make the app slower, so faulty memory allocation can cause performance issues.

An app can run slower if it doesn't optimize its allocation of data in the memory. If the app requires more memory than the system provides, the app will stop working and throw an error. Thus, side effects of poor memory management are slowness in execution and even total app crashes. It's essential we write app capabilities that make the best use of their allocated memory.

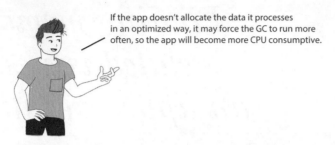

If the app doesn't allocate the data it processes in an optimized way, it may force the GC to run more often, so the app will become more CPU consumptive.

An app should be as efficient as possible in managing its resources. When we discuss the resources of an app, we mainly think about CPU (processing power) and memory. In chapters 7 to 10, we discussed how to investigate issues with CPU consumption. In this chapter, we'll focus on identifying problems with how an app allocates data in memory.

We'll start the chapter by discussing execution sampling and profiling for memory usage statistics in section 11.1. You'll learn how to identify if an app has issues with memory usage and how to find which part of the application causes them.

Then, in section 11.2, we'll discuss how to get a complete dump (i.e., heap dump) of the allocated memory to analyze its contents. In certain cases, when the app crashes entirely because of faulty memory management, you cannot profile the execution. But getting and analyzing the contents of the app's allocated memory at the moment the problem appears can help you to identify the problem's root cause.

You need to remember a few basic concepts about the way in which a Java app allocates and uses memory before continuing with this chapter. If you need a refresher, appendix E provides all the information you need to properly understand the ideas in this chapter.

11.1 Sampling and profiling for memory issues

In this section, we use a small application that simulates a faulty implemented capability that uses too much of the allocated memory. We use this app to discuss investigation techniques you can use to identify issues with memory allocation or places in code that can be optimized to use the system's memory more efficiently.

Suppose you have a real application, and you notice that some feature runs slowly. You use the techniques we discussed in chapter 6 to analyze resource consumption and find that although the app doesn't "work" very often (consume CPU resources), it uses a large amount of memory. When an app uses too much memory, the JVM can trigger the garbage collector (GC), which will further consume CPU resources also.

Remember that the GC is the mechanism that automatically deallocates unneeded data from memory (see appendix E for a refresher).

Look at figure 11.1. When discussing how to analyze resource consumption in chapter 6, we used the Monitor tab in VisualVM to observe what resources the app consumes. You can use the memory widget in this tab to find when the app uses an extensive amount of memory.

Under the Monitor tab, you find the widget that allows you to monitor the app's memory usage.

Note a large increase in the used memory when calling the app's endpoint. The JVM also adjusted the heap max size as a result of the increased memory usage.

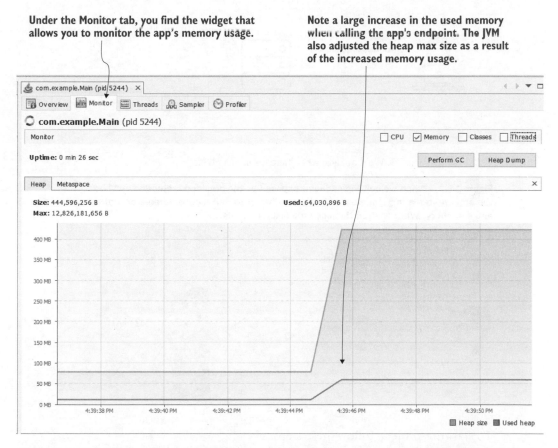

Figure 11.1   **The memory widget in the Monitor tab in VisualVM helps you to identify if the app spends more memory than usual at any given time. Often, widgets in the Monitor tab, such as CPU and memory consumption, give us clues on how to continue our investigation. When we see that the app consumes an abnormal amount of memory, we may decide to continue with memory profiling the execution.**

The application we use in this chapter is in project da-ch11-ex1. This small web application exposes an endpoint. When calling this endpoint, we give a number, and the endpoint creates that many object instances. We basically make a request to create one million objects (a large enough number for our experiment) and then look at what a profiler tells us about this request execution. This endpoint execution simulates what happens in a real-world situation when a given app capability spends a lot of the app's memory resources (figure 11.2).

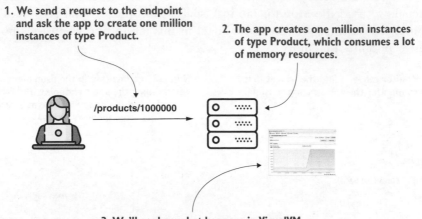

1. We send a request to the endpoint and ask the app to create one million instances of type Product.

2. The app creates one million instances of type Product, which consumes a lot of memory resources.

/products/1000000

3. We'll analyze what happens in VisualVM.

Figure 11.2   When we call the endpoint exposed by the provided project da-ch11-ex1, the app creates a large number of instances that consume a considerable part of the app's memory. We'll analyze this scenario using a profiler.

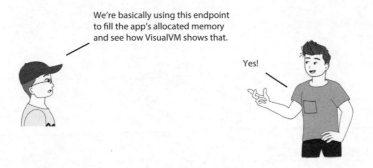

We're basically using this endpoint to fill the app's allocated memory and see how VisualVM shows that.

Yes!

To start the project, follow these steps:

1 Start project da-ch11-ex1.
2 Start VisualVM.
3 Select a process for project da-ch11-ex1 in VisualVM.
4 Go to the Monitor tab in VisualVM.
5 Call the /products/1000000 endpoint.
6 Observe the memory widget in the Memory tab in VisualVM.

In the Monitor tab in the memory widget, you can see that the app uses a lot of memory resources. The widget looks similar to figure 11.1. What should we do when we suspect some app capability doesn't optimally use the memory resources? The investigation process follows two major steps:

1 Use memory sampling to get details about the object instances the app stores.
2 Use memory profiling (instrumentation) to get additional details about a specific part of the code in execution.

Let's follow the same approach you learned in chapters 7 to 9 for CPU resource consumption: get a high-level view of what happens using sampling. To sample an app execution for memory usage, select the Sampler tab in VisualVM. Then select the Memory button to start a memory usage sampling session. Call the endpoint and wait for the execution to end. The VisualVM screen will display the objects the app allocates.

We are looking for what occupies most of the memory. In most cases, that will be one of these two situations:

- Many object instances of certain types are created and fill up the memory (this is what happens in our scenario).
- There are not many instances of a certain type, but each instance is very large.

Many instances filling up the allocated memory makes sense, but how could a small number of instances do this? Imagine this scenario: your app processes large video files. The app loads maybe two or three files at a time, but since they are large, they fill the allocated memory. A developer can analyze whether the capability can be optimized. Maybe the app doesn't need the full files loaded in memory but just fragments of them at a time.

When we start our investigation, we don't know which scenario we'll fall into. I usually sort, in descending order, by the amount of memory occupied and then by the number of instances. Notice in figure 11.3 that VisualVM shows you the memory spent and the number of instances for each sampled type. You need to sort, in descending order, by the second and the third columns in the table.

In figure 11.3, you clearly see that I sorted the table in descending order by Live Bytes (space occupied). We can then look for the first type in our app's codebase that appears in the table. Don't look for primitives, strings, arrays of primitives, or arrays of strings. These are usually at the top since they are created as a side effect. However, in most cases, they don't provide any clues about the problem.

In figure 11.3, we clearly see that type Product is causing trouble. It occupies a large part of the allocated memory, and in the Live Objects column, we see that the app created one million instances of this type.

If you need the total number of instances of the type created throughout execution, you must use profiling (instrumentation) techniques. We'll do this later in this chapter.

This app is just an example, but in a real-world app, simply sorting by the occupied space may not be enough. We need to figure out whether the problem is a large number of instances or whether each instance takes a lot of space. I know what you're thinking: isn't it clear in this case? Yes, but in a real-world app it may not be, so I always recommend that developers also sort in descending order by the number of instances

2. Find the first object type that belongs to your codebase or a library that your app uses. Don't look for types coming from the JDK.

1. Sort in descending order by allocated memory.

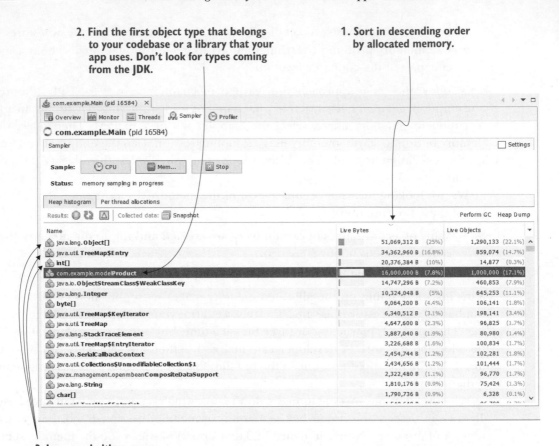

3. Ignore primitives, arrays of primitives, or JDK objects.

Figure 11.3 We sort the sampled results in descending order by memory occupied. This way, we can see which objects consume most of the memory. We don't usually look for primitives, strings, and arrays of strings or JDK objects in general. We are mostly interested in finding the object, directly related to our codebase, that is causing the problem. In this case, the `Product` type (which is part of our codebase) occupies a large part of the memory.

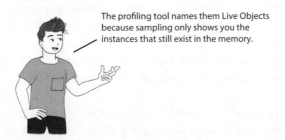

The profiling tool names them Live Objects because sampling only shows you the instances that still exist in the memory.

to make sure. Figure 11.4 shows the sampled data sorted in descending order by the number of instances the app created for each type. Again, type `Product` is at the top.

2. Find the first object type that belongs to your codebase or a library that your app uses. Don't look for types coming from the JDK.

1. Sort in descending order by the number of object instances (live objects).

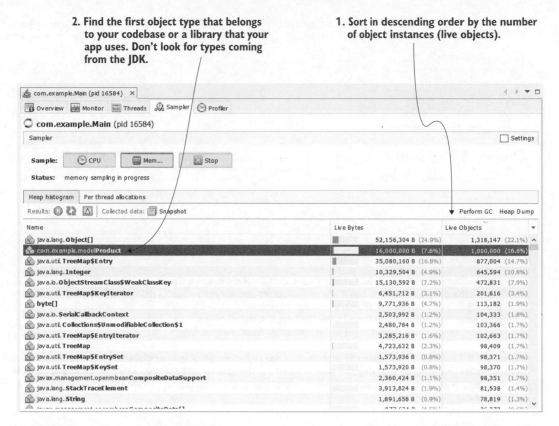

Figure 11.4 We can sort the sampled results by the number of instances (live objects). This gives us clues on whether some capability creates a large number of objects that are negatively affecting the memory allocation.

Sometimes sampling is enough to help you identify the problem. But what if you can't figure out what part of the app creates these objects? When you can't find the problem just by sampling the execution, your next step is profiling (instrumentation). Profiling gives you more details, including what part of the code created the potentially problematic instances. But remember the rule of thumb: when you use profiling, you need to first know what to profile. That's why we always begin by sampling.

Since we know the problem is with the Product type, we will profile for it. Like you did in chapters 7 to 9, you must specify which part of the app you want to profile using an expression. In figure 11.5, I profile only for the Product type. I do this by using the fully qualified name (package and class name) of the class in the Memory settings textbox on the right side of the window.

2. Start profiling, and then call the app's endpoint.

1. Specify the expression that defines which objects you want to profile for memory usage.

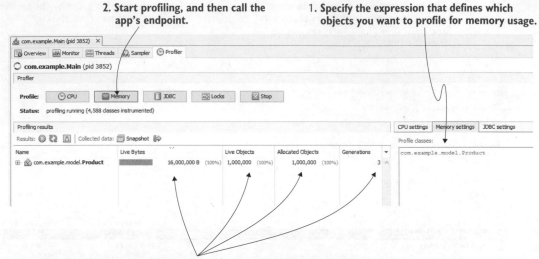

3. The profiler will indicate details about each object involved in execution during the profiling session. You'll find the allocated memory per object, the number of instances in memory for each object, how many objects have been garbage collected, how many still exist in the memory, and how many times the GC tried to remove them from the memory.

Figure 11.5   To profile for memory allocation, first specify which packages or classes you want to profile, and then start the profiling by pressing the Memory button. The profiler will give you relevant details about the profile types, including used memory, number of instances, the total number of allocated objects, and the number of GC generations.

Just as in the case of CPU profiling (chapter 8), you can profile for more types at a time or even specify entire packages. Some of the most commonly used expressions are as follows:

- *Strict-type, fully qualified name (e.g.,* `com.example.model.Product`*)*—Only searches for that specific type
- *Types in a given package (e.g.,* `com.example.model.*`*)*—Only searches for types declared in the package `com.example.model` but not in its subpackages
- *Types in a given package and its subpackages (e.g.,* `com.example.**`*)*—Searches in the given package and all its subpackages

Always remember to restrict the types you profile as much as possible. If you know Product causes the problem, then it makes sense to profile only this type.

In addition to the live objects (which are the instances that still exist in memory for that type), you will get the total number of instances of that type that the app created. Moreover, you will see how many times those instances "survived" the GC (what we call *generations*).

These details are valuable, but finding what part of the code creates the objects is often even more useful. As shown in figure 11.6, for each profiled type, the tool displays where the instances were created. Click the plus sign (+) on the left side of the line in the table. This capability quickly shows you the root cause of the problem.

For each profiled object type, the profiler indicates the part of code that created it during execution. This way, you can find the potential problem.

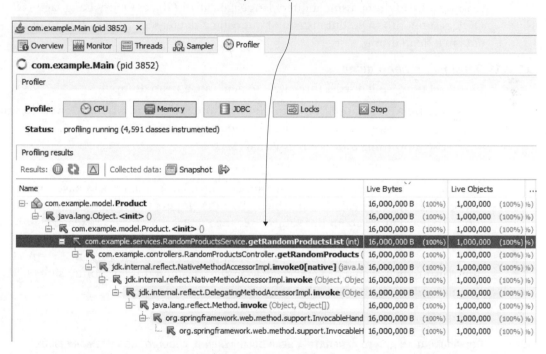

Figure 11.6 The profiler shows the stack trace of the code that created the instances of each of the profiled types. This way, you can easily identify what part of the app created the problematic instances.

11.2 Using heap dumps to find memory leaks

If the app is running, you can profile to identify any capability that can be optimized. But what if the app crashed and you suspect this happened due to a memory allocation issue? In most cases, app crashes are caused by capabilities with memory allocation problems such as memory leaks—the app doesn't deallocate the objects it creates in memory even after it doesn't need them. Since the memory is not infinite, continuously allocating objects will fill the memory at some point, causing the app to crash. In a JVM app, this is signaled with an `OutOfMemoryError` thrown at run time.

If the app is not running, you can't attach a profiler to investigate the execution. But, even so, you have other alternatives to investigate the problem. You can use a *heap dump*, which is a snapshot of what the heap memory looked like when the app crashed. Although you can collect a heap dump anytime, it is most useful when you can't profile the app for some reason—maybe because the app crashed or you simply don't have access to profile the process and you want to determine whether it suffers from any memory allocation issues.

In the next section, we'll discuss three possible ways to get a heap dump, and in section 11.2.2, I'll show you how to use the heap dump to identify memory allocation issues and their root causes. In section 11.2.3, we'll discuss a more advanced way of reading a heap dump using a query language called Object Query Language (OQL). OQL is similar to SQL, but instead of querying a database, you use OQL to query the data in a heap dump.

11.2.1 Obtaining a heap dump

In this section, we'll discuss three ways to generate a heap dump:

- Configure the application to generate one automatically in a given location when the app crashes because of a memory issue.
- Use a profiling tool (such as VisualVM).
- Use a command-line tool (such as `jcmd` or `jmap`).

You can even get a heap dump programmatically. Some frameworks have capabilities that can generate a heap dump, which allow developers to integrate app-monitoring tools. To learn more about this subject, see the `HotSpotDiagnosticMXBean` class in the Java official API documentation (http://mng.bz/19XZ).

Project da-ch11-ex1 implements an endpoint you can use to generate the heap dump using the `HotSpotDiagnosticMXBean` class. Calling this endpoint using cURL or Postman will create a dump file:

```
curl http://localhost:8080/jmx/heapDump?file=dump.hprof
```

CONFIGURING AN APP TO GENERATE A HEAP DUMP WHEN IT ENCOUNTERS A MEMORY ISSUE

Developers often use a heap dump to investigate an app crash when they suspect faulty memory allocation is causing a problem. For this reason, apps are most often configured to generate a heap dump of what the memory looked like when the app crashed. You should always configure an app to generate a heap dump when it stops due to a memory allocation problem. Fortunately, the configuration is easy. You just need to add a couple of JVM arguments when the app starts:

```
-XX:+HeapDumpOnOutOfMemoryError
-XX:HeapDumpPath=heapdump.bin
```

The first argument, -XX:+HeapDumpOnOutOfMemoryError, tells the app to generate a heap dump when it encounters an OutOfMemoryError (the heap gets full). The second argument, XX:HeapDumpPath=heapdump.bin, specifies the path in the filesystem where the dump will be stored. In this case, the file containing the heap dump will be named heapdump.bin and will be located close to the executable app, from the root of the classpath (because we used a relative path). Make sure the process has "write" privileges on this path to be able to store the file in the given location.

The following snippet shows the full command for running an app:

```
java -jar -XX:+HeapDumpOnOutOfMemoryError
➥ -XX:HeapDumpPath=heapdump.bin app.jar
```

We'll use a demo app named da-ch11-ex2 to demonstrate this approach. You can find this app in the projects provided with the book. The app in the following listing continuously adds instances of type Product to a list until the memory fills.

Listing 11.1 Generating a large numbers of instances that can't be deallocated

```
public class Main {

  private static List<Product> products = new ArrayList<>();

  public static void main(String[] args) {
    Random r = new Random();
    while (true) {                        ⟵── The loop iterates forever.
      Product p = new Product();
      p.setName("Product " + r.nextInt());
      products.add(p);                    ⟵────────── Adds instances to the list
    }                                                 until the memory gets full
  }
}
```

The next code snippet shows what the simple Product type looks like:

```
public class Product {

  private String name;

  // Omitted getters and setters

}
```

Maybe you're wondering why there is a random name for the product instances. We'll need that later when we discuss reading a heap dump in section 11.2.2. For the moment, we're only interested in how to generate a heap dump to figure out why this app is filling its heap memory in seconds.

You can use the IDE to run the app and set the arguments. Figure 11.7 shows you how to set the JVM arguments in IntelliJ. I also added the -Xmx argument to limit the

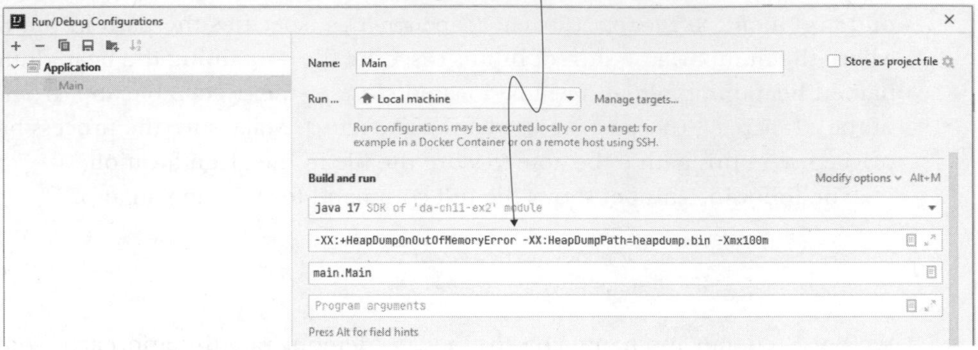

Set the JVM arguments in the Run/Debug Configuration window.

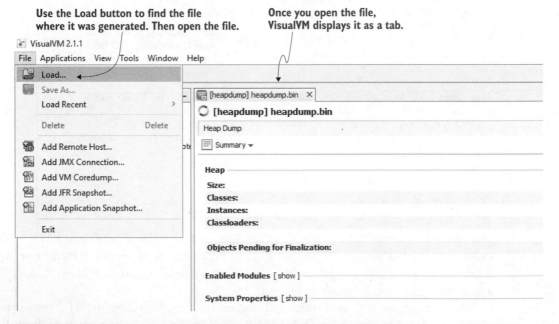

Figure 11.7   You can configure the JVM arguments from your IDE. Add the values in the Run/Debug Configurations before starting the application.

heap memory of the app to just 100 MB. That will make the heap dump file smaller and our example easier.

When you run the application, wait a moment, and the app will crash. With only 100 MB of heap space, the memory shouldn't take more than a few seconds to get full. The project folder contains a file named heapdump.bin, which includes all the details about the data in the heap the moment the app stopped. You can open this file with VisualVM to analyze it, as presented in figure 11.8.

Use the Load button to find the file where it was generated. Then open the file.

Once you open the file, VisualVM displays it as a tab.

Figure 11.8   You can use VisualVM to open the heap dump file for analysis. Use the Load button in the menu to find the file. Open the file, and VisualVM will display the heap dump as a tab.

OBTAINING A HEAP DUMP USING A PROFILER

Sometimes you need to get a heap dump for a running process. In this case, the easiest solution is to use VisualVM (or a similar profiling tool) to generate the dump. Getting a heap dump with VisualVM is as easy as clicking a button. Just use the Heap Dump button in the Monitor tab, as shown in figure 11.9.

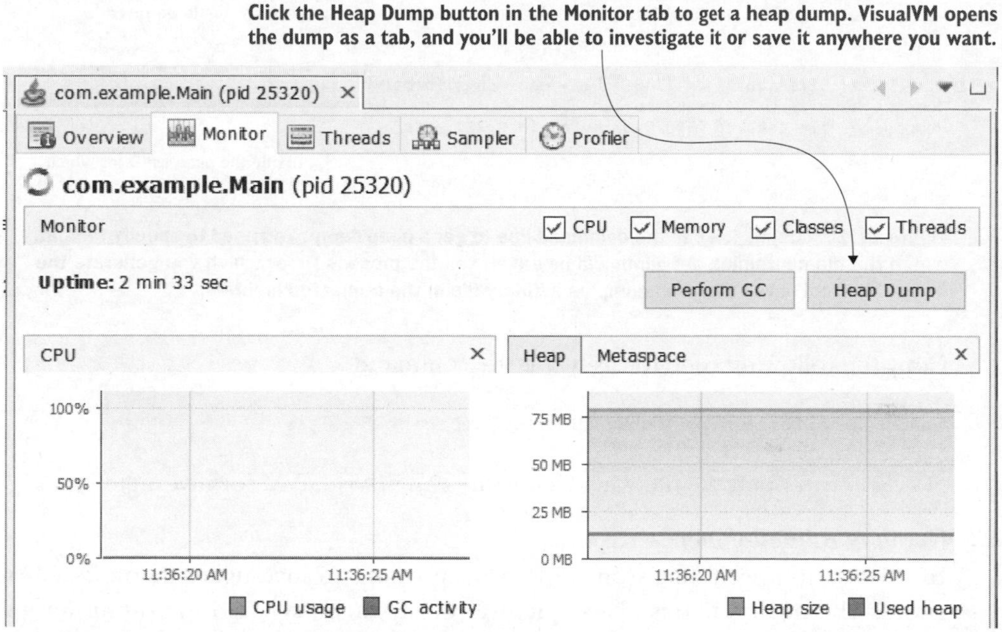

Figure 11.9   Press the Heap Dump button in VisualVM's Monitor tab to get a heap dump for the selected process. VisualVM opens the dump as a tab, and you can further investigate it or save it anywhere you want.

OBTAINING A HEAP DUMP WITH THE COMMAND LINE

If you need to get a heap dump for a running process, but your app is deployed in an environment in which you don't have access to connect a profiler to it, don't panic; you still have options. You can use jmap, a command-line tool provided with the JDK, to generate the heap dump.

There are two steps for collecting a heap dump with jmap:

1   Find the process ID (PID) of the running app for which you want to get the heap dump.
2   Use jmap to save the dump into a file.

To find the running-process PID, you can use jps, as we did in chapter 10:

```
jps -l
25320 main.Main
132 jdk.jcmd/sun.tools.jps.Jps
25700 org.jetbrains.jps.cmdline.Launcher
```

The second step is using jmap. To call jmap, specify the PID and the location where the heap dump file will be saved. You must also specify that the output is a binary file using the -dump:format=b parameter. Figure 11.10 shows the use of this tool in the command line.

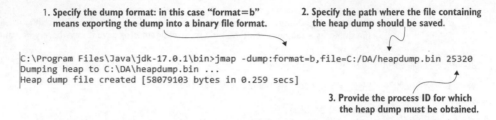

1. Specify the dump format: in this case "format=b" means exporting the dump into a binary file format.

2. Specify the path where the file containing the heap dump should be saved.

```
C:\Program Files\Java\jdk-17.0.1\bin>jmap -dump:format=b,file=C:/DA/heapdump.bin 25320
Dumping heap to C:\DA\heapdump.bin ...
Heap dump file created [58079103 bytes in 0.259 secs]
```

3. Provide the process ID for which the heap dump must be obtained.

Figure 11.10   Using jmap in the command line to get a heap dump. You need to specify the path where the file containing the dump will be saved and the process ID for which you generate the dump. The tool saves the heap dump as a binary file in the requested location.

Copy the following code to easily use the command:

```
jmap -dump:format=b,file=C:/DA/heapdump.bin 25320
```

Now you can open the file you saved with jmap in VisualVM for investigation.

11.2.2 Reading a heap dump

In this section, we'll focus on using a heap dump to investigate memory allocation issues. The heap dump is like a "picture" of the memory when the dump was generated. It contains all the data the app had in the heap, which means you can use it to examine the data and the way it was structured. This way, you can determine which objects occupied a big part of the allocated memory and understand why the app couldn't deallocate them.

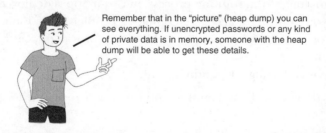

Remember that in the "picture" (heap dump) you can see everything. If unencrypted passwords or any kind of private data is in memory, someone with the heap dump will be able to get these details.

Unlike a thread dump, you cannot analyze a heap dump as plain text. Instead, you must use VisualVM (or any profiling tool in general). In this section, we'll use VisualVM to analyze the heap dump we generated for project da-ch11-ex2 in section 11.2.1. You'll learn to utilize this approach to find the root cause of an OutOfMemoryError.

When you open a heap dump in VisualVM, the profiling tool displays a summary view of the heap dump (figure 11.11), which provides quick details on the heap dump

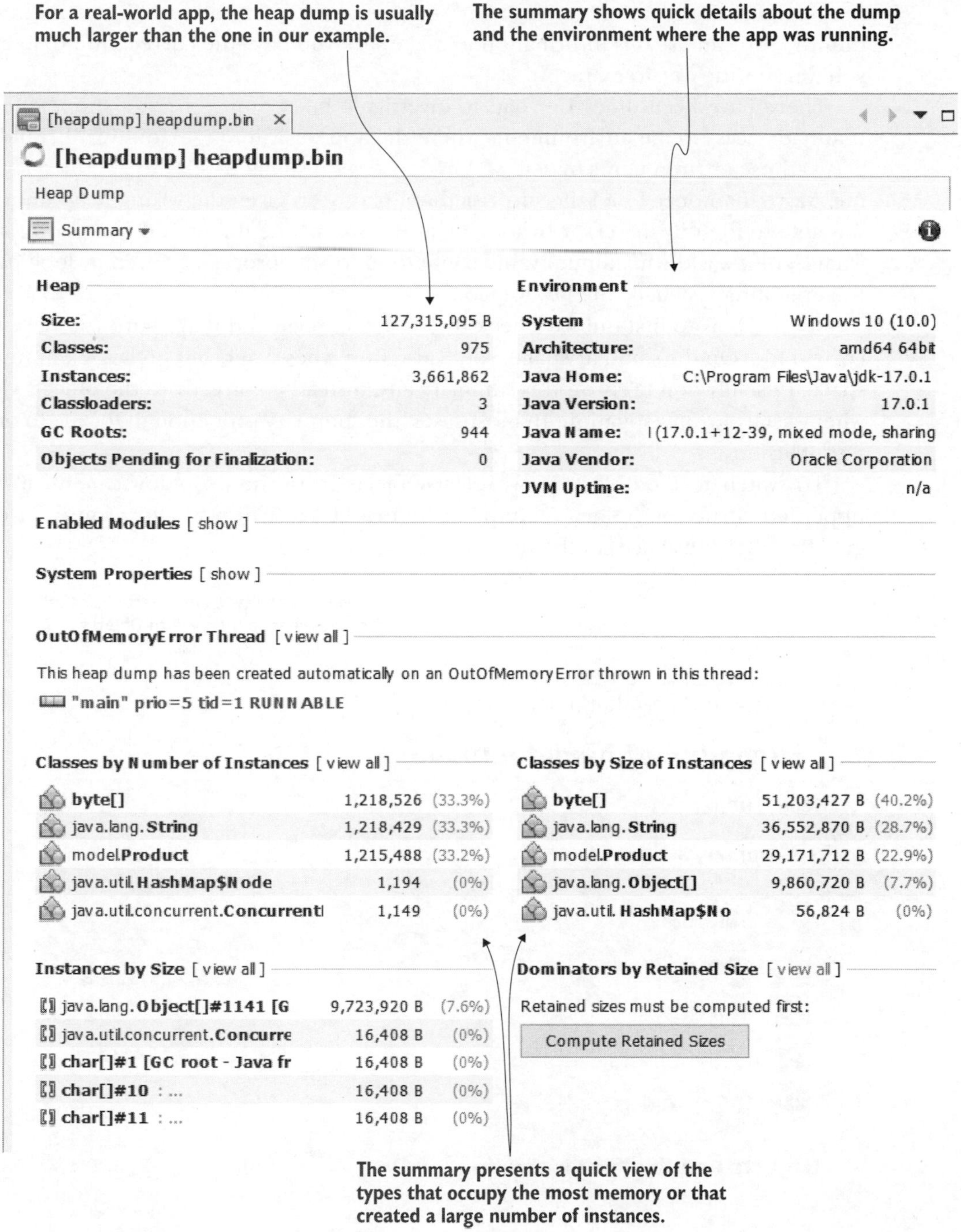

For a real-world app, the heap dump is usually much larger than the one in our example.

The summary shows quick details about the dump and the environment where the app was running.

[heapdump] heapdump.bin ✕   ◀ ▶ ▼ ☐

○ **[heapdump] heapdump.bin**

Heap Dump

▤ Summary ▼   ❶

Heap

Size:	127,315,095 B
Classes:	975
Instances:	3,661,862
Classloaders:	3
GC Roots:	944
Objects Pending for Finalization:	0

Environment

System	Windows 10 (10.0)
Architecture:	amd64 64bit
Java Home:	C:\Program Files\Java\jdk-17.0.1
Java Version:	17.0.1
Java Name:	I (17.0.1+12-39, mixed mode, sharing
Java Vendor:	Oracle Corporation
JVM Uptime:	n/a

Enabled Modules [show]

System Properties [show]

OutOfMemoryError Thread [view all]

This heap dump has been created automatically on an OutOfMemoryError thrown in this thread:

▭ "main" prio=5 tid=1 RUNNABLE

Classes by Number of Instances [view all]

🍂 byte[]	1,218,526	(33.3%)
🍂 java.lang.**String**	1,218,429	(33.3%)
🍂 model.**Product**	1,215,488	(33.2%)
🍂 java.util.**HashMap$Node**	1,194	(0%)
🍂 java.util.concurrent.**Concurrent**	1,149	(0%)

Instances by Size [view all]

〔I〕 java.lang.**Object[]#1141 [G**	9,723,920 B	(7.6%)
〔I〕 java.util.concurrent.**Concurre**	16,408 B	(0%)
〔I〕 char[]#1 [GC root - Java fr	16,408 B	(0%)
〔I〕 char[]#10 : ...	16,408 B	(0%)
〔I〕 char[]#11 : ...	16,408 B	(0%)

Classes by Size of Instances [view all]

🍂 byte[]	51,203,427 B	(40.2%)
🍂 java.lang.**String**	36,552,870 B	(28.7%)
🍂 model.**Product**	29,171,712 B	(22.9%)
🍂 java.lang.**Object[]**	9,860,720 B	(7.7%)
🍂 java.util.**HashMap$No**	56,824 B	(0%)

Dominators by Retained Size [view all]

Retained sizes must be computed first:

[Compute Retained Sizes]

The summary presents a quick view of the types that occupy the most memory or that created a large number of instances.

Figure 11.11   In the initial screen after opening a heap dump, VisualVM provides a summary of the heap dump, which includes information about the dump itself and the system where the app was running. The view also shows the types that occupy the largest amount of memory.

file (e.g., the file size, the total number of classes, the total number of instances in the dump). You can use this information to make sure you have the correct dump, in case you weren't the one to extract it.

There have been times I've had to investigate heap dumps from a support team that had access to the environments where the app was running. However, I couldn't access those environments myself, so I had to rely on someone else to get the data for me. More than once I had the surprise that I had been given the wrong heap dump. I was able to identify the error by looking at the size of the dump and comparing it to what I knew was the maximum value configured for the process, or even by looking at the operating system or the Java version.

My advice is to first quickly check the summary page and make sure you have the correct file. On the summary page, you'll also find types that occupy a large amount of space. I usually don't rely on this summary and instead go directly to the objects view, where I start my investigation. In most cases, the summary isn't enough for me to draw a conclusion.

To switch to the objects view, select Objects from the drop-down menu in the upper-left corner of the heap dump tab (figure 11.12). This will allow you to investigate the object instances in the heap dump.

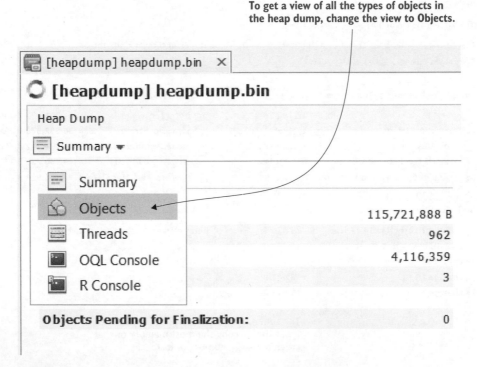

Figure 11.12   You can switch to the Objects view, which makes it easier to investigate the instances in the heap dump.

Just as with memory sampling and profiling, we're searching for the types that use the most memory. The best approach is to sort, in descending order, by both instances and occupied memory and look for the first types that are part of the app's codebase. Don't look for types such as primitives, strings, or arrays of primitives and strings. There are usually a lot, and they won't give you many clues as to what is wrong.

In figure 11.13, you can see, after sorting, that the `Product` type seems to be involved in the problem. The `Product` type is the first type that is part of the app's codebase, and it uses a large part of the memory. We need to figure out why so many instances have been created and why the GC can't remove them from the memory.

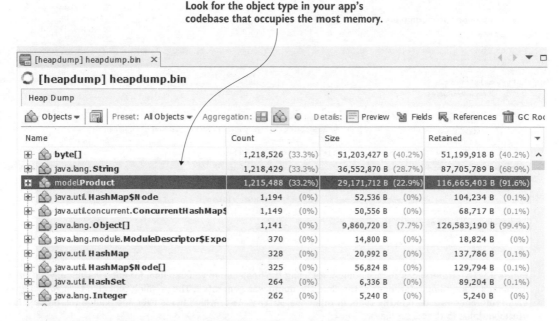

Look for the object type in your app's codebase that occupies the most memory.

Figure 11.13 **Use sorting on columns to identify which type created a large number of instances or takes up a lot of space. Always look for the first object in your app codebase. In this case, both in number of instances and size, the `Product` type is the first in the list.**

You can select the small plus sign (+) on the left side of the row to get details about all the instances for that type. We already know there are more than one million `Product` instances, but we still need to find

- What part of the code creates those instances
- Why the GC can't remove them in time to avoid the app's failure

You can find what each instance refers to (through fields) and what refers to that instance. Since we know the GC cannot remove an instance from the memory unless it has no referrers, we look for what refers the instance to see whether it is still needed in the processing context or if the app forgot to remove its reference.

Figure 11.14 shows the expanded view for the details of one of the Product instances. We can see that the instance refers to a String (the product name), and its reference is kept in an Object array, which is part of an ArrayList instance. Moreover, the ArrayList instance seems to keep a large number of references (over one million). This is usually not a good sign, as either the app implements an unoptimized capability or we found a memory leak.

The object referencing this Product instance is an ArrayList that holds 1,215,487 other references.

Figure 11.14   References to an instance. By using the heap dump, you can find, for each instance, what other instances were being referenced at the time the dump was generated. The profiling tool also tells you where a given reference is stored in the code. In this case, ArrayList, which holds over one million references, is a static variable in the Main class.

To understand which is the case, we need to investigate the code using the debugging and logging techniques we discussed in chapters 2 to 5. Fortunately, the profiler shows you exactly where to find the list in the code. In our case, the list is declared as a static variable in the Main class.

Using VisualVM, we can easily understand the relationships between objects. By combining this technique with other investigation techniques you've learned throughout the book, you have all the tools you need to address these kinds of issues. Complex problems (and apps) may still require significant effort, but using this approach will save you a lot of time.

11.2.3 *Using the OQL console to query a heap dump*

In this section, we'll discuss a more advanced way of investigating a heap dump. We use a querying language similar to SQL to retrieve details from the heap dump. The simple approaches we discussed in section 11.2.2 are usually enough to identify memory allocation problems' root causes. But they aren't sufficient when we need to compare the details of two or more heap dumps.

Suppose you want to compare the heap dumps provided for two or more versions of an app to determine whether something faulty or unoptimized was implemented between the version releases. You can investigate them manually, one by one. But I'll teach you how to write queries that you can easily run on each of them, which will save you time. That's where OQL is an excellent approach. Figure 11.15 shows you how to change the view to the OQL console, where you can run queries to investigate the heap dump.

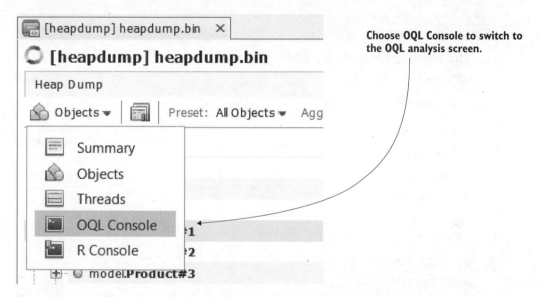

Figure 11.15   To switch to the OQL view in VisualVM, choose OQL Console from the drop-down menu in the upper-left corner of the heap dump tab.

We'll discuss a few examples I find most useful, but remember that OQL is more complex. (You can find more information on its functions at http://mng.bz/Pod2.)

Let's start with a simple one: selecting all the instances of a given type. Say we want to get all the instances of type `Product` from the heap dump. To use a SQL query to get all the product records from a table in a relational database, we would write something like this:

```
select * from product
```

To query all the `Product` instances in a heap dump using OQL, you need to write this:

```
select p from model.Product p
```

 **NOTE** For OQL, keywords such as "select," "from," or "where" are always written in lowercase. The types are always given with their fully qualified name (package + class name).

Figure 11.16 shows the result of executing the simple query that retrieves all the Product instances from the heap dump.

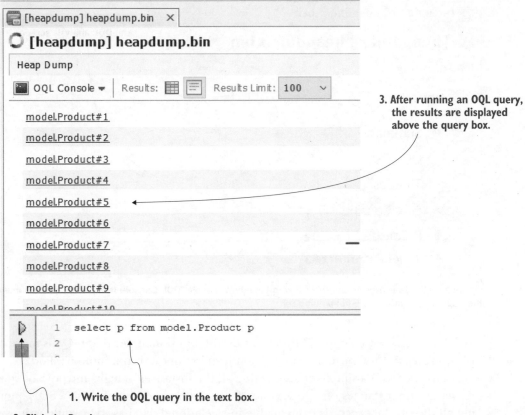

Figure 11.16   Running an OQL query with VisualVM. In the OQL console, write the OQL query in the textbox on the bottom of the window and click the Run button (the green arrow on the left of the text box) to run the query. The results will appear above the text box.

NOTE When learning OQL, use small heap dumps.
Real-world heap dumps are usually large (4 GB or larger).
The OQL queries will be slow. If you are studying only,
generate and use small-sized heap dumps like we do
in this chapter.

You can select any of the queried instances to get its details. You can find what keeps a
reference to that instance, what that instance refers to, and its values (figure 11.17).

**Selecting any of the rows in the result
(which represents an object instance)
gives you details about that instance.**

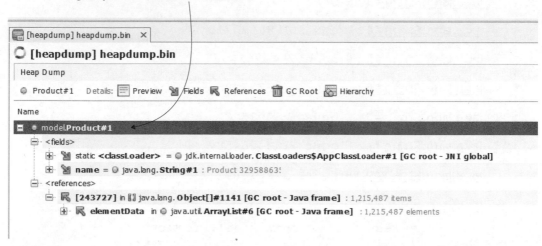

Figure 11.17   You can access the details about a queried instance (referees and referrers) by clicking it.

You can also select values or references referred from certain instances. For example,
if we want to get all the product names instead of the product instances, we can write
the following query (figure 11.18):

```
select p.name from model.Product p
```

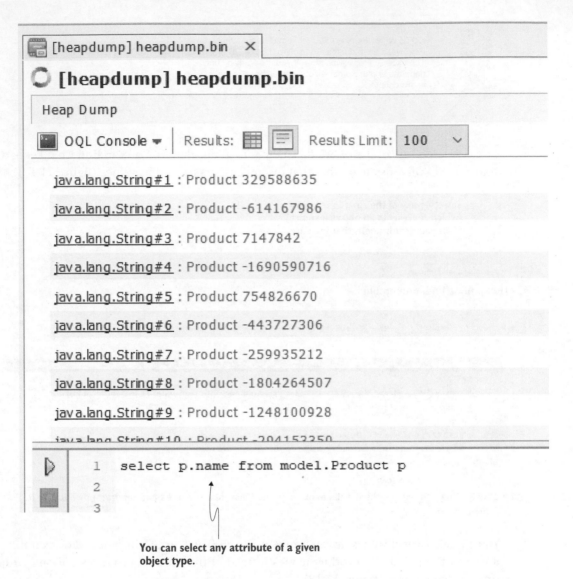

You can select any attribute of a given
object type.

**Figure 11.18   Selecting an attribute of a given object type. Just as in Java, you can use the standard dot
operator to refer to an attribute of an instance.**

With OQL, you can extract multiple values at the same time. To do so, you need to format them as JSON, as in the next listing.

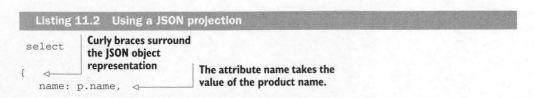

Listing 11.2   Using a JSON projection

```
        name_length: p.name.value.length
}

from model.Product p
```

> The attribute **name_length** takes the value of the number of characters in the product name.

Figure 11.19 shows you the result for running this query.

To more clearly see the results, use the formatter display.

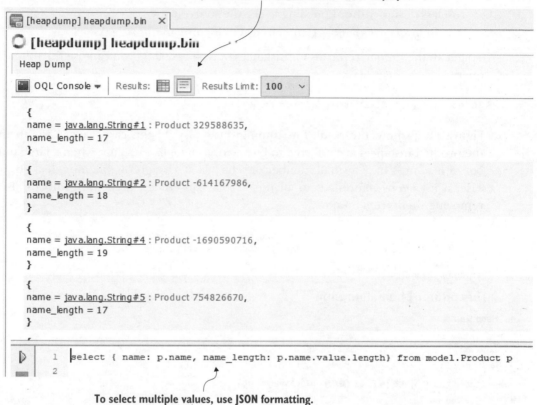

To select multiple values, use JSON formatting.

Figure 11.19 Selecting multiple values. You can use JSON formatting to obtain multiple values with one query.

You can change this query to, for example, add conditions on one or more of the selected values. Say you want to select only the instances that have a name longer than 15 characters. You could write a query as presented in the next snippet:

```
select { name: p.name, name_length: p.name.value.length}
from model.Product p
where p.name.value.length > 15
```

Let's move on to something slightly more advanced. A query I often use when looking into memory issues employs the `referrers()` method to get the objects that refer to instances of a specific type. By using built-in OQL functions such as this one, you can do plenty of helpful things:

- *Find or query instance referees*—Can tell you if the app has memory leaks
- *Find or query instance referrals*—Can tell you if specific instances are the cause of memory leaks
- *Find duplicates in instances*—Can tell you if specific capabilities can be optimized to use less memory
- *Find subclasses and superclasses of certain instances*—Gives you insight into an app's class design without needing to see the source code
- *Identify long life paths*—Can help you to identify memory leaks

To get all the unique referrals for instances of type `Product`, you can use the following query:

```
select unique(referrers(p)) from model.Product p
```

Figure 11.20 shows the result for running this query. In this case, we can see that all the product instances are referred to by one object—a list. Usually, when a large number of instances have a small number of referrals, it's a sign of a memory leak. In our case, a list keeps references to all the `Product` instances, preventing the GC from removing them from memory.

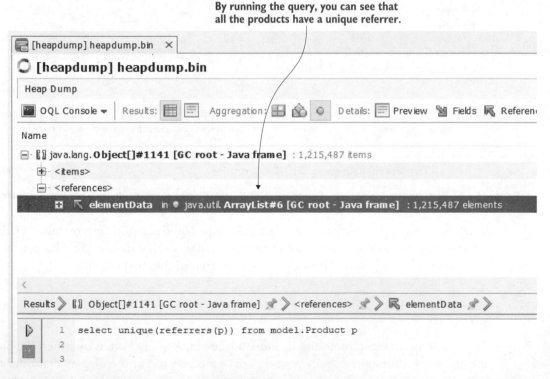

By running the query, you can see that all the products have a unique referrer.

Figure 11.20 Selecting all the unique referrers for instances of a type shows you if there's one object that prevents the GC from removing the instances from memory. This can be a quick way to identify a memory leak.

If the result is not unique, you can count the referrals by instance using the next query to find the instances that are potentially involved in a memory leak:

```
select { product: p.name, count: count(referrers(p))} from model.Product p
```

The OQL queries provide a lot of opportunities, and once you write a query, you can run it as many times as you need and on different heap dumps.

Summary

- An app with capabilities that are not optimized for memory allocation can cause performance problems. Optimizing the app to wisely allocate (avoid spending unnecessary memory space) the data in memory is essential to an app's performance.
- A profiling tool allows you to sample and profile how the memory gets occupied during an app's execution. This can help you identify unoptimized parts of your app and provides you with details on what can be improved.
- If new object instances are continuously added to the memory during execution but the app never removes the references to new instances, the GC won't be able to delete the references and free the memory. When the memory gets fully occupied, the app cannot continue its execution and stops. Before stopping, the app throws an OutOfMemoryError.
- To investigate an OutOfMemoryError, we use heap dumps. A heap dump collects all the data in the app's heap memory and allows you to analyze it to figure out what went wrong.
- You can start your app using a couple of JVM arguments to instruct it to generate a heap dump at a given path if the app fails with an OutOfMemoryError.
- You can also get a heap dump by using a profiling tool or a command-line tool such as jmap.
- To analyze a heap dump, load it in a profiling tool such as VisualVM, which allows you to investigate the instances in the dump and their relationships. This way, you can figure out what part of the app is not optimized or has memory leaks.
- VisualVM offers more advanced ways to analyze the heap dump, such as OQL queries. OQL is a querying language similar to SQL that you use to retrieve data from a heap dump.

Part 3

Finding problems in large systems

Today, most apps are part of large systems that use various architectural styles. Issues can sometimes be challenging to find in such systems, and evaluating a single process is not enough. Imagine you have a car, and you have ways to analyze independent parts of it, but not a way to evaluate how these parts interact with one another. Would you be able to find all the problems your car may have?

In part 3, we'll discuss techniques that apply to investigating systems composed of multiple apps. We'll focus on investigating the way these apps "speak" with one another, how they are affected by the environment in which they are deployed, and what to consider when implementing the systems.

Investigating apps' behaviors in large systems

12

This chapter covers

- Investigating app communication issues
- Using log-monitoring tools in your system
- Taking advantage of deployment tools

In this chapter, we go beyond the border of a single app and discuss how to investigate situations caused by apps working together in systems. Today, many systems are composed of multiple apps that communicate with one another. Large business systems leverage various apps, and they are often implemented with different technologies and on different platforms. In many cases, the maturity of these apps also varies from new services to old and messy scripts.

Debugging, profiling, and logs aren't always enough. Sometimes you need to find bigger clues. An app can work well independently but not correctly integrate with other apps or the environment it's deployed into.

We'll start in section 12.1 with ways to investigate communication between the services of a system. In section 12.2, we'll focus our attention on the relevance of implementing monitoring for apps in a system and how to use the information a monitoring tool provides. We'll end this chapter's discussion in section 12.3, where we'll discuss how to take advantage of deployment tools.

12.1   Investigating communication between services

In this section, we discuss investigating communication between apps. In a system, apps "talk" to one another to fulfill their responsibilities. Thus far, we have focused on investigating the interior workings of an app and the communication between an app and a database management system. But what about apps that talk to one another? Is there a way to monitor the events throughout an entire system composed of many apps (figure 12.1)?

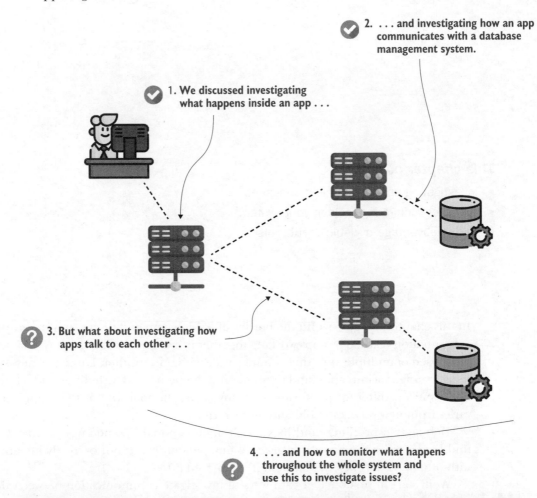

2. . . . and investigating how an app communicates with a database management system.

1. We discussed investigating what happens inside an app . . .

3. But what about investigating how apps talk to each other . . .

4. . . . and how to monitor what happens throughout the whole system and use this to investigate issues?

Figure 12.1   In many cases, an investigation stays within the boundaries of an app. But you may need to go beyond what happens inside a given process. Issues or strange behavior can be caused by apps that have problems communicating with each other, and implementing a monitoring tool will make investigating these types of issues easier.

Let's discuss how to use a profiling tool to investigate issues regarding how apps "talk" to each other. We'll use JProfiler to observe communication for a simple app (project da-ch12-ex1) to expose an endpoint you can call (/demo endpoint). When you send an HTTP request to this endpoint, the app sends a request to an endpoint exposed by httpbin.org, which delays the response for 5 seconds and then responds with a 200 OK HTTP status.

As you'll learn in this section, JProfiler offers a set of tools you can use to observe both the requests an app receives and the requests an app sends. Moreover, you can investigate low-level communication events on sockets. Such approaches can help you to identify the root cause of communication problems.

In section 12.1.1, we'll use JProfiler to observe the requests an app receives. In section 12.1.2, we'll investigate details about the requests an app sends, and in section 12.1.3, we'll focus on investigating low-level communication events on sockets.

Microservices

Let's talk frankly about microservices. Many systems you'll work on claim they are microservices. Most often this is not true; they are simply service-oriented architectures. Microservices have become (for some reason I can't say I fully understand) a brand that sells quite well:

- Do you want to employ someone faster? Tell them they're going to work with microservices.
- Do you want to impress a customer during a presales meeting? Tell them you do microservices.
- Do you want more people to attend your presentation? You guessed it: just add microservices in the title.

But microservices are more difficult than what I feel the majority of developers understand. You'll find plenty of literature out there if you want to better understand what microservices are. You can start with *Microservices Patterns* by Chris Richardson (Manning, 2018) and then read *Monolith to Microservices* by Sam Newman (O'Reilly Media, 2018) or *Building Microservices: Designing Fine-Grained Systems*, second edition (O'Relly Media, 2021), also by Sam Newman.

Whether they are real microservices systems or not, you still need to know how to investigate problems and how to quickly understand what the system does in given scenarios. In this chapter, we will discuss investigation techniques that apply to microservices, but not just to microservices. I prefer to use the simple term *service* instead of *microservice*. Sometimes I'll just use *app* or *application*.

12.1.1 Using HTTP server probes to observe HTTP requests

When two apps communicate, the data flows in two directions. An app either sends or receives a request. When an app sends a request, we say it acts as a *client*; when it receives a request, we say it's the *server*. In this section, we focus on the HTTP requests an app receives (as a server). We'll use a simple app provided with the book (project da-ch12-ex1) to understand how to monitor such events with JProfiler.

Open project da-ch12-ex1 in your IDE and start the application. Using JProfiler, connect to the app and start recording the received HTTP requests going to HTTP Server > Events, and then press the star icon to record single events. Figure 12.2 shows you how to start recording the events. We want to learn what HTTP requests the app receives and what information these requests can provide.

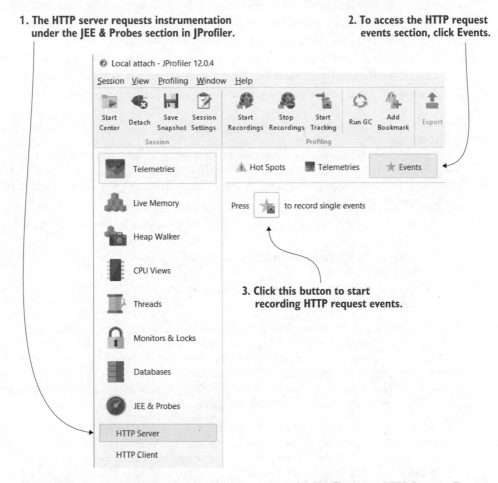

Figure 12.2   To start recording received HTTP requests with JProfiler, go to HTTP Server > Events, and then press the star icon to record single events. Now, whenever the profiled app receives HTTP requests, JProfiler will display the details.

Let's call the only endpoint this demo app exposes:

```
curl http://localhost:8080/demo
```

As presented in figure 12.3, JProfiler shows the request the server received. First, you can easily determine when the event ends: the displayed status will be "completed." If the operation never ends, meaning for some reason either the request wasn't fully processed or the response wasn't sent back to the client, the status will be "in progress." This way, you can determine whether the request takes too long or if it has been delayed or interrupted by something.

The HTTP server events table also displays the event duration. If the event is completed but takes a long time, you need to determine what caused the delay. It may be faulty communication, which you will observe using socket events, discussed in section 12.1.3, or you may need to sample and profile the execution, as discussed in chapters 7 to 9.

It's also important to see how many events the app gets. In some cases, one request won't cause trouble, but I remember a situation in which an app was affected by one of the clients *polling* (repeatedly sending requests over a short time) one of the endpoints. If a client sends a high number of requests in a short interval and there's nothing preventing them from reaching the app, the app may have trouble responding to all the requests and even crash.

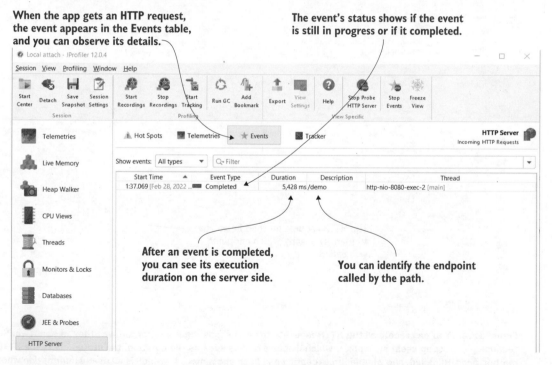

Figure 12.3 After starting to record the HTTP server events (HTTP requests the app receives), the profiling tool shows details of all the received events on the page. You can easily see if an event ended and the time it took to complete.

12.1.2 *Using HTTP client probes to observe HTTP requests the app sends*

Similar to HTTP server events (HTTP requests the app receives), you can profile the HTTP client events (HTTP requests the app sends). In this section, we'll discuss profiling HTTP requests the app sends to identify potential issues they can cause. To do this, we'll continue using the app provided with project da-ch12-ex1, the same one we used in section 12.1.1. This app sends a request to an endpoint of httpbin.org when you call the /demo endpoint it exposes. Let's start the app, call the /demo endpoint, and find out if we can observe the HTTP requests this app sends.

After starting the app, begin recording the HTTP client events in JProfiler (figure 12.4), and call the /demo endpoint:

```
curl http://localhost:8080/demo
```

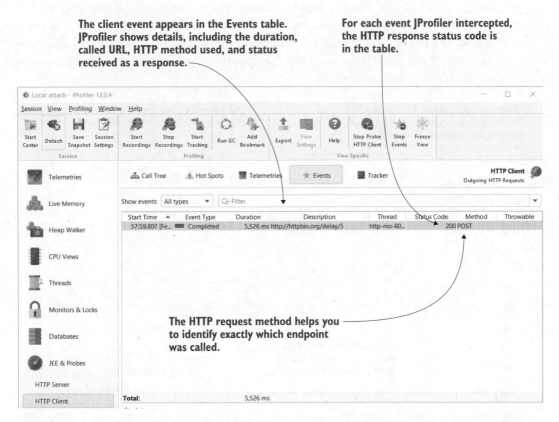

Figure 12.4   You can record all the HTTP requests the app sends regardless of the way they're sent (what technology your app uses) in JProfiler, which displays details such as the duration, the status code, the HTTP method and URI called, and whether an exception has been encountered—which is all useful information when investigating specific scenarios that involve HTTP requests an app sends.

Look at the information this tool provides (figure 12.4). You're first interested in the description and method columns since they help you to identify what endpoint the app calls. Once you know this, the details that give the most insight are the call duration, the response status code, and whether an exception has been encountered.

If you find that a call takes a long time to execute (more than you expect), you'll want to figure out why. First, try to determine whether the problem is caused by the data exchange (over the network) or something inside the app (e.g., deserializing the response or processing it).

As you'll see in section 12.1.3, investigating low-level events on sockets can tell you whether the problem is the communication itself or whether you should look at something your app does. If you discover that the data exchange is not causing the problem, you can apply the profiling techniques we discussed in chapters 7 to 9 to discover what affects the app's execution performance.

Just as with the HTTP requests an app gets (as discussed in section 12.1.1), it is important to consider the event count (how many lines appear in the events table) of HTTP requests an app sends. Does your app send too many requests, causing the other service to be slower to respond? In an app I implemented some time ago, I found that the app was sending frequent requests because of a faulty retry mechanism. The problem was difficult to spot up front since the requests were made to retrieve some data and were not changing anything or resulting in a wrong output. In this case, the supplementary requests only affected the app's performance.

12.1.3   *Investigating low-level events on sockets*

In this section, we discuss investigating low-level communication events on sockets to see whether a communication problem is caused by the communication channel (e.g., the network) or by something faulty inside the app. To observe these low-level events, you can use JProfiler: go to the Sockets > Events section.

Start the application, begin registering the events in JProfiler, and then send a request to the /demo endpoint:

```
curl http://localhost:8080/demo
```

JProfiler intercepts all the events on sockets and displays them in a table, as presented in figure 12.5.

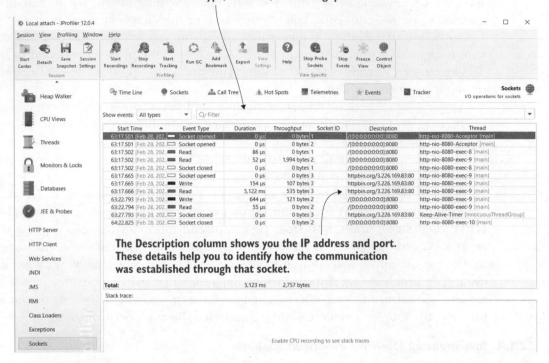

JProfiler intercepts all the socket events and displays their details. The most important details are the event type, duration, and throughput.

The Description column shows you the IP address and port. These details help you to identify how the communication was established through that socket.

Figure 12.5   Any message an app exchanges through the network level uses sockets behind the scenes. You can use a profiling tool such as JProfiler to observe all the low-level events at the sockets level. To monitor these events, use the Sockets > Events section. These events can help you to understand whether the app faces networking issues or if it simply doesn't correctly manage the communication.

A socket is a gateway to another process your app communicates with. When establishing communication, your app will execute the following socket events (figure 12.6):

1 Open a socket to establish the communication (handshake with the app it needs to talk to).

2 Read from the socket (receive data) or write through it (send data).

3 Close the socket.

Let's discuss these kinds of events in more detail and understand what can they tell you about your app's behavior.

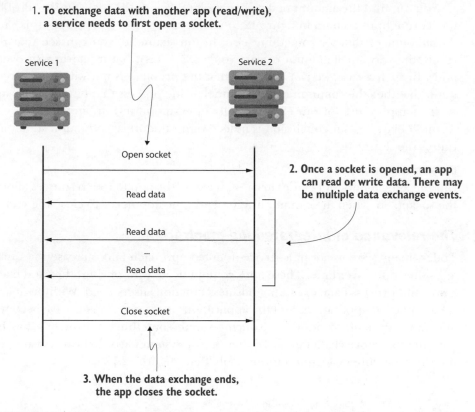

**1. To exchange data with another app (read/write),
a service needs to first open a socket.**

Service 1

Service 2

Open socket

**2. Once a socket is opened, an app
can read or write data. There may
be multiple data exchange events.**

Read data

Read data

...

Read data

Close socket

**3. When the data exchange ends,
the app closes the socket.**

**Figure 12.6 When an app starts a data exchange, it first opens a socket. To exchange the data,
the app can execute multiple data exchange events (read or write data events). When the data
exchange ends, the app closes the socket.**

OPENING A SOCKET TO ESTABLISH COMMUNICATION

One thing that should draw your attention is a long execution time for the open
socket event. Opening a socket shouldn't take a long time. If it does, this indicates a
problem with the communication channel. For example, the system or virtual
machine on which the app runs may not be properly configured, or the network
could have issues. When the open socket event takes a long time, it is usually not
caused by a problem with your code.

WRITING DATA THROUGH THE SOCKET OR READING DATA FROM IT

Reading or writing data through the socket is the actual process of communication.
The two apps are connected to each other, and they exchange data. If this operation is
slow, it can be because either a large amount of data is transferred or the communication channel is slow or faulty.

You can find the amount of data being sent through the socket using JProfiler (see the Throughput column in figure 12.5) so you can decide if the slowness is caused by the amount of data or something else. In our example, you can see that the app received a very small amount of data (only 535 bytes), but it had to wait over 5 seconds. In such a case, we can conclude that the problem is not with the current app, but with either the communication channel or the process that our app talks to.

The app we use for our example calls an endpoint in httpbin.org that causes a 5 second delay. So, our conclusion is indeed right: the other communication endpoint causes the slowness.

CLOSING THE SOCKET

Closing a socket doesn't cause slowness. It allows the app to free resources allocated to the socket. So, when the communication ends, the app needs to close the socket.

12.2 *The relevance of integrated log monitoring*

Today, many systems adopt a service-oriented approach and increase the number of apps they offer over time. These apps communicate with one another and exchange, store, and process data, executing business functions users need. With the increase in the number of applications and the applications' sizes, the systems have become more and more difficult to monitor. Noticing where something goes wrong has become considerably more challenging. To identify the system parts that cause issues, you can use the capabilities a log-monitoring tool offers (figure 12.7).

DEFINITION   A log-monitoring tool is software you can integrate with apps to see exceptions happening throughout the whole system.

The tool observes the executions of all apps and collects data whenever an app throws a run-time exception. It then displays this information in a user-friendly way to help you to more quickly identify the problem's cause.

We'll use a simple tool you can configure with your system to collect the exception events and present them in an easy-to-read way. Sentry (https://sentry.io) is a log-monitoring tool that I've used in many of the systems I've worked with, and it has proved to be extremely useful throughout both the production and development of apps. Sentry has a free plan you can use for learning purposes (like the examples in this chapter).

Let's create an app that throws an exception on purpose and integrate it with Sentry. This app is in project da-ch12-ex2.

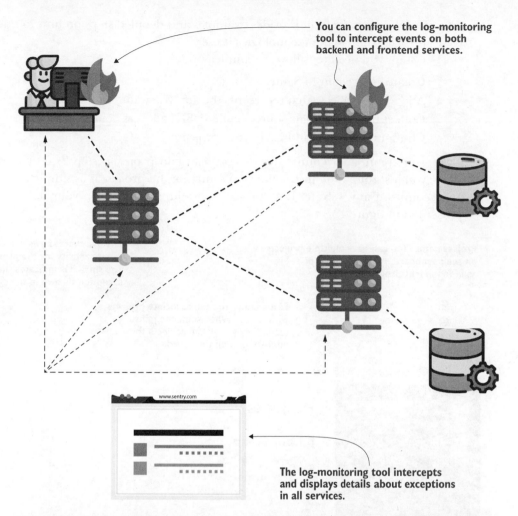

You can configure the log-monitoring tool to intercept events on both backend and frontend services.

The log-monitoring tool intercepts and displays details about exceptions in all services.

Figure 12.7 A log-monitoring tool helps you to easily collect and visualize events throughout the whole system. You can use these details to investigate issues and specific app behavior.

The next code snippet shows you the simple implementation of this app. We want to use Sentry to observe the exceptions caused by this app.

```
@RestController
public class DemoController {

  @GetMapping                          Defines an endpoint you
  public void throwException() {       call using HTTP GET
    throw new RuntimeException("Oh No!");
  }                                    Throw an exception when you
}                                      send a request to the endpoint
```

Integrating an app with Sentry is straightforward. Sentry provides APIs that allow you to integrate apps developed in a large variety of platforms with just a few lines of code.

The official documentation provides examples and detailed steps on how to integrate your app according to the technologies it uses.

The steps you need to follow are simple:

1 Create an account in Sentry.
2 Add a new project (that represents the app you want to monitor).
3 Collect the project data source name (DSN) address Sentry provides.
4 Configure the DSN address in your project.

Once you create an account (step 1), you can add projects (step 2). For these two steps, you just follow the instructions on sentry.io; the process is as simple as creating an account on any website. Each project you add will appear in your dashboard, as presented in figure 12.8.

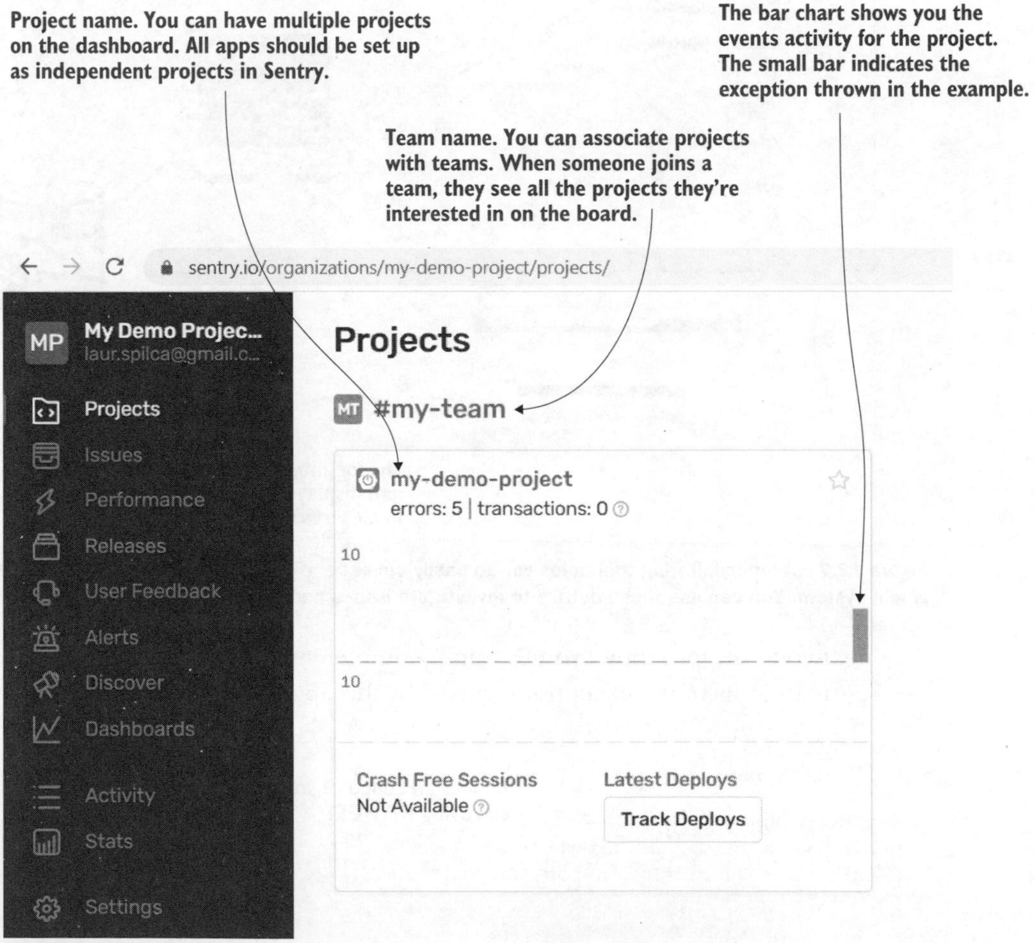

Project name. You can have multiple projects on the dashboard. All apps should be set up as independent projects in Sentry.

The bar chart shows you the events activity for the project. The small bar indicates the exception thrown in the example.

Team name. You can associate projects with teams. When someone joins a team, they see all the projects they're interested in on the board.

sentry.io/organizations/my-demo-project/projects/

MP My Demo Projec...
laur.spilca@gmail.c...

Projects
Issues
Performance
Releases
User Feedback
Alerts
Discover
Dashboards

Activity
Stats

Settings

Projects

MT #my-team

my-demo-project
errors: 5 | transactions: 0 ⓘ

10

10

Crash Free Sessions   Latest Deploys
Not Available ⓘ   **Track Deploys**

Figure 12.8 Sentry independently monitors the logs of each service in your system and displays a short overview of the events for each service in the initial dashboard. Services (named projects) are allocated to teams, and Sentry can be configured to send email notifications for events to the team members.

I created my-demo-project. One or multiple projects can be added to a team. In this case, Sentry created my-team by default when I added the first project. You can rename it if you like and add others if needed. When you have more apps, you can allocate them to teams. Each user can be part of one or multiple teams and can monitor the events of the apps allocated to their teams. Teams in Sentry are a simple way to organize who takes care of what and make developers accountable for monitoring certain services.

Since your app didn't send any events yet to Sentry, your project won't show a bar on the bar chart (as presented in figure 12.8). You first need to tell your app where to send the events. To do this, you need to configure the DSN address that Sentry provides, as shown in figure 12.9. You find the DSN address in the project settings, in the Client Keys section (step 3).

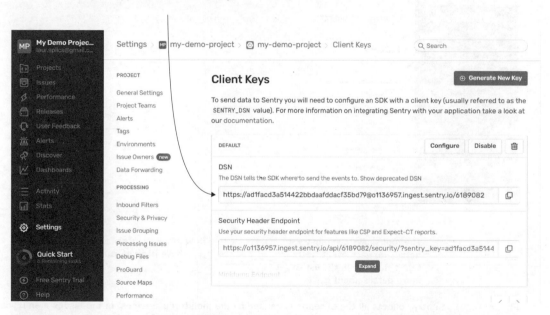

Figure 12.9   In the project settings, in the Client Keys section, you find the DSN value, which is a URL. The application uses this URL to send the events to Sentry.

Depending on the app type, Sentry offers different ways to set up the configuration (step 4). You can find detailed steps on the official page for each platform: https://docs.sentry.io/platforms/.

Because our project uses Spring Boot as a platform, we can just add the DSN value to the property sentry.dsn in the application.properties file. You find this configuration in the next snippet. Although optional in Sentry, I always recommend specifying the name of the environment in which the app runs. This allows you to filter the events later so that you get only the ones you're interested in:

```
sentry.dsn=https://ad1facd3a514422bbdaafddacf…
sentry.environment=production
```

Figure 12.10 shows you how to get details about exception events in your app. Select the Issues menu on the left to access a board where you can browse all the events that Sentry caught from the apps it integrates with. You can filter which apps you want to see events for, which environment, and the period of time in which you're interested.

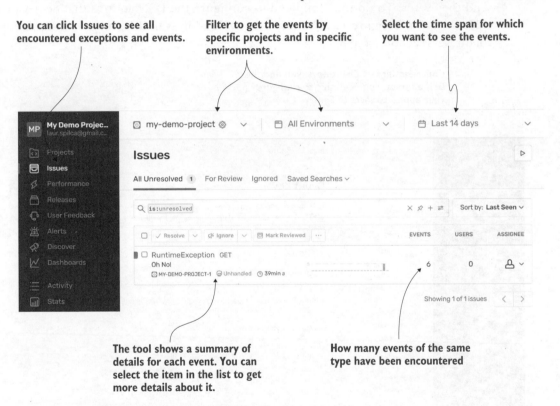

Figure 12.10   Sentry collects all the exceptions caused by the monitored services. In the Issues menu, you can browse a list of these issues. You can filter them based on the time the events happened, the environment, and specific services that cause the events, which helps you to more easily identify an issue.

This board is the key starting point for an investigation. If you use Sentry and need to analyze something happening with a service in the system, first check the events in the issues board. Using Sentry to find exception events is much faster than searching these events in logs, as we discussed in chapter 5.

The first thing you find on the board is a list with short details for each audited event. The exception type, its message, and the number of occurrences are the most important details.

Another essential detail you find about each event is the last time the event was encountered and the first time it appeared. You can use this information to figure out if the problem is a recurrent one, if it happens frequently, or if it's an isolated case. If the event is isolated, you may find that it's caused by a sporadic problem in the environment, but bugs generated by the app logic are recurrent and more frequent. As presented in figure 12.10, all these details are in the main issues board.

If you are interested in more information on a specific event, select the event you need to investigate in the main issues board. Sentry collects the following useful details (figure 12.11):

- The exception stack trace
- Environment details such as the operating system, runtime JVM, and server name
- Client details, in case the exception was caused during an HTTP request
- Information sent on the request, in case the exception happened during an HTTP request

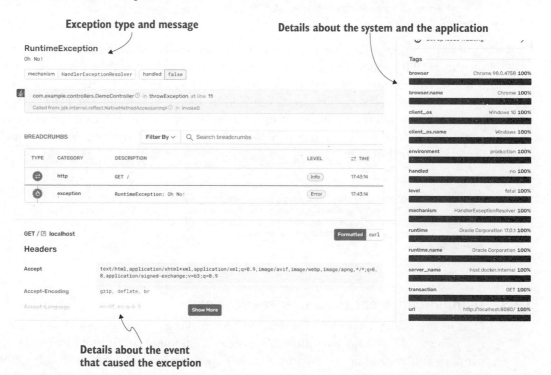

Figure 12.11   Each of the events Sentry collects—the event stack trace, details about the server and client environments, and even details about the request (headers, HTTP method, etc.)—provides information that can help you to identify the problem's root cause.

Using Sentry in team management

Even though Sentry is a tool mainly used in auditing, monitoring, and investigating issues with apps, there is an alternative use for it that I consider quite helpful.

As a development lead, I am both the team lead and the technical lead. Before the COVID-19 pandemic, when we all used to work in the office, close to each other, knowing when someone was struggling with something was much easier for me, and vice versa: it was much easier to throw a ball of paper toward me to get my attention when they needed me. But things changed with remote, online work. One of the things that added delays to the team was simply the difficulty in communication between team members.

Sentry can be configured to send emails for the events it encounters, so I configured it to get emails, even for events coming from local environments, to see what difficulties team members encountered. And since I know my team well, I knew if someone was stuck with a specific problem. In some cases, two or more team members experienced the same problem, but because communication was flawed, they both spent time investigating it.

Using Sentry, I was able to act right away and help someone before they spent too much time trying to investigate an error and was able to plan team tasks more efficiently. I could also stop them from working when I saw they ran over schedule or worked at the same time. Pretty cool, isn't it?

One of the things I find particularly useful is that Sentry automatically collects details on the HTTP request in case the exception happened on a thread serving such a request. You can use this information to replicate the problem in a development environment or try to determine whether any of the data sent through the HTTP request could have caused the exception event. While Sentry doesn't indicate the cause of a problem, it does provide more pieces of the puzzle, helping you to more quickly understand its root cause.

NOTE In many cases today, apps talk to each other over HTTP, and it's very likely that exception events happen as a consequence. Sentry takes the details of the HTTP request and associates them with the event.

12.3   *Using deployment tools in investigations*

One of the things I learned with time and by working on many projects is that environments that host apps are different and evolve. An important lesson I learned is that properly understanding the environment my apps run in can be tremendously helpful when investigating why an app behaves in a specific way. Let's discuss one of the latest ways of deploying service-oriented architectures and how this can be helpful when investigating issues your apps might encounter: *service meshes.*

A service mesh is a way to control how different apps in a system communicate with one another, and they can be extremely helpful from many points of view, including making your apps easier to monitor and to investigate when they have issues. The service mesh tool I use and like the most is Istio (https://istio.io); for more details, I recommend you read *Istio in Action* by Christian E. Posta and Rinor Maloku (Manning, 2022).

I'll provide an overview of how a service mesh works, and then we'll discuss a couple of ways they are helpful when investigating app executions:

- *Fault injection*—A way you can force the app communication to fail to create a specific scenario you need to investigate
- *Mirroring*—A way to replicate events from a production application to investigate them in a testing environment

Figure 12.12 visually shows you three services deployed in a service mesh. Each service is accompanied by an app that intercepts the data that app exchanges with other apps.

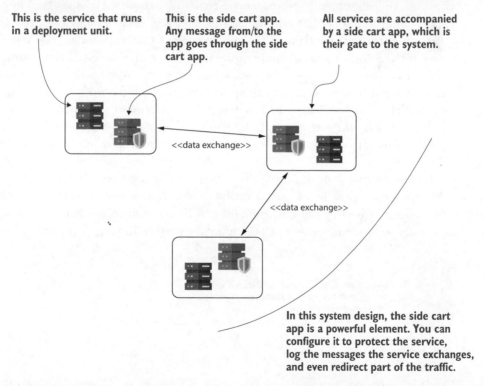

This is the service that runs in a deployment unit.

This is the side cart app. Any message from/to the app goes through the side cart app.

All services are accompanied by a side cart app, which is their gate to the system.

<<data exchange>>

<<data exchange>>

In this system design, the side cart app is a powerful element. You can configure it to protect the service, log the messages the service exchanges, and even redirect part of the traffic.

Figure 12.12 In a service mesh deployment, communication from and to each app is intercepted by a side cart app (a separate application). Since the side cart app intercepts the data exchanged, you can configure it to log details you need and even alter the communication to force the system into scenarios you want to investigate.

Because the side cart app intercepts the communication between the service it's linked to as well as other apps, you can configure it to manage that data in a way that is completely transparent to the service. We'll discuss this further in sections 12.3.1 and 12.3.2.

12.3.1 *Using fault injection to mimic hard-to-replicate issues*

Some of the most challenging scenarios to investigate are the ones that are hard to replicate in your local environment or in an environment where you have more access to debugging or profiling. In my experience, the environment can create some of the most difficult-to-replicate scenarios. Events such as the following can give you terrible headaches and make investigating an app's behavior quite challenging:

- Some faulty device causes network failures.
- Some additional software running where your app is installed makes the whole environment faulty or unstable.

However, there's something important to remember about such issues: your app should expect them to happen. The network is never 100% reliable, and you can't trust the environment completely. If your app fails because of a network spike, your app isn't reliable enough; don't try to sweep the problem under someone else's rug—solve it!

You need to design apps to be robust and expect them to know how to act upon an external event that doesn't allow them to execute a normal flow. But designing a system in such a way is no easy job. As a developer, you should anticipate that, but even if you made great efforts to cover all the bases, problems can still occur. You need to be ready to investigate where these problems come from and implement solutions to solve them.

I've made this point multiple times throughout the book, but it bears repeating here: the best way to investigate a problem is to find a way to replicate it. Although some issues caused by the environment can be difficult to replicate, some scenarios can easily be re-created when you use a service mesh with your deployment.

NOTE The best way to investigate a scenario is to replicate the app's or system's behavior in a test environment first.

One of the easiest and most useful things to do is simulate a faulty communication scenario. In a service-oriented or microservices system, the whole system relies on the way the apps communicate, one with another. For this reason, it is extremely important to be able to test what happens when a certain service in the system can't be accessed. You need to simulate faulty behavior for testing or for investigation purposes.

Since with a service mesh the communication to and from an app is managed by the side cart app, you can configure the side cart app to act abnormally, on purpose, to simulate faulty communication (figure 12.13). This way, you can investigate how the system behaves in such a case.

1. Service A sends requests to service B. You want to investigate what happens if service B takes too long to respond or doesn't respond at all.

2. To simulate this behavior in a development environment, you can configure the side cart app to reject the call or respond to the call more slowly.

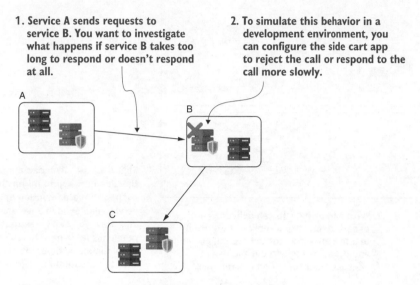

Figure 12.13 **You can use the side cart app of a service mesh to force the system into scenarios you want to investigate. Say you want to replicate a production case in which the communication is often disrupted between two services. You can easily configure a service mesh side cart app to force the execution into such a scenario to allow you to investigate.**

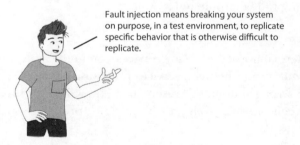

Fault injection means breaking your system on purpose, in a test environment, to replicate specific behavior that is otherwise difficult to replicate.

12.3.2 *Using mirroring to facilitate testing and error detection*

When using service meshes, one technique you can use to replicate a problem in a different environment is mirroring. *Mirroring* is configuring the side cart app to send a copy of the same requests the service sends to a replica of the app it communicates with. This replica may run in a different environment that you use for testing (figure 12.14), which allows you to use the app running in the test environment to debug or profile the communication between services.

1. You investigate a problem in production and suspect that the root cause is somewhere in the communication between services A and B.

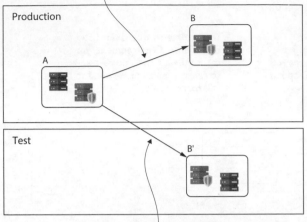

Figure 12.14   **You can configure the side cart app to mirror the events from a production app to a service deployed in development. This way, you can investigate a problem that is hard to replicate in development without interfering with the production environment.**

2. With mirroring, you can deliver a copy of each request to a replica of service B in a test environment to have full access and debug or log without the risk of affecting the production environment.

Mirroring is a really useful investigation tool, but remember that even if your system uses a service mesh for deployment, it's possible you won't be able to use mirroring. In many systems, the data used in the production environment is private and can't simply be copied to a test environment. If your system doesn't allow copying data from production to test, then mirroring will be prohibited as well.

Summary

- Systems today are often composed of many services communicating with one another. Faulty communication between services can cause issues such as bad performance or even wrong output. It's essential to know how to investigate communication between services using tools such as profiling or service meshes.

- You can use JProfiler to intercept the HTTP requests a server app receives and the event duration. You can then use this information to observe whether a given endpoint is called too many times or takes too long to execute, causing stress on the app instance.

- You can use JProfiler to observe the behavior of an app as an HTTP client. You can intercept all the requests an app sends, as well as details such as duration, HTTP response status code, and encountered exceptions. This information can help you to figure out if something is wrong with how the app integrates with other services.

- JProfiler gives you excellent tools to observe low-level communication established by an app by directly investigating the socket events, which allows you to isolate the problem and determine whether the issues are related to either the communication channel or some part of your application.

- With large, service-oriented systems, using a log-monitoring tool is an excellent way to observe issues and put puzzle pieces together faster to find a problem's root cause. A log-monitoring tool is software that collects exceptional events in each app in the system and displays the information you need to understand the problem and where it comes from. Sentry is an excellent tool you can use for system log monitoring.

- In some cases, you can take advantage of tools used to deploy apps. For example, if your service deployments rely on a service mesh, you can use service mesh capabilities to reproduce scenarios you want to investigate. You can configure
  - Fault injection to simulate a service that doesn't work properly and investigate how other services are affected in this case.
  - Mirroring to get a copy of all the requests an app sends to a replica of the receiver service. This replica is installed in a test environment, where you can investigate a scenario using debugging and profiling techniques without affecting the production system.

appendix A
Tools you'll need

In this appendix, you find links to installation instructions for all the recommended tools for the examples discussed in the book.

To open and execute the projects provided with the book, you need to install an IDE. I used IntelliJ IDEA: https://www.jetbrains.com/idea/download/. Alternatively, you can use Eclipse IDE: https://www.eclipse.org/downloads/. Otherwise, you can use Apache Netbeans: https://netbeans.apache.org/download/index.html.

To run the Java projects provided with the book, you need to install JDK version 17 or higher. I recommend using the OpenJDK distribution: https://jdk.java.net/17/.

To discuss profiling techniques and reading heap dumps and thread dumps, we use VisualVM: https://visualvm.github.io/download.html. For some techniques we'll discuss, VisualVM will not be enough. For these we'll use JProfiler: https://www.ej-technologies.com/products/jprofiler/overview.html.

A tool that will help you investigate thread dumps is fastThread, which we use in chapter 9: https://fastthread.io/.

Throughout the book, we'll use Postman to call endpoints to demonstrate investigation techniques: https://www.postman.com/downloads/.

In chapter 12, we discuss monitoring log events with Sentry: https://sentry.io.

appendix B
Opening a project

In this appendix, you find the steps for opening and running an existing project. The projects provided with the book are Java apps that use Java 17. We use these projects to demonstrate the use of several techniques and tools.

First, you need to have an IDE such as IntelliJ IDEA, Eclipse, or Apache Netbeans installed. For the examples, I used IntelliJ IDEA: https://www.jetbrains.com/idea/download/.

To run the projects provided with the book, you need to install JDK version 17 or higher. You can use any Java distribution. I use the OpenJDK distribution: https://jdk.java.net/17/.

Figure B.1 shows you how to open an existing project in IntelliJ IDEA. To select the project you want to open, choose File > Open.

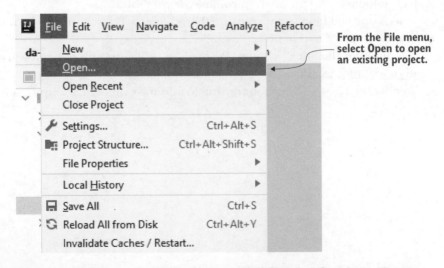

Figure B.1   To open an existing project in IntelliJ IDEA, select Open in the File menu.

Click File > Open, and a pop-up window appears. Select the project you want to open. Figure B.2 shows this pop-up window.

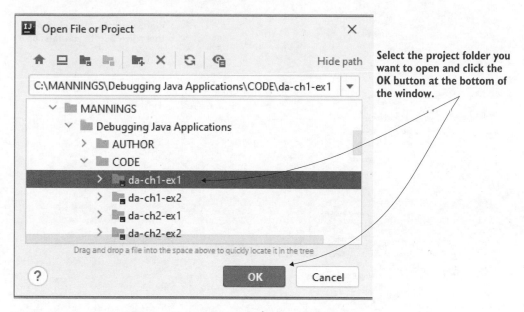

Select the project folder you want to open and click the OK button at the bottom of the window.

Figure B.2   After selecting Open in the File menu, a pop-up window appears. In this window, select the project you want to open from the file system and click the OK button.

To run the application, right-click the class containing the main() method. For the projects provided with the book, the main() method is defined in a class named Main. Right-click this class, as presented in figure B.3, and select Run.

If you want to run the app with a debugger, right-click the Main class > Debug.

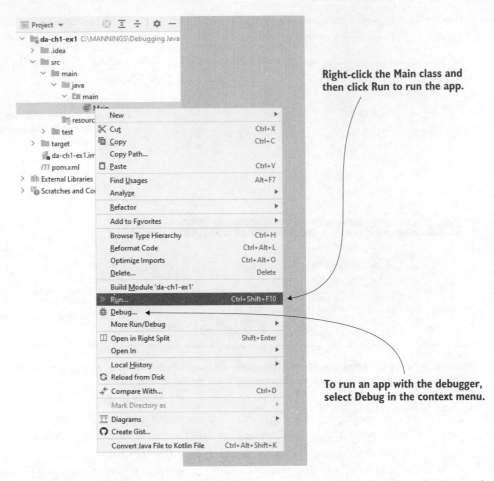

Right-click the Main class and then click Run to run the app.

To run an app with the debugger, select Debug in the context menu.

Figure B.3   Once you open an app, you can run it. To run the app, right-click the `Main` class and select the Run menu item. If you want to run the app with a debugger, click Debug.

appendix C
Recommended
further reading

This appendix recommends some books related to this book's subject that you may find useful and interesting:

- *The Programmer's Brain* by Felienne Hermans (Manning, 2021) explores how a developer's brain works when they investigate code. Reading the code is part of understanding software, and it's something we do before applying investigation techniques. A better understanding of these aspects will also help you with investigating code.

- *Monolith to Microservices* by Sam Newman (O'Reilly Media, 2019) is a recommendation I made in chapter 12 for studying microservices as an architectural style. This book focuses on the difference between a monolithic approach and microservices and where and how to use each of the two architectural styles.

- *Building Microservices: Designing Fine-Grained Systems, Second Edition* (O'Reilly Media, 2021) is another book by Sam Newman that focuses on designing systems composed of fine-grained services. The author analyzes the pros and cons of the presented techniques with clear and detailed examples.

- *Microservices Patterns* by Chris Richardson (Manning, 2018) is one of the books I consider a must-read for anyone working with microservices architectures. The author details, with clear examples, the most essential techniques used in large-scale microservices and service-oriented systems.

- *Five Lines of Code* by Christian Clausen (Manning, 2021) teaches you clean coding practices. Many apps today are unstructured and challenging to understand. I designed many of the code listings you find throughout the examples of the book to be realistic, so they don't always follow clean coding principles. But after you understand how a piece of unclean code works, you should refactor it to make it easier to understand. Developers call this principle the "Boy Scout rule." In many cases, debugging is followed by refactoring to make code easier to understand in the future.

- *Good Code, Bad Code* by Tom Long (Manning, 2021) is an excellent book that teaches high-quality code-writing principles. I also recommend you read this to upskill in refactoring and writing easier-to-understand apps.

- *Software Mistakes and Tradeoffs* by Tomasz Lelek and Jon Skeet (Manning, 2022) discusses, with excellent examples, how to make difficult decisions, make compromises, and optimize decisions in software development.

- *Refactoring: Improving the Design of Existing Code* by Martin Fowler with Kent Beck (Addison-Wesley Professional, 2018) is another must-read for any software developer wanting to improve their skills in designing and building clean and maintainable applications.

appendix D
Understanding
Java threads

In this appendix, we'll discuss the basics of threads in a Java app. A thread is an independent sequential set of instructions your app runs. Operations on a given thread run concurrently with those on other threads. Any Java app today relies on having multiple threads, so it's almost impossible not to get into investigation scenarios where you have to more deeply understand why specific threads don't do what they should or don't easily collaborate with other threads. That's why you'll find threads in several discussions throughout this book (especially chapters 7 to 9, but also here and there in the first half of the book when we discuss debugging). To properly understand these discussions, you need to know some basics about threads. This appendix teaches you those elements that are essential for understanding other discussions we have throughout the book.

We'll start with section D.1, where I'll remind you of the threads' big picture and why we use them in apps. We'll continue in section D.2 with more details on how a thread executes by discussing its life cycle. Knowing the states of a thread's life cycle and the possible transitions is necessary for investigating any thread-related issue. In section D.3, we'll discuss thread synchronization, which is a way to control the executing threads. Faulty synchronization implementations introduce most of the problems you need to investigate and solve. In section D.4, we'll discuss the most common thread-related issues.

Threads are a complex subject, so I'll only focus on the topics you need to know to understand the techniques presented in this book. I can't promise to make you an expert in the subject in only a few pages, so you'll find a few resources I recommend at the end of this appendix.

D.1   *What is a thread?*

In this section, we discuss what threads are and how using multiple threads helps an app. A *thread* is an independent sequence of operations in a running process. Any process can have multiple threads that run concurrently, enabling your app to solve multiple tasks, potentially, in parallel. Threads are an essential component of how a language handles concurrency.

I like to visualize a multithreaded app as a group of sequence timelines as presented in figure D.1. Notice that the app starts with one thread (the main thread). This thread launches other threads, which can start others, and so on. Remember that each thread is independent of the others. For example, the main thread can end its execution long before the app itself. The process stops when all its threads stop.

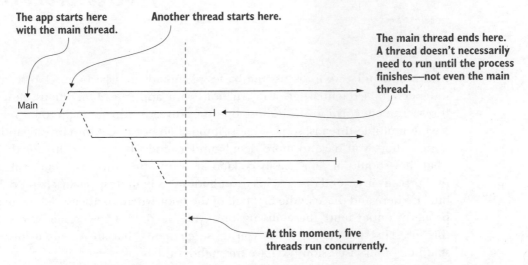

The app starts here with the main thread.

Another thread starts here.

The main thread ends here. A thread doesn't necessarily need to run until the process finishes—not even the main thread.

Main

At this moment, five threads run concurrently.

Figure D.1   A multithreaded app visualized as a group of sequence timelines. Each arrow in the figure represents the timeline of a thread. An app starts with the main thread, which can launch other threads. Some threads run until the process ends, while others stop earlier. At a given time, an app can have one or more threads running in parallel.

Instructions on a given thread are always in a defined order. You always know that A will happen before B if instruction A is before instruction B on the same thread. But since two threads are independent of one another, you can't say the same about two instructions A and B, each on a separate thread. In such a case, either A can execute before B, or vice versa (figure D.2). Sometimes we say that one case is more probable than another, but we can't know how one flow will consistently execute.

In many cases, you'll see thread execution visually represented by tools as sequence timelines. Figure D.3 shows the way VisualVM (a profiler tool we use throughout the book) presents the thread execution as sequence timelines.

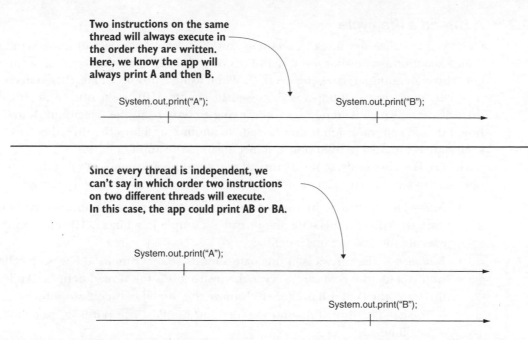

Two instructions on the same thread will always execute in the order they are written. Here, we know the app will always print A and then B.

System.out.print("A");

System.out.print("B");

Since every thread is independent, we can't say in which order two instructions on two different threads will execute. In this case, the app could print AB or BA.

System.out.print("A");

System.out.print("B");

Figure D.2 With two instructions on one thread, we can always know the exact order of execution. But because two threads are independent, if instructions are on different threads, we can't know the order in which they will execute. At most, we can say that one scenario is more likely than another.

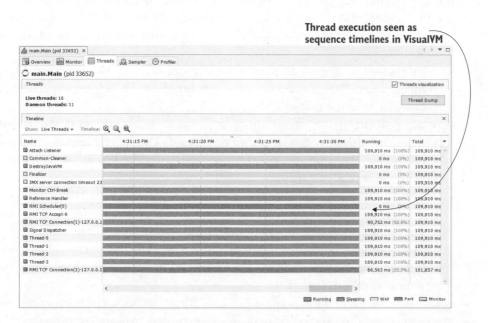

Thread execution seen as sequence timelines in VisualVM

Figure D.3 VisualVM shows thread execution as sequence timelines. This visual representation makes the app's execution easier to understand and helps you to investigate possible problems.

D.2   *A thread's life cycle*

Once you visualize the thread execution, another essential aspect in understanding their execution is knowing the thread life cycle. Throughout its execution, a thread goes through multiple states (figure D.4). When using a profiler (as discussed in chapters 6–9) or a thread dump (as discussed in chapter 10), we'll often refer to the thread's state, which is important when trying to figure out the execution. Knowing how a thread can transition from one state to another and how the thread behaves in each state is essential to following and investigating the app's behavior.

Figure D.4 visually presents the thread states and how a thread can transition from one state to another. We can identify the following main states for a Java thread:

- *New*—The thread is in this state right after its instantiation (before being started). While in this state, the thread is a simple Java object. The app can't yet execute the instructions it defines.
- *Runnable*—The thread is in this state after its start() method has been called. In this state, the JVM can execute the instructions the thread defines. While in this state, the JVM will progressively move the thread between two substates:
  - *Ready*—The thread doesn't execute, but the JVM can put it in execution at any time.
  - *Running*—The thread is in execution. A CPU currently executes instructions it defines.
- *Blocked*—The thread was started, but it was temporarily taken out of the runnable state, so the JVM can't execute its instructions. This state helps us to control the thread execution by allowing us to temporarily "hide" the thread from the JVM so that it can't execute it. While blocked, a thread can be in one of the following substates:
  - *Monitored*—The thread is paused by a monitor of a synchronized block (object controlling the access to a synchronized block) and waits to be released to execute that block.
  - *Waiting*—During the execution, a monitor's wait() method was called, which caused the current thread to be paused. The thread remains blocked until the notify() or notifyAll() methods are called to allow the JVM to release the thread in execution.
  - *Sleeping*—The sleep() method in the Thread class was called, which paused the current thread for a defined time. The time is given as a parameter to the sleep() method. The thread becomes runnable after this time passes.
  - *Parked*—Almost the same as waiting, a thread will show as parked after someone calls the park() method, which blocks the current thread until the unpark() method is called.
- *Dead*—A thread is dead or terminated after it finishes its set of instructions, an Error or Exception halted it, or it was interrupted by another thread. Once dead, a thread cannot be started again.

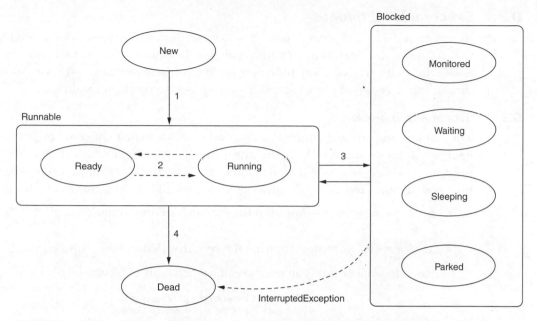

Figure D.4 **A thread life cycle. During its life, a thread goes through multiple states. First, the thread is new, and the JVM cannot run the instructions it defines. After starting the thread, it becomes runnable and starts to be managed by the JVM. The thread can be temporarily blocked during its life, and at the end of its life it goes to a dead state, from which it can't be restarted.**

Figure D.4 also shows the possible transitions between thread states:

- The thread goes from new to runnable once someone calls its start() method.
- Once in the runnable state, the thread oscillates between ready and running. The JVM decides which thread is executed and when.
- Sometimes, the thread gets blocked. It can go into the blocked state in several ways:
  - The sleep() method in the Thread class is called, putting the current thread into a temporary blocked state.
  - Someone called the join() method, causing the current thread to wait for another one.
  - Someone called the wait() method of a monitor, pausing the execution of the current thread until the notify() or notifyAll() methods are called.
  - A monitor of a synchronized block paused the execution of a thread until another active thread finished the execution of the synchronized block.
- The thread can go into a dead (terminated) state either when it finishes its execution or when another thread interrupts it. The JVM considers transitioning from the blocked state to the dead state unacceptable. If a blocked thread is interrupted by another, the transition is signaled with an InterruptedException.

D.3   *Synchronizing threads*

In this section, we'll discuss approaches to synchronizing threads, which developers use to control the threads in a multithreaded architecture. Incorrect synchronization is also the root cause of many problems you'll have to investigate and solve. We'll go through an overview of the most common ways used to synchronize threads.

D.3.1   *Synchronized blocks*

The simplest way to synchronize threads, and usually the first concept any Java developer learns about synchronizing threads is using a synchronized block of code. The purpose is to allow only one thread at a time through the synchronized code—to prohibit concurrent execution for a given piece of code. There are two options for this:

- *Block synchronization*—Applying the synchronized modifier on a given block of code
- *Method synchronization*—Applying the synchronized modifier on a method

The next code snippet shows an example of a synchronized block:

The object between the parentheses is the monitor of the synchronized block.

```
synchronized (a) {
    // do something
}
```

The synchronized block of instructions is defined between the curly braces.

The next code snippet shows you a method synchronization:

Synchronized modifier applied to the method

```
synchronized void m() {
    // do something
}
```

The whole block of code of the method defined between the curly braces is synchronized.

Both ways of using the synchronized keyword work the same, even if they look a bit different. You'll find two important components of each synchronized block:

- *The monitor*—An object managing the execution of the synchronized instructions
- *The block of instructions*—The actual instructions, which are synchronized

The method synchronization seems to be missing the monitor, but for this syntax the monitor is actually implied. For a nonstatic method, the instance "this" will be used as a monitor, while for a static method, the synchronized block will use the class's type instance.

The monitor (which cannot be null) is the object that gives sense to a synchronized block. This object decides whether a thread can enter and execute the synchronized instructions. Technically, the rule is easy: once a thread enters the synchronized block, it acquires a lock on the monitor. No other thread will be accepted in the synchronized block until the one that has the lock releases it. To simplify things, let's assume that a thread releases the lock only when it exits the synchronized block. Figure D.5 shows a visual example. Imagine the two synchronized blocks are in different

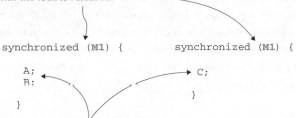

Both synchronized blocks use the same monitor. For this reason, when one thread acquires a lock on M1, no other thread can enter the two synchronized blocks until the lock is released.

```
synchronized (M1) {            synchronized (M1) {

    A;                             → C;
    B;
                                   }
}
```

A, B, and C are common code instructions. None can be executed at the same time because only one thread can be active throughout the two synchronized blocks.

Figure D.5   An example of using synchronized blocks. Multiple synchronized blocks of the app can use the same object instance as a monitor. When this happens, all threads are correlated such that only one active thread executes in all. In this image, if one thread enters the synchronized block, defining instructions A and B, no other thread can enter in the same block or in the one defining instruction C.

parts of the app, but because they both use the same monitor, M1 (the same object instance), a thread can execute in only one of the blocks at a time. None of the instructions, A, B, or C, will be called concurrently (at least not from the presented synchronized blocks).

However, the app may define multiple synchronized blocks. The monitor links multiple synchronized blocks, but when two synchronized blocks use two different monitors (figure D.6), these blocks are not synchronized. In figure D.6, the first and

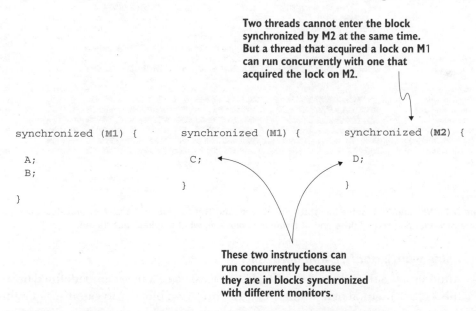

Two threads cannot enter the block synchronized by M2 at the same time. But a thread that acquired a lock on M1 can run concurrently with one that acquired the lock on M2.

```
synchronized (M1) {        synchronized (M1) {          synchronized (M2) {

    A;                         C;  ←             →  D;
    B;
                               }                            }
}
```

These two instructions can run concurrently because they are in blocks synchronized with different monitors.

Figure D.6   When two synchronized blocks don't use the same object instance as the monitor, they are not synchronized. In this case, the second and the third synchronized blocks use different monitors. That means instructions from these two synchronized blocks can execute simultaneously.

the second synchronized blocks are also synchronized with each other since they use the same monitor. But these two blocks aren't synchronized with the third. The result is that instruction D, defined in the third synchronized block, can execute concurrently with any of the instructions of the first two synchronized blocks.

When investigating issues using tools such as a profiler or a thread dump, you need to understand the way in which a thread has been blocked. This information can shed light on what happens, why, or what causes a given thread not to execute. Figure D.7 shows how VisualVM (the profiler we use in chapters 7–9) shows that the monitor of a synchronized block blocked a thread.

In this example, VisualVM shows certain threads that are blocked by a monitor of a synchronized block of code. When investigating an app's behavior, knowing what this state means helps you to understand what executes and may reveal certain problems.

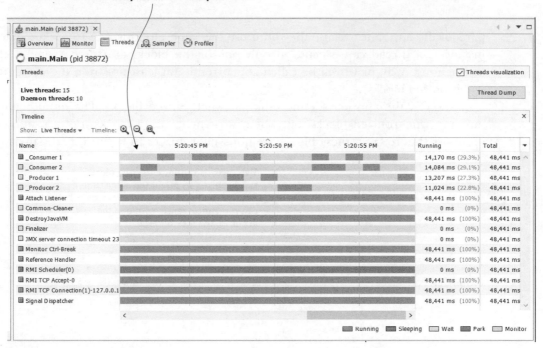

Figure D.7   VisualVM indicates the state of a thread. The Threads tab in the profiler provides a complete picture of what each thread does and, if a thread is blocked, what blocked that thread.

D.3.2   Using wait(), notify(), and notifyAll()

Another way a thread can be blocked is if it is asked to wait for an undefined time. Using the wait() method of a monitor of a synchronized block, you can instruct a thread to wait indefinitely. Some other thread can then "tell" the one that's waiting to continue its work. You can do this with the notify() or notifyAll() methods of the monitor. These methods are often used to improve an app's performance by preventing a thread from executing if it doesn't make sense to execute. At the same time, the wrong use of these methods can lead to deadlocks or situations where threads wait indefinitely without ever being released to execution.

Remember that `wait()`, `notify()`, and `notifyAll()` make sense only when they are used in a synchronized block. These methods are behaviors of the synchronized block's monitor, so you can't use them without having a monitor. With the `wait()` method, the monitor blocks a thread for an undefined time. When blocking the thread, it also releases the lock it acquired so that other threads can enter blocks synchronized by that monitor. When the `notify()` method is called, the thread can again be executed. Figure D.8 summarizes the `wait()` and `notify()` methods.

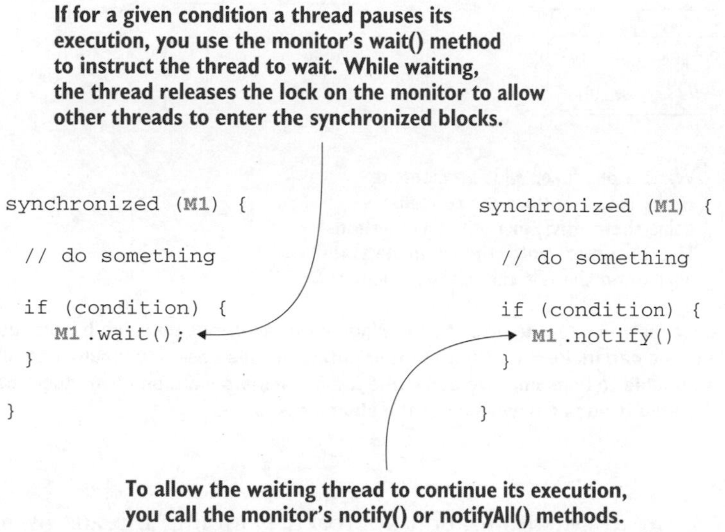

If for a given condition a thread pauses its execution, you use the monitor's wait() method to instruct the thread to wait. While waiting, the thread releases the lock on the monitor to allow other threads to enter the synchronized blocks.

```
synchronized (M1) {

  // do something

  if (condition) {
    M1 .wait();
  }

}
```

```
synchronized (M1) {

  // do something

  if (condition) {
    M1 .notify()
  }

}
```

To allow the waiting thread to continue its execution, you call the monitor's notify() or notifyAll() methods.

Figure D.8   In some cases, a thread should pause from executing and wait for something to happen. To make a thread wait, the monitor of a synchronized block can call its `wait()` behavior. When the thread becomes executable again, the monitor can call the `notify()` or `notifyAll()` methods.

Figure D.9 shows a more particular scenario. In chapter 7, we used an example of an app implementing a producer-consumer approach, in which multiple threads share a resource. The producer threads add values to the shared resource, and the consumer threads consume those values. But what happens if the shared resource no longer has value? The consumers would not benefit from executing at this time. Technically, they can still execute, but they have no value to consume, so allowing the JVM to execute them would cause unneeded resource consumption on the system. A better approach would be to "tell" the consumers to wait when the shared resource has no value and to continue their execution only after a producer added a new value.

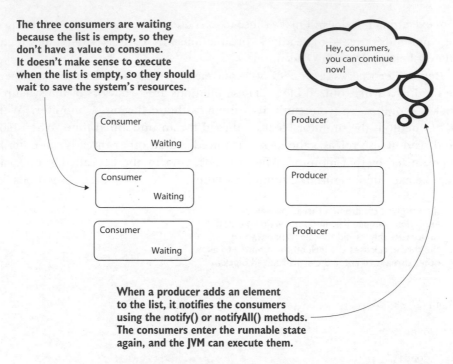

The three consumers are waiting because the list is empty, so they don't have a value to consume. It doesn't make sense to execute when the list is empty, so they should wait to save the system's resources.

Hey, consumers, you can continue now!

When a producer adds an element to the list, it notifies the consumers using the notify() or notifyAll() methods. The consumers enter the runnable state again, and the JVM can execute them.

Figure D.9   A use case for `wait()` **and** `notify()`. **When a thread brings no value by executing in the current conditions, we can make it wait until further notice. In this case, a consumer should not execute when it has no value to consume. We can make the consumers wait, and a producer can tell them to continue only after it adds a new value to the shared resource.**

D.3.3   Joining threads

A quite common thread synchronization approach is joining threads by making a thread wait until another has finished its execution. What's different from the wait/notify pattern is that the thread doesn't wait to be notified. The thread simply waits for the other to finish its execution. Figure D.10 shows a scenario that could benefit from this synchronization technique.

Suppose you have to implement some data processing based on data retrieved from two different independent sources. Usually, retrieving the data from the first data source takes about 5 seconds, and getting the data from the second data source takes about 8 seconds. If you execute the operations sequentially, the time needed to get all the data for processing is 5 + 8 = 13 seconds. But you know a better approach. Since the data sources are two independent databases, you can get the data from both at the same time if you use two threads. But then you need to make sure the thread that processes the data waits for both threads that retrieve data to finish before it can start. To achieve this, you make the processing thread join the threads that retrieve the data (figure D.10).

Joining threads is, in many cases, a necessary synchronization technique. But when not used well, it can also cause problems. For example, if one thread is waiting for another, is stuck, or never ends, the one joining it will never execute.

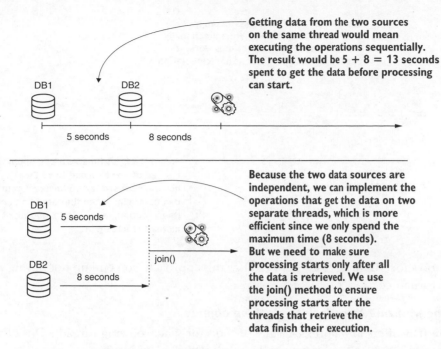

Getting data from the two sources on the same thread would mean executing the operations sequentially. The result would be 5 + 8 = 13 seconds spent to get the data before processing can start.

Because the two data sources are independent, we can implement the operations that get the data on two separate threads, which is more efficient since we only spend the maximum time (8 seconds). But we need to make sure processing starts only after all the data is retrieved. We use the join() method to ensure processing starts after the threads that retrieve the data finish their execution.

Figure D.10   In some cases, you can improve the app's performance using multiple threads. But you need to make some threads wait for others since they depend on the execution result of those threads. You can make a thread wait for another using a join operation.

D.3.4   *Blocking threads for a defined time*

Sometimes a thread needs to wait for a given amount of time. In this case, the thread is in a "timed waiting" state or "sleeping." The following operations are the most common to cause a thread to be timed waiting:

- sleep()—You can always use the static sleep() method in the class Thread to make the thread currently executing the code wait for a fixed amount of time.

- wait(long timeout)—The wait method with a timeout parameter can be used the same as the wait() method without any parameters, as discussed in section D.3.2. However, if you provide a parameter, the thread will wait the given time if not notified earlier.

- join(long timeout)—This operation works the same as the join() method we discussed in section D.3.3, but waits for the maximum timeout, which is given as a parameter.

A common antipattern I often find in apps is the use of sleep() to make a thread wait instead of the wait() method we discussed in chapter 4. Take the producer-consumer architecture we discussed as an example. You could use sleep() instead of wait(), but how long should a consumer sleep to ensure the producer has time to run and add values to the shared resource? We don't have an answer to this question. For example, making the thread sleep for 100 milliseconds (as shown in figure D.11) can be too long

Sometimes timed waiting is wrongly
used instead of waiting. While functionally
this approach might sometimes work, it
usually is a less performant implementation.

```
synchronized (M1) {

 // do something

 if (condition) {
    Thread.sleep(100);
 }

}
```

Figure D.11 A timed waiting approach
instead of wait() and notify() is usually
not the best strategy. Whenever your code
can determine when the thread can continue
its execution, use wait() and notify()
instead of sleep().

or too short. In most cases, if you follow this approach, you end up not having the best performance.

D.3.5   *Synchronizing threads with blocking objects*

The JDK offers an impressive suite of tools for synchronizing threads. Out of these, a few of the best-known classes used in multithreaded architectures are

- Semaphore—An object you can use to limit the number of threads that can execute a given block of code
- CyclicBarrier—An object you can use to make sure at least a given number of threads are active to execute a given block of code
- Lock—An object that provides more extensive synchronization options
- Latch—An object you can use to make some threads wait until certain logic in other threads is performed

These objects are higher-level implementations, each deploying a defined mechanism to simplify the implementation in certain scenarios. In most cases, these objects cause trouble because of the improper way they are used, and in many cases, developers overengineer the code with them. My advice is to use the simplest solution you can find to solve a problem and, before using any of these objects, make sure you properly understand how they work.

D.4   *Common issues in multithreaded architectures*

When investigating multithreaded architectures, you'll identify common problems, which are root causes of various unexpected behavior (be it an unexpected output or a performance problem). Understanding these problems up front will help you to more quickly identify where a problem comes from and fix it. These issues are as follows:

- *Race conditions*—Two or more threads compete for modifying a shared resource.
- *Deadlocks*—Two or more threads stick while waiting for each other.

- *Livelocks*—Two or more threads fail to meet the conditions to stop and continuously run without executing any useful work.
- *Starvation*—A thread is continuously blocked while the JVM executes other threads. The thread never gets to execute the instructions it defines.

D.4.1 Race conditions

Race conditions happen when multiple threads try to change the same resource concurrently. When this happens, we can encounter either unexpected results or exceptions. Generally, we use synchronization techniques to avoid these situations. Figure D.12 visually shows such a case. Threads T1 and T2 simultaneously attempt to change the value of variable x. Thread T1 tries to increment the value, while thread T2 tries to decrement it. This scenario may result in different outputs for repeated executions of the app. The following scenarios are possible:

- *After the operations execute, x may be 5*—If T1 changed the value first, and T2 read the already changed value of the variable, or the other way around, the variable will still have a value of 5.
- *After the operations execute, x may be 4*—If both threads read the value of x at the same time, but T2 wrote the value last, x will be (the value T2 read, 5, minus 1).
- *After the operations execute, x may be 6*—If both threads read the value of x at the same time, but T1 wrote the value last, x will be 6 (the value T1 read, 5, plus 1).

Such situations usually lead to unexpected output. With a multithreaded architecture where multiple execution flows are possible, such scenarios can be challenging to reproduce. Sometimes, they happen only in specific environments, which makes investigations difficult.

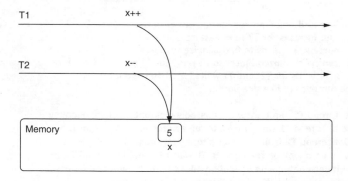

Figure D.12 A race condition. Multiple threads concurrently try to change a shared resource. In this example, threads T1 and T2 try to change the value of variable *x* simultaneously, which can result in different outputs.

D.4.2 Deadlocks

Deadlocks are situations in which two or more threads pause and then wait for something from each other to continue their execution (figure D.13). Deadlocks cause an app, or at least part of it, to freeze, preventing certain capabilities from running.

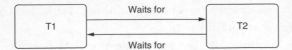

Figure D.13   Example of a deadlock. In a case in which T1 waits for T2 to continue the execution and T2 waits for T1, the threads are in a deadlock. Neither can continue because they are waiting for the other.

Figure D.14 illustrates the way a deadlock can occur with code. In this example, one thread acquired a lock on resource A, and another, on resource B. But each thread also needs the resource acquired by the other thread to continue its execution. Thread T1 waits for thread T2 to release resource A, but at the same time, thread T2 waits for T1 to release resource B. Neither of the threads can continue since both wait for the other to release the resources they need, resulting in a deadlock.

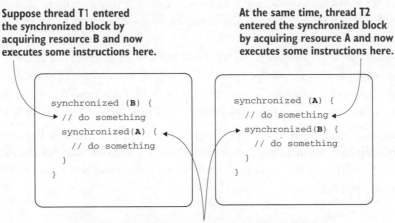

Figure D.14   A deadlock. Thread T1 can't enter the nested synchronized block because T2 has a lock on resource A. Thread T1 waits for T2 to release resource A so that it can continue its execution. But thread T2 is in a similar situation: it cannot continue its execution because T1 acquired a lock on resource B. Thread T2 waits for thread T1 to release resource B so that it can continue its execution. Since both threads wait for each other and neither can continue its execution, the threads are in a deadlock.

The example presented in figure D.14 is simple, but it's just a didactic one. A real-world scenario is usually much more difficult to investigate and understand and can involve more than two threads. Beware that synchronized blocks are not the only way threads can get stuck in a deadlock. The best way to understand such scenarios is using the investigation techniques you learned in chapters 7 to 9.

D.4.3 Livelocks

Livelocks are more or less the opposite of deadlocks. When threads are in a livelock, the condition always changes in such a way that the threads continue their execution even though they should stop on a given condition. The threads can't stop, and they continuously run, usually consuming the system's resources without reason. Livelocks can cause performance issues in an app's execution.

Figure D.15 demonstrates a livelock with a sequence diagram. Two threads, T1 and T2, run in a loop. To stop its execution, T1 makes a condition true before its last iteration. The next time T1 comes back to the condition, it expects it to be true and to stop. However, this doesn't happen since another thread, T2, changed it back to false. T2 finds itself in the same situation. Each thread changes the condition so that it can stop, but at the same time, each change in the condition causes the other thread to continue running.

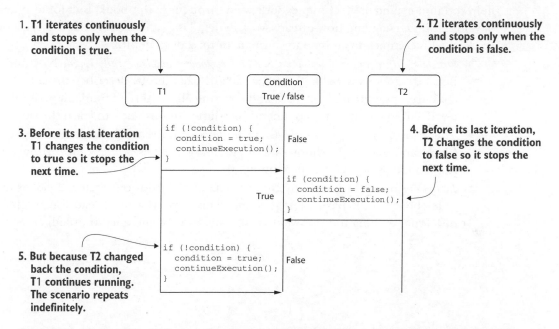

Figure D.15 An example of a livelock. Two threads rely on a condition to stop their execution. But when changing the value of the condition so that they can stop, each thread causes the other to continue running. The threads cannot stop, and thus unnecessarily spend the system's resources.

Just as with the deadlock example in chapter 4 (section 4.4.2), remember this is a simplified scenario. Livelocks can be caused by more complex scenarios in the real world, and more than two threads can be involved. Chapters 7 to 9 address several ways you can approach the investigation of such scenarios.

D.4.4   *Starvation*

Another common problem, although less likely to occur in today's apps, is starvation. Starvation is caused by a certain thread being constantly excluded from the execution even if it is runnable. The thread wants to execute its instructions, but the JVM continuously allows other threads to access the system's resources. Because the thread cannot access the system's resources and execute its defined set of instructions, we say that it is starving.

In the early JVM versions, such situations occurred when the developer set a much lower priority to a given thread. Today, the JVM implementations are much smarter in treating these cases, so (at least in my experience) starvation scenarios are less likely.

D.5   *Further reading*

Threads are complex, and in this appendix we discussed the essential topics that will help you understand the techniques addressed throughout this book. But, for any Java developer, understanding how threads work in detail is a valuable skill. Here is a list of resources I recommend you read to learn about threads in depth:

- *Oracle Certified Professional Java SE 11 Developer Complete Study Guide* by Jeanne Boyarsky and Scott Selikoff (Sybex, 2020). Chapter 18 describes threads and concurrency, starting from zero and covering all the thread fundamentals OCP certification requires. I recommend you start with this book to learn threads.
- The second edition of *The Well-Grounded Java Developer* by Benjamin Evans, Jason Clark, and Martijn Verburg (Manning, 2022) teaches concurrency, from the fundamentals to performance tuning.
- *Java Concurrency in Practice* by Brian Goetz et al. (Addison-Wesley, 2006) is an older book, but it hasn't lost its value. This book is a must-read for any Java developer wanting to improve their threads and concurrency knowledge.

appendix E
Memory management
in Java apps

In this appendix, we discuss how the Java Virtual Machine (JVM) manages the memory of a Java app. Some of the most challenging problems you'll have to investigate in Java apps are related to the way the apps manage memory. Fortunately, we can use several techniques to analyze such problems and find their root causes, with minimal time invested. But to benefit from those techniques, you first need to know at least some basics about how a Java app manages its memory.

An app's memory is a limited resource. Even if today's systems can offer a large amount of memory for an app to use during its execution, we still need to be careful with how an app spends this resource. No system can offer unlimited memory as a magical solution (figure E.1). Memory issues lead to performance problems (the app becomes slow, it's more costly to deploy, it starts more slowly, etc.) and sometimes can even bring the entire process to a complete stop (e.g., in the case of an OutOfMemoryError).

We'll cover the essential aspects of memory management. In section E.1, we'll discuss how the JVM organizes the memory for an executing process. You'll learn about three ways of allocating the app's memory: the stack, the heap, and the metaspace. In section E.2, we'll discuss the stack, the memory space a thread uses to store locally declared variables and their data. Section E.3 discusses the heap and the way an app stores object instances in memory. We'll end our discussion in section E.4 with the metaspace, a memory location where an app stores the object types' metadata.

Be aware that a Java app's memory management is complex. In this appendix, I'll present only the details you need to understand the discussions you'll find throughout the book.

Figure E.1 An app's memory is a limited resource. There's no magical solution that allows us to allocate infinite memory to an app. When building apps, we need to treat memory consumption with consideration and avoid spending it for no reason. Apps may sometimes have memory issues. If a certain capability uses too much memory, it can cause performance problems or even a complete failure. You need to be ready to find the causes of such issues and solve them properly.

E.1   *How the JVM organizes an app's memory*

In this section, we'll discuss how the JVM organizes data in different memory locations, which are each managed differently. Understanding how the JVM manages memory is essential for investigating issues related to memory. We'll use some visuals to discuss the main aspects related to memory management, and you'll learn which data goes where in a Java app's memory. Then, we'll detail the memory management in each memory location.

For the moment (to simplify the discussion), let's assume that a Java app has two ways to manage the data it stores during its execution: the stack and the heap. Depending on how the data is defined, the app will manage it in either the stack or the heap. But before discussing which data goes where, remember one essential detail: an app has more than one thread, allowing it to concurrently process data. The heap is a singular memory location, and all the app's threads use it. However, each thread has its own memory location, called a *stack*. This can create confusion when developers first learn about memory management. Figure E.2 presents these details visually.

The stack is a memory location owned by a thread. Each thread owns a particular stack that is not shared with other threads. The thread stores any data locally declared in a block of code and executed by that thread in this memory location. Say you have a method like the one presented in the next code snippet. The parameters x and y

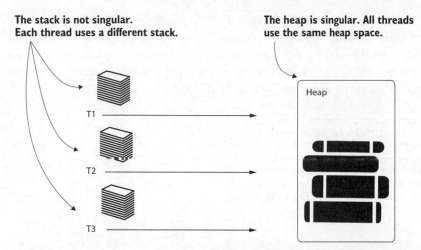

The stack is not singular. Each thread uses a different stack.

The heap is singular. All threads use the same heap space.

Heap

T1

T2

T3

Figure E.2 T1, T2, and T3 are all threads of a Java app. All these threads use the same heap. The heap is a memory location where the app stores object instances' data. However, each thread uses its own memory location, called a stack, to store data locally declared.

and the variable sum, declared inside the method's code block, are local variables. These values will be stored in the thread's stack when the method executes:

```
public int sum(int x, int y) {      Variables x, y, and sum will
    int sum = x + y;                be stored in the stack.
    return sum;
}
```

The heap is a memory location where the app stores object instances' data. Suppose your app declares a class, Cat, such as the one shown in the next code snippet. Any time you create an instance using the class's constructor, new Cat(), the instance goes to the heap:

```
public class Cat {
}
```

If the class declares instance attributes, the JVM stores these values in the heap too. For example, if the Cat class looks like the one in the next code snippet, the JVM will store the name and age of each instance in the heap:

```
public class Cat {

    private String name;      The object's attributes
    private int age;          are stored in the heap.

}
```

Figure E.3 visually presents an example of data allocation. Notice that the locally declared variables and their values (x and c) are stored in the thread's stack, while the Cat instance and its data go in the app's heap. A reference to the Cat instance will be stored in the thread's stack in variable c. Even the method's parameter that stores a reference to a String array will be part of the stack.

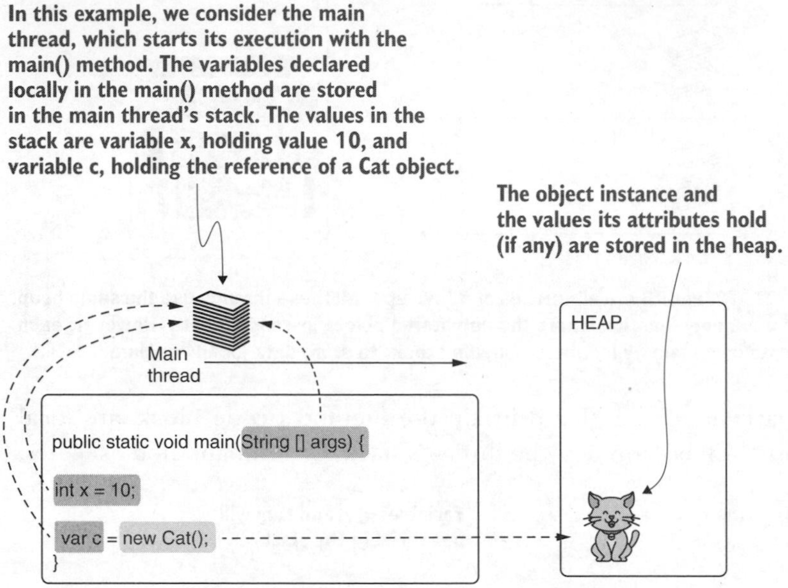

In this example, we consider the main thread, which starts its execution with the main() method. The variables declared locally in the main() method are stored in the main thread's stack. The values in the stack are variable x, holding value 10, and variable c, holding the reference of a Cat object.

The object instance and the values its attributes hold (if any) are stored in the heap.

Main thread

HEAP

```
public static void main(String [] args) {

int x = 10;

var c = new Cat();
}
```

Figure E.3   The app reserves the locally declared variables in the thread's stack and the data defining an object instance in the heap. A variable in one thread's stack may refer to an object in the heap. In this example, variable x, holding value 10, and variable c, holding the reference to the Cat instance, are part of the thread's stack.

E.2   *The stack used by threads to store local data*

In this section, we'll analyze the mechanics behind the stack in more depth. In section E.1, you learned that local values are stored in a stack and that each thread has its own stack location. Let's find out now how these values are stored and when the app removes them from memory. We'll use visuals to describe this process step by step with a short code example. Once we clarify the mechanics behind the stack's memory management, we'll discuss what could go wrong and cause problems related to it.

First, why is this memory location called "a stack"? A thread's stack uses the principles of a stack data structure. A *stack* is an ordered collection in which you can always remove the most recently added element. We usually visualize such a collection as a stack of layers, where each layer is stored above another. You can only add a new layer on top of all the existing ones, and you can only remove the top layer. This method of adding and removing elements is also called *last in, first out* (LIFO). Figure E.4 demonstrates how a stack works with a series of add-and-remove steps. To make the example simpler, numbers are the values in the stack.

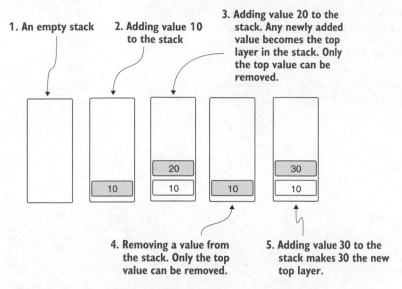

1. An empty stack

2. Adding value 10 to the stack

3. Adding value 20 to the stack. Any newly added value becomes the top layer in the stack. Only the top value can be removed.

4. Removing a value from the stack. Only the top value can be removed.

5. Adding value 30 to the stack makes 30 the new top layer.

Figure E.4 Adding and removing values from a stack. The stack is an ordered collection working on the LIFO principle. When you add a value to the stack it becomes the top layer—the only one you can remove.

You will recognize the same behavior in how the app manages the data in a thread's stack. Whenever the execution reaches the start of a code block, it creates a new layer in the thread stack. Following a common stack principle, any new layer becomes the top layer and is the first to be removed. In figures E.5, E.6, E.7, and E.8, we follow the execution of a simple code snippet step by step to observe how the thread's stack changes:

```
public static void main(String [] args) {
   int x = 10;
   a();
   b();
}

public static void a() {
   int y = 20;
}

public static void b() {
   int y = 30;
}
```

The execution starts with the main() method (figure E.5). When the execution reaches the start of the main() method, the first layer is added to the thread's stack. This layer is a memory location where every local value declared in the code block is stored. In this case, the code block declares a variable, x, and initializes the variable

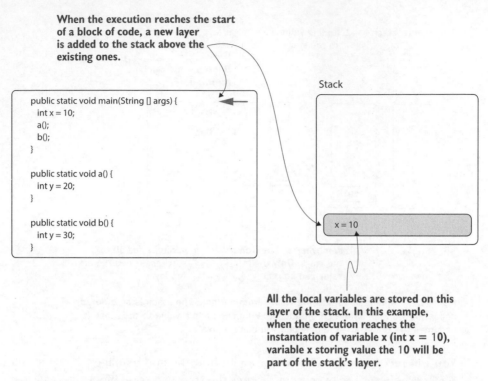

When the execution reaches the start of a block of code, a new layer is added to the stack above the existing ones.

Stack

```
public static void main(String [] args) {
  int x = 10;
  a();
  b();
}

public static void a() {
  int y = 20;
}

public static void b() {
  int y = 30;
}
```

x = 10

All the local variables are stored on this layer of the stack. In this example, when the execution reaches the instantiation of variable x (int x = 10), variable x storing value the 10 will be part of the stack's layer.

Figure E.5   When the execution reaches the start of a block of code, a new layer is created in the thread's stack. All the variables the block of code defines are stored in this new layer. The layer is removed when the block of code ends. This way, we know that the values in this part of the memory are released when they're no longer needed.

with the value 10. This variable will be stored in this newly created layer of the thread's stack. This layer will be removed from the stack when the method ends its execution.

A code block can call other code blocks. For example, in this case, method main() calls methods a() and b(), which work similarly. When the execution reaches the start of their blocks of code, a new layer is added to the stack. That new layer is the memory location where all the data that is declared local is stored. Figure E.6 shows what happens when the execution reaches method a().

When method a() ends its execution and returns to main(), the layer reserved in the thread's stack is also removed (figure E.7)—meaning the data it stored is no longer in the memory. This way, the memory that is not needed is deallocated to allow space for new data to be stored. A code block ends when the execution reaches its last instruction, gives a return instruction, or throws an exception. Notice that when a code block ends, its layer is always the top one in the stack, fulfilling the LIFO principle.

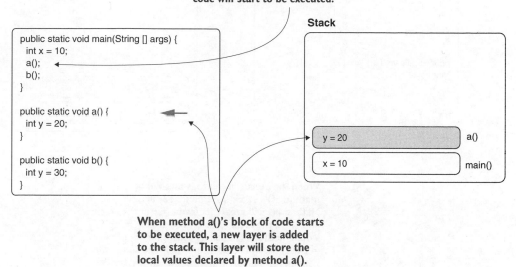

When the execution reaches the call to method a(), that block of code will start to be executed.

When method a()'s block of code starts to be executed, a new layer is added to the stack. This layer will store the local values declared by method a().

Figure E.6   Another block of code can be called from one in execution. In this case, method `main()` calls method `a()`. Since `main()` didn't finish, its layer is still part of the stack. Method `a()` creates its own layer where the local values it defines are stored.

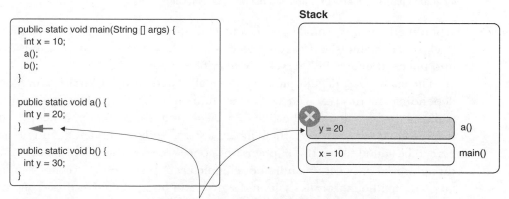

When the execution reaches the end of a block of code (or if the method returns or throws an exception), the layer in the stack and all of its content are removed.

Figure E.7   When the execution reaches the end of a block of code, the stack layer opened for that block is removed with all the data it contains. In this case, when method `a()` returns, its stack layer is removed. This way, we make sure the unneeded data is removed from the memory.

Method `main()` continues its execution by calling method `b()`. Just like method `a()` did, method `b()` reserves a new layer in the stack to store the local data it declares (figure E.8).

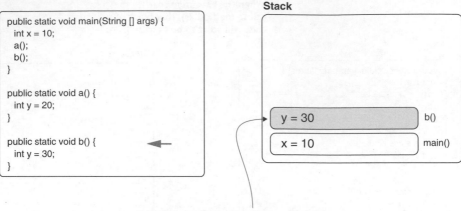

```
public static void main(String [] args) {
  int x = 10;
  a();
  b();
}

public static void a() {
  int y = 20;
}

public static void b() {
  int y = 30;
}
```

Stack

| y = 30 | b() |
| x = 10 | main() |

When the execution reaches method b(),
method a()'s stack layer no longer exists.
Method b() will create its own layer in the stack
and store the local values it declares in it.
When method b() ends its execution, its layer
in the stack will also be removed. The same will
happen for main(). In the end, when the thread
ends its execution, the stack will be empty.

Figure E.8   Just like with method a(), when method b() is called and the execution reaches the start of its block of code, a new layer is added to the stack. The method can use this layer to store local data until the method returns and the layer is removed.

When method main() finally reaches its end, the thread ends its execution, and the stack remains empty and is completely removed. At the same time, the thread goes into the dead state of its life cycle, as described in appendix D.

The stack has a default memory space allocated. You can find the precise values depending on the JVM you use here: http://mng.bz/JVYp. This limit can also be adjusted, but you wouldn't be able to make it infinite. A common issue with the stack is the StackOverflowError, which means a stack is filled completely, and no more layers can be added. When this happens, the code throws a StackOverflowError, and the thread whose stack became full stops completely. A recursion (or recursive implementation), a method that calls itself until a given condition is filled, with a wrong stop condition usually causes such a problem. If this condition is missing or allows the method to call itself too many times, the stack may get filled with the layers the method creates every time it begins its execution. Figure E.9 visually presents the stack created by an infinite recursion caused by two methods that call one another.

Since each thread has its own stack, a StackOverflowError affects only the thread whose stack becomes full. The process can continue its execution, and other threads will not be affected. Also, a StackOverflowError produces a stack trace, which you can use to identify the code that caused the problem. Figure E.10 shows an example of what this type of stack trace looks like. You can use project da-app-e-ex1 provided with the book to replicate this stack trace.

Because the beginning of any new block of code execution creates a new layer in the stack, any uncontrolled recursion can cause a stack overflow: the stack fills and the app cannot allocate more layers to store the local values. In this example, method a() calls method b() and method b() calls method a(), without any condition for this cycle to stop at some point.

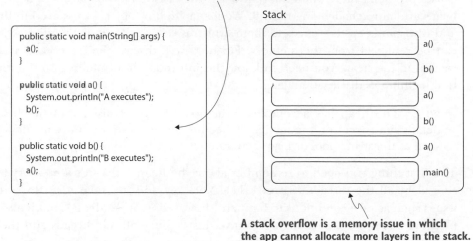

```
public static void main(String[] args) {
  a();
}

public static void a() {
  System.out.println("A executes");
  b();
}

public static void b() {
  System.out.println("B executes");
  a();
}
```

Stack

a()
b()
a()
b()
a()
main()

A stack overflow is a memory issue in which the app cannot allocate more layers in the stack.

Figure E.9   Every new execution of a method creates a new layer in the stack. In case of a recursion, a method may fill the stack if it's called too many times. When the stack gets full, the app throws a `StackOverflowError`, and the current thread stops.

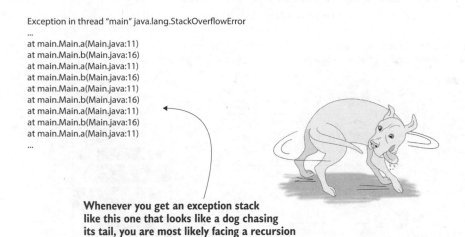

```
Exception in thread "main" java.lang.StackOverflowError
...
at main.Main.a(Main.java:11)
at main.Main.b(Main.java:16)
at main.Main.a(Main.java:11)
at main.Main.b(Main.java:16)
at main.Main.a(Main.java:11)
at main.Main.b(Main.java:16)
at main.Main.a(Main.java:11)
at main.Main.b(Main.java:16)
at main.Main.a(Main.java:11)
...
```

Whenever you get an exception stack like this one that looks like a dog chasing its tail, you are most likely facing a recursion with a wrong condition.

Figure E.10   The stack trace caused by a `StackOverflowError`. Usually, a `StackOverflowError` is easy to identify. The stack trace shows a method calling itself repeatedly or a group of methods that call each other, as in this example. You can go directly to these methods to figure out how they started infinitely calling each other.

E.3   *The heap the app uses to store object instances*

In this section, we'll discuss the heap: a memory location shared by all threads of a Java app. The heap stores object instance data. As you'll see in this section, the heap causes problems more often than the stack does. Also, the root causes of heap-related issues are more challenging to find. We'll analyze how objects are stored in the heap and who can keep references to them, which is relevant to understanding when they can be removed from the memory. Further, we'll discuss the main causes of issues related to the heap. You need to know this information to understand the investigation techniques discussed in chapters 7 to 9.

> **NOTE**   The heap has a complex structure. We won't discuss all the heap details since you won't immediately need them. We also won't discuss details such as the string pool or heap generations.

The first thing you need to remember about the heap is that it's a memory location shared by all the threads (figure E.11). Not only does this allow for thread-related issues such as race conditions to happen (discussed in appendix D), but it also makes memory issues more challenging to investigate. Since all the threads add the object instances they create in the same memory location, one thread may impact the execution of others. If one thread suffers from a memory leak (which means it adds instances in the memory but never removes them), it affects the whole process because other threads will also suffer from the lack of memory.

In most cases, when an `OutOfMemoryError` occurs, as shown in figure E.11, the situation is signaled by a different thread than the one affected by the root cause of the

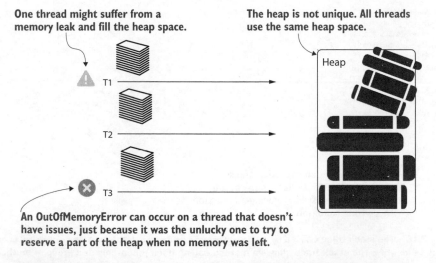

One thread might suffer from a memory leak and fill the heap space.

The heap is not unique. All threads use the same heap space.

Heap

T1

T2

T3

An OutOfMemoryError can occur on a thread that doesn't have issues, just because it was the unlucky one to try to reserve a part of the heap when no memory was left.

Figure E.11   All threads use the same heap location. If one of the threads has an issue that causes the heap to become full (memory leak), another thread may signal the problem. This scenario happens quite often because the problem will be reported by the first thread unable to store data in the heap. Because any thread can signal the problem and it's not necessarily the one causing the problem, heap-related issues are more challenging to solve.

problem (the memory leak). The OutOfMemoryError is signaled by the first thread that tries to add something in the memory but cannot because there is no more free space.

The garbage collector (GC) is the mechanism that frees the heap by removing unneeded data. The GC knows that an object instance is no longer needed when nothing references it. Thus, if an object isn't needed but the app fails to remove all the references, the GC won't remove that object. When an app continually fails to remove references to newly created objects until at some point they fill the memory (causing an OutOfMemoryError), we say that the app has a memory leak.

An object instance may be referred to from another object in a heap (figure E.12). A common example of a memory leak is a collection in which we continuously add object references. If these references aren't removed, then, as long as the collection is in the memory, the GC won't remove them; they become a memory leak. You should pay special attention to static objects (object instances referred to from static variables). These variables don't disappear once they are created, so unless you explicitly remove the reference, you can assume that an object referred to from a static variable will stay for the whole life of the process. If that object is a collection that refers to other objects that are never removed, it can potentially become a memory leak.

The objects in a heap may refer to one another. In this case, the cat instance can't be removed by the garbage collector until the reference made by the person instance is removed or the person is removed.

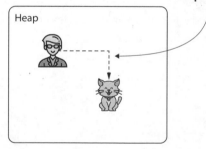

Figure E.12   Any object in the heap can keep references to other objects in the heap. The GC can remove an object only when no reference to it exists.

An object instance can also be referred to from the stack (figure E.13). Usually, references from the stack don't cause memory leaks since (as discussed in section E.2) a stack layer automatically disappears when the execution reaches the end of the code block for which the app created the layer. But in specific cases, when combined with other issues, references from the stack can also cause trouble. Imagine a deadlock that keeps the execution from running through a whole block of code. The layer in the stack won't be removed, and if it keeps references to objects, this may also become a memory leak.

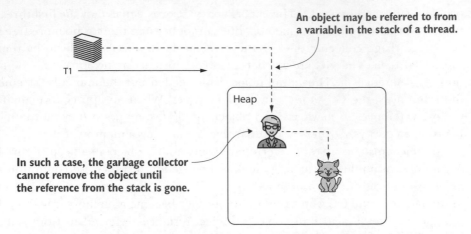

Figure E.13 A variable in the stack can also refer to an instance in the heap, which cannot be removed until all its references are gone (including the ones in the stack).

E.4   *The metaspace memory location for storing data types*

The metaspace is a memory location the JVM uses to store the data types used to create instances stored in the heap (figure E.14). The app needs this information to handle the object instances in the heap. Sometimes, in specific conditions, an `OutOfMemoryError` can also affect the metaspace. If the metaspace becomes full and there's no more space for the app to store new data types, the app throws an `OutOf-MemoryError`, announcing that the metaspace is full. In my experience, these errors are rare, but I would like you to be aware of them.

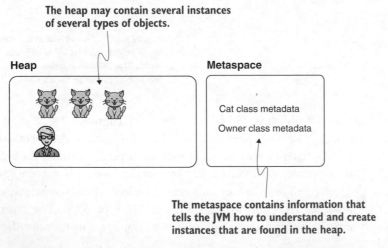

Figure E.14 The metaspace is a memory location where the app stores the data types' descriptors. It holds the blueprints used to define the instances stored in the heap.

index

A new online reading experience

liveBook, our online reading platform, adds a new dimension to your Manning books, with features that make reading, learning, and sharing easier than ever. A liveBook version of your book is included FREE with every Manning book.

This next generation book platform is more than an online reader. It's packed with unique features to upgrade and enhance your learning experience.

- Add your own notes and bookmarks
- One-click code copy
- Learn from other readers in the discussion forum
- Audio recordings and interactive exercises
- Read all your purchased Manning content in any browser, anytime, anywhere

As an added bonus, you can search every Manning book and video in liveBook—even ones you don't yet own. Open any liveBook, and you'll be able to browse the content and read anything you like.*

Find out more at www.manning.com/livebook-program.

*Open reading is limited to 10 minutes per book daily